WOMEN EDUCATION THROUGH THE AGES

By the Same Author

- ★ Crosscultural Communication: Global Perspective, 1998.
- ★ Encyclopaedic Survey of Oriental Thought (Three Volumes), 1998.
- ★ Neo-Humanism and Human Values, 1998.
- ★ Phonology of Banda Dialect, 1996.
- ★ Equality of Religions, 1995.
- ★ Creativity and Values, 1992.
- ★ A Search for Human Values, 1992.
- ★ New Education Policy, 1987.
- ★ Value Education: Theory and Practice, 1986.
- ★ Current Trends and Problems of Progressive Education, 1985.
- ★ Anglo-Hindi-Sanskrit Practical Grammar, 1967.

About the Author

Dr. N.L. Gupta (*b.* 1940) is the first scholar to obtain a Ph.D. from two different faculties of Nagpur University. He has a series of Postgraduate degrees and many firsts at his credit. He is the first candidate to submit a thesis for D.Litt. in R.S. University Raipur. He is the first writer to get subsidy for a Hindi book *Berar Ke Sufi Shayar* from Governor of Maharashtra, which is oftly quoted by Urdu scholars. Recently he has been awarded by Maharashtra Hindi Granth Academy for the best work on Literary criticism styled as "Nav-Manavatavadi Chintan" (Neo-humanistic Thought).

Dr. Gupta is a prolific writer. Besides many research papers, he has 35 books in both Hindi and English at his credit. Dr. Gupta's writings have a very broad spectrum of themes which include Literature, History, Culture, Education, Sociology, Philosophy, Theology and so on. He is considered to be the authority on 'Value Education' on which he has contributed as many as six books with different angles. Latest in the series was *Education and Values in the Mahabharata, Mulya Parak Shiksha* of about 400 pages published from Ajmer, has been profusely quoted by the scholars.

Presently Dr. Gupta is working as Assistant Commissioner, Kendriya Vidyalaya Sangathan, Bhopal, Madhya Pradesh.

WOMEN EDUCATION THROUGH THE AGES

N.L. GUPTA
Assistant Commissioner
Kendriya Vidyalaya Sangathan, Bhopal (M.P.)

CONCEPT PUBLISHING COMPANY, NEW DELHI-110059

ISBN 81-7022-826-3

First Published 2000

Published and Printed by
Ashok Kumar Mittal
Concept Publishing Company
A/15-16, Commercial Block, Mohan Garden
NEW DELHI-110059 (India)

Phones : 5648039, 5649024
Fax : 091-11-5648053
E-mail: publishing@conceptpub.com

PREFACE

It was a long-felt need to highlight the historical development of Women's Education from *Vedic* time to the Post-Independence Era in a single volume. Definitely it was a stupendous task; but my previous background and works pave the path of this difficult task. Besides many reference books in Sanskrit, English and Hindi the following books authored by the author himself had been of immense help to him:

1. *Educational Ideals and Institutions in Mahabharata* (Mohit).
2. *Education and Values in Mahabharata* (Concept).
3. *Jain-Buddha Shikshan Paddhati* (Vishva Bharati)
4. *New Education Policy* (Krishna Bros.)
5. *Oriental Thoughts*, Vol. I (Anmol)
6. *Value Education: Theory and Practice* (Krishna Bros.)

Seeing the increasing number of various types of crimes (rapes, assaults, battering, dowry-deaths, incest, etc.) One is constrained to think that the age-old attitude towards women still prevails considering them second class citizen or 'Second Sex' instead of 'fair six'. But now, with the active intervention and attention of international bodies towards emancipation and empowerment of women, the tide may turn soon in favour of women and make them *Nari-Shakti* in real sense of the term. "It was during U.N. Women's Development Decade (1975-85), Major emphasis was given to women's status. International bodies such as UNICEF, UNESCO, UN and various Non-Governmental Organisations (NGOs) have been playing a major role in this regard."

A significant landmark began in the history of Indian women with the Constitution of India, guaranteeing equal opportunity to men and women, this was, no doubt, a silver lining in the dark clouds. The UN Charter Declaration on the right to development, equal remuneration against women, etc., ensure equal rights to women. For protection of women rights a number of acts were passed, such as the Hindu Marriage Act, Hindu Succession Act 1956, Sati Prevention Act 1929, Dowry Prevention Act 1961. As a matter of fact these Acts have little or no effect in reality. The year 1989 was declared as year of the girl child by

SAARC countries. UNESCO also brought the issue of girls and women on National and International agendas. One of the objectives of WARLAT (Women Action Research and Legal Action Trust) established in 1992 is asserting of gender equality and taking recourse to the special protection laws already designed to empower women, the other objectives, to examine factors, which perpetuate the inferior status of women; to promote conception of Human Rights established in the Universal Declaration of Human Rights 1948 and other related international conventions; and to work towards the elimination of discrimination against women.

Women's Conference held in Beijing in 1995 discussed important issues of women Human Rights, property rights, etc. Reproduction rights were broadly discussed. But in spite of all these provisions, violation of Human Rights of Women are on the rampant and a strong and urgent growth of NGOs to create awareness of the Human Rights and also to sensitize the need of exercising one's rights alongwith duties is very much needed.

Efforts have been made to cover all the topics befitting to the title of the volume in the most precise manner in the following chapters:

1. Women Education: Genesis and Dimensions.
2. Historical Development of Women Education.
3. Socio-cultural Status: Through the Ages (I-Hindu Legacy).
4. Socio-cultural Status: Through the Ages (II-Customs and Problems).
5. Women Education under Jain-Buddha System.
6. Women Education under Islamic System.
7. Women Education under British Rule.
8. Commissions and Committees on Women Education.
9. Constitutional Provisions for Sex-Equality and Betterment.
10. Empowerment of Women.
11. Changing Scenario and Future Prospects.

Besides Bibliography, there are three appendices—'Thought of Mahatma Gandhi on Women', 'Women Education for Equality' and 'Women Fighters of Freedom'—which may interest the readers.

In the perspective of the changing scenario when many of the universities have already introduced independent Postgraduate Department for 'Women Studies', and many proposals for this purpose are in the process and all-around awareness is rising with unforeseen rapidity at national and international level as well, present study will definitely help the scholars as well as general readers to systematize their ideas and have a comprehensive picture of women's education from ancient time to the post-Independent era.

I am thankful to Dr. D.K. Bhattacharya, Principal, Regional Institution of Education, Bhubaneswar, for inspiring me to complete this volume, and also to Ms. Singh for extending necessary help by providing books and magazines from time to time. I take this opportunity to extend my hearty thanks to Shri Ashok Kumar Mittal of Concept Publishing Company, New Delhi, who has recently brought out my voluminous book on 'Crosscultural Communication', for having accepted this volume on 'Women Studies' very enthusiastically.

N.L. GUPTA

Laxmisagar
Bhubaneswar

CONTENTS

LIST OF TABLES

1

WOMEN EDUCATION
Genesis and Dimensions

The Urgency of the Need

In a developed society women's education is as necessary as that of men; but in the developing and under-developed societies it has become more so for several socio-economic reasons. As far as refinement of generation is concerned women's education has been considered to be more necessary. If a woman is educated, she can benefit the children with her enlightenment and learning experiences. In her guidance entire family may be educated. According to an American survey, the more educated the mother, the easier it will be for her children to win higher education diplomas. Conversely, if left in ignorance, women will hamper the progress that needs to be made in hygiene, dietary habits, child care, health and so on.

Regarding the need and importance of women's education, the University Education Commission (1948-49) has rightly observed:

> "There cannot be an educated people without educated women. If general education had to be limited to men or to women, that opportunity should be given to women, for then it would most surely be passed on to the next generation. General education is very important not only for men but also for women; because it is the education that makes men's or women's living interesting and intelligent. It also makes a person a good, useful and productive citizen of his society." According to Anderson (1956), "General education is concerned with the development of a balanced individual who can take his place as a well-adjusted person in society and who can approach with intelligence the social and cultural problems of his day."

On 7th November 1967 the United Nations adopted the 'Declaration of the Elimination of Discrimination against Women'. Article 3 stipulates: "All appropriate measures shall be taken to educate public opinion and to direct national aspirations towards the eradication of prejudice and the abolition of customary and all other practices which are based on the idea of the inferiority of women."

According to Jacueline Chabaud,

> "The education of women has become a world-wide need. It is not a question of providing the rudiments of an education of humanitarian grounds; women must be given all the means of participating in the building of the world. The urgency of the need is thus linked with the desire for justice and with respect for the individual—which make the idea of the inferiority of women intolerable. Woman is as much a human being as a man; she is equally entitled to develop her abilities, all her abilities, to choose the sort of life she wishes to lead and carry on all the activities and assume all the responsibilities that go to make up human dignity.
>
> "Like work or scientific and economic progress, education is a matter for the whole mankind, for men and women alike and not for one of the two sexes only. This is the truth worth remembering when, as so often happens, the human personality of the individual is crushed by the economic machine. Instead of this machine being harnessed to serve the development of humanity, it is man who serves it. And woman, too."[1]

Therefore, women need to be viewed not as beneficiaries; but as active participants in the process of development and change of the society they live in. Her capacity to work, her knowledge and her skills are often the only resources to call upon for survival in poor households. Thus, women become the critical actors in the process of moving their families out of poverty. It may be proper to refer to the conclusion drawn by the World Bank Report (1991):

> "What emerges most forcefully from the review is that efforts to improve the position of Indian women need to focus on women as economic actors. . . . Women are central to the success of poverty alleviation efforts in the short and medium as in the long-term."

Women's Studies Defined

The focal point of women's studies is, of course, women; but is linked with men by choice or compulsion, by nature or by heredity. Therefore, alike men, women are related with so many socio-cultural and economic factors? Therefore, all these aspects including social or man-made environment are very much part of women's studies. The founders of US National Women's Studies Association defined Women's Studies as *An Educational Strategy for Change* owning its existence to the Women's Liberation Movement, it is important to stress that Women's Studies consist of both teaching and research. It is the interaction between feminist scholarship and learning that takes place in the classrooms which respectively inspires, probes, reinforces, expands and develops them. Rather than transmitting knowledge as 'the truth' from 'the expert' to 'the ignorant' students and teachers in women's studies attempt to create knowledge in an environment in which all are learners. Some, usually the teachers, are more familiar with the existing scholarship on a topic and make this resource then contribution to the classroom. Others being their life experiences as a resource, and, as many students in women's studies are mature women, their contribution is just as pertinent in gaining and understanding of a phenomenon and developing and analysis. It is here that 'the personal becomes the intellectual and the intellectual the personal'. The enthusiasm that most students and teachers display in women's studies courses stem from the attempt to blend theory and practice, a rare happening in other disciplines. Whether the topic is work, health, politics or literature, discussing it from a perspective that puts women at its centre allows us to compare and contrast our own experiences with the given facts and figures.

The study of women's education is our major concern. The past decade had witnessed a proliferation of excellent research studies on very important topics concerning women—their roles and relative status, their participation in the work force and in politics, their contribution to economic development, and so forth. This scholarship is rich and highly relevant for understanding the significance of women's education. However, most of it does not directly consider education. We learn little from this body of knowledge about why women attend school, what they learn in school, how education affects them or whether education makes a contribution to improving their lives apart from class, ethnicity, and other socio-cultural factors.

Dimensions of Women Studies

Women's studies programme has four dimensions: *teaching, research, training* and *extension.* National Policy on Education (NPE) 1986 suggests the following activities in *teaching:*

1. Incorporation of issues relating to women's status and role in the foundation course proposed to be introduced by University Grants Commission all undergraduate students;
2. Incorporation of the women's dimension into courses in different disciplines; and
3. Elimination of sexist bias and sex stereo-types from text-books.

Under *research*, following steps are suggested:

(i) Encouraging research on identified areas and subjects which are crucial in advancing knowledge in this area and to expand the information base; and
(ii) Critical appraisal of existing tools and techniques which have been responsible for the disadvantages suffered by them and where necessary reformation of research methodology.

The following measures are suggested under *training:*

(i) Dissemination of information and interaction through seminars/ workshops on the need for women's studies and its role in University education;
(ii) Orientation of teachers and researchers to handle women related topics and to incorporate women's dimension into general topics; and
(iii) Workshops for restructuring the curriculum.

Under *extension* the following proposals have been made:

(i) To encourage educational institutions to take up programmes which directly benefit the community and bring about the empowerment of women; and
(ii) These would include actual implementation of development programmes directly aimed at women's empowerment such as adult education, awareness building, legal literacy, informational and training support for socio-economic programmes of women's development, media, etc.[2]

Education and Women

According to Confucious knowledge is both—"It is to know both—what one knows and what one does not know."[3] In answer to FanHsu's question the master said, "To love one's fellow-men is Manhood-at-his-best. To know them is to have knowledge." In Hindu scriptures knowledge is said to be the most pious, most powerful and like the third eye of a man. In the orient thought knowledge has been roughly divided into two kind—Material knowledge and Spiritual knowledge. Max Weber describes these two types of knowledge as following :

> "A careful examination would reveal the fact that 'knowledge' does not mean knowing the things of this world, nature, social life, or laws regulating both nature and man. Rather, it is the philosophical knowledge of the 'meaning' of world and life. It is naturally understood that such knowledge cannot be replaced by Western empirical learning, and that it should never be sought by empirical means, if we are to do justice to the purpose to that learning."[4]

The word 'education' implies the characteristics of both the types of knowledge, *viz.*, material and spiritual. That is why Mahatma Gandhi said that "By education, I mean an all-round drawing out of the best in child and man—body, mind and spirit." Literacy is not the end of education nor even the beginning. It is one of the means whereby man and woman can be educated. Thus, Gandhi's concept of education stands for the balanced and harmonious development of all the aspects of human personality. This concept of education can be called more or less the representative Indian thought on the subject of education. Education is the key which opens the door to life by widening one's vision, develops the sense of concerns towards the fellow-being and thus promotes national development.

The Government of India has endorsed the need for promotion of women education not only through its constitutional provisions but also in plans, policies and programmes launched at different points of time. Article 15 of the Constitution prohibits any discrimination on ground of sex. In 1958 the Government of India appointed a National Committee on Women's Education in order to recommend special measures to bridge the gap between the education of girls and boys at the primary and secondary levels. Almost all Five Year Plans have laid emphasis on removal of disparities in educational opportunities to women. While, the Seventh Five Year Plan which was co-terminus with the National Policy on Education (NPE) 1986 gave overriding priority to the removal of women illiteracy and obstacles inhibiting their access to and retention in elementary education. Further the Plan also aimed at removing traditional gender discrimination and sex stereotyping.

In the Action Plan of National Policy on Education 1986 greater emphasis has been given on education for women's equality. It says:

> Provision of educational opportunities to women has been an important programme in the education sector since independence. Between 1951 and 1981, the percentage of literacy amongst women improved from 7.93 per cent to 24.82 per cent. However, in absolute numbers, illiterate women have increased during this period from 158.7 million excluding Assam. Women comprise 57 per cent of the illiterate population and 70 per cent of the non-enrolled children of school stage are girls. In spite of the efforts made so far, the education system has not been able to make sufficient contribution towards women's equality."[5]

The NPE (1986) and the programme of Action for 1992 on women empowerment also advocated that education can be an effective tool for women's empowerment with the following parameters:

1. Enhance self-esteem and self-confidence of women;
2. Building a positive image of women by recognising their contribution to the society, polity and the economy;
3. Developing ability to think critically;
4. Fostering decision-making and action through collective processes;
5. Enable to make informed choices in areas like education, employment and health;
6. Ensuring equal participation and developmental processes;
7. Providing information, knowledge and skill for economic independence; and
8. Enhancing access to legal literacy and information relating to their rights and entitlements in society with a view to enhancing their participation on an equal footing in all areas.[6]

The Eighth Five Year Plan focussed in women's literacy which has a beneficial impact on children's literacy as well as other national objectives like population control and family welfare. Nation Policy on Education (NPE) 1986 had resolved that it will "give the highest priority to solve the problem of children dropping out of school and adopt an array of meticulously formulated strategies based on micro-planning, and applied at the grassroot level all over the country, to ensure children's retention at school. This effort will be fully coordinated with the network of non-formal education. It shall be ensured that all children who attain the age of about 11 years by 1990 will have had five years of schooling, or its equivalent through the non-formal stream. Likewise, by 1995 all children will be provided free and compulsory education up to 14 years of age."[6]

Because of so many socio-economic factors the above premise of NPE-1986 could not be fulfilled to the fullest extent; but it succeeded in charging the entire environment with desired enthusiasm and awareness for universalisation of primary education through various incentives like mid-day meals, scholarship, etc. In our policy documents there is lot of emphasis on the "Education for women's equality." The NPE envisages that education would be used as a strategy for achieving a basic change in the status of women. The National education system would—(i) play a positive interventionist role in the empowerment of women, (ii) contribute towards development of new values through redesigned curricula and text-books, and (iii) women's studies will be promoted as part of various courses. The main features of the targets and implementation strategy will consist the following:

(i) to gear the entire education system to plan a positive interventionist role in the empowerment of women;
(ii) to promote women's studies as a part of various courses and encouragement to educational institutions to take up active programme to further women's development;
(iii) to widen the access of women in programmes of vocational, technical and professional education; and
(iv) to create dynamic managerial structure to cope with the targets envisaged.[7]

To translate into action the above policy-parameters into action, it is needless to say that inter-institutional and inter-departmental coordination is a must. Production of new text-books and other training material is one of the significant works which may enable us to remove the sex-bias and prejudices between the two sexes. In this regard Prof. M.S. Gore has rightly observed:

> Of late there has been some active discussion of the problem of sex-bias in our text-books. Two approaches have been suggested to overcome this limitation. One is to request organisations like NCERT to prepare new text-books wherein this bias would be eliminated. It would not be possible to remove sex-bias in materials that deal with

historical or even contemporary social facts, but certainly this should be possible where new models for man-woman interaction or male-female status are likely to be discussed, suggested or created. The other way is to help teachers to handle existing text-books in a manner that through discussion children can see how sex-bias enter almost unconsciously or as a reflection of social reality in the material of the text-book. Both these are complementary approaches. In either case, it is important that teachers themselves first overcome their own biases so that they can become instruments of change. As in the area of family planning or removal of caste discrimination so in the area of sex equality one cannot begin with the assumption that teachers are already free from traditional biases.[8]

REFERENCES

1. Jacqueline Chabaud, *The Education and Advancement of Women*, UNESCO, 1970.
2. *Programme of Action*, p. 106.
3. *Sayings of Confucious*, II, 17.
4. Max Weber, *Aufsatze Religion Sogiologie*, II, pp. 364-65
5. *Programme of Action*, p. 105.
6. *Ibid.*
7. *Ibid.*, pp. 105-6.
8. M.S. Gore, *Indian Education: Process and Structures*, p. 117.

2

HISTORICAL DEVELOPMENT OF WOMEN EDUCATION
Through the Ages

The tender regard for womenhood is one of the distinguishing characteristics of the *Vedas* and as such women enjoyed a fair amount of personal freedom and equality with men. The courteous address for a woman is the same as for Goddess—Subhage! 'O graceful one!' (*e.g.*, *Rigveda*, X.10.12). She is often described as '*kalyani*, the blissful one'. The woman's smile has been treated as a mark of divine beauty. The mother's kiss for the child is invested with divine loveliness (*Rigveda*, X.114.4). There are great goddesses, like Usha, Saraswati and Aditi, etc. among the *Vedic* seers. It is remarkable that in such a remote age women had an exalted position not attained by her under later civilization for long ages either in the East or in the West. Radha Kamal Mukherjee has rightly said, "Women had free access to education and training in their learning and participation in religious ceremonies and functions."[1] However, it appears that the prevalence of learning among women was restricted only to the seers or the Brahmins.

Due to stratification of the society into four *varnas*—Brahmin, Kshatriya, Vaishya, and Shudra—and division of their social rights and duties; only Brahminas were having the privilege and access to education. A.S. Altekar, in his book titled as *Position of Women in Hindu Civilization*, has observed,

> "In the *Vedic* period among the higher section of society, the sacred initiation (*upnayan*) of girls was common and they used to go through a regular course of education. Some attained distinction in the realm of theology and philosophy and a considerable number of women used to follow the teaching career."[2]

As the religion played an important role in the life of men in

Ancient India, the *Vedas* and the literature that interpreted the *Vedas* were the principal topic of study during the *Vedic* period. In addition to the sacred hymns which the students had to memorise, a number of historical poems had to be studied by them. These poems, which were of a secular nature, depicted in the growth and evolution of the times during which they were composed. They also recorded contemporary events. Religion was one of the bed-rocks of Ancient Indian Education. Music also played an important role in spiritualising the nature of man. It was, therefore, regarded as one of the most indispensable adjuncts of education. *Sama Veda*, which is called the Veda of Music, reveals the divine harmony of music. Some of the hymns, when set to music, become really soul-elevating. Therefore, music is called "the companion of religion and the child of the prayer." It played a significant role in spiritualising education in Ancient India as it did in idealising education in Ancient Greece.

In the post-Vedic period our hermitages were situated in the far-flung forest areas, and as such for security purpose the practice of sending women out to great scholars and to centres, situated in the remote forests, began to be looked upon with disfavoured. It was preferred that women should receive training at home from father, brothers and members of kin groups. Such a practice made it obvious that tradition of imparting learning to women remain restricted to high-up Brahmin families only. This limited access of women to learning, also curtailed their religious rights and privileges. In general, girls used to have non-formal education from elder brothers, parents, learned guests, etc. The King Drupad had appointed a learned Brahmin to teach state-craft to his son. His daughter (Draupadi) also learnt Brihaspati-*Arthashastra* from the learned Brahmin at home.[3] Shakuni, the prince of Gandhar king and Gandhari (sister of Shakuni) both were well-versed in *Arthashastra*. Though the girls were not sent to hermitages; but in the families of hermits some female members used to live including the Acharya's wife (*guru-patni*), daughter, etc.[4]

Women used to take keen interest in narrating and listening to the stories. This was not only a source of entertainment for them but also a tool of knowledge. Brihannala (name adopted by Arjuna in disguise in the kingdom of Virata) used to narrate various interesting stories and amuse the persons in the *harem* (inner apartment) of the king Virata. Thus, we see the deteriorating trends in the education of women in the post-Vedic as well as in the epic-age, *i.e.*, the age of *Ramayana* and *Mahabharata*, exact time of which still stands as disputed among the scholars. According to Altekar, "The cause of women education suffered a good deal after 300 B.C. on account of the new fashion of child-marriage that then began to come into vogue."[5]

Buddhism and Jainism which came into existence in the form of a revolt against Brahminism, tried to assign an important and honourable place to women in society. Many women achieved distinctions as teachers and scholars. There may be discrimination between man and woman; but at the religious level there was no discrimination—this is what the Jain and Buddha proclaim. But as a matter of practice the scenario was different, which we will discuss in a separate chapter. In the *Sanghas* (communities) there was an apparent subordination of nuns as compared to the monks in both the religions. This subordination is so supreme that a monk of three years' standing could become the *Upadhyaya* or a nun of thirty years' standing. Thus for the position in *Sangha* sex was considered more rather than seniority or merit. It is reported that Mahavira had established Sangha for nuns like that of *monks* (*Shravakas*).

According to A.S. Altekar,

> "Nuns continued to figure in the Buddhist monastic life down to the 3rd century A.D., but do not seem to have distinguished themselves as authoresses or preachers. Nunneries went out of vogue in Buddhism from about the 4th century A.D.; neither Buddhist nuns, nor scholars, nor authoresses are mentioned either by Fa Hien or by Yuan Chuang, who have given a detailed account of Buddhism of India of their time. Female education, therefore, received no helping hand from Buddhism during the period 300 B.C. to 800 A.D. It is interesting to note that in modern Burma and Ceylon nunneries do not impart education to girls as monasteries do to boys."[6]

Thus, we see that with the diminishing influence of Buddhism, the educational position of women further deteriorated and remained shaky as is evident from the interpretation of religious dicta as given by various law-givers, Manu, a famous law-giver observed that at one place that a maiden should be protected by her father, a wife by her husband and a widow by her sons. The total Hindu period is charged with the authoritarian rule of the patriarch.

During the age of later *Smritis*, commentators and digest-writers adopted benevolent attitude towards women. Though in the field of education no social effort were was registered, but on the legal front some rights like proprietary rights, etc. were given to women by the law-givers. According to Altekar,

> "The only sphere in which the position of women improved in this age was the one of proprietary rights; otherwise she continued to lose all along the line. The right of the widow to inherit the share of her husband came to be eventually recognised all over the country by 1200 A.D. In Bengal the position was further improved by conceding her this right even when her husband had not separated from the joint family at the time of his death. The scope of the *Stridhana* was further extended by the Mitakshara School by including in it property acquired even by inheritance and partition. The widow's estate continued to be a limited one, but in some parts of south India she was allowed to gift it away for religious purposes without the consent of the reversioners."[7]

Proprietary rights apart, in all other spheres the position of women continued to deteriorate in this period. Most of the causes for women's degradation during the last period continued to operate in this age also. The *Upnayan* (initiation) went completely out of vogue. From the theological point of view the woman, therefore, came naturally to be regarded as of the same status as the *Shudras*. This inflicted an incalculable harm on their general status and prestige.

The Muslim rulers of India generally took a keen interest in education, and many of them founded schools, colleges and libraries in various places in their dominions. The example of rulers was followed by many of their influential subjects, scholars, poets, and other literary men were often encouraged by the patronage of the courts or of private individuals. Stipends and scholarships were often given to pupils and in many places orphanages were established. The permanent settlement of Muslims in India, and conversion of some of the inhabitants to Islam, meant the establishment of mosques, and as in other Muslim countries, the mosques, especially in towns, was a centre of instruction and of literary activities. Muslim educational institutions are distinguished as *maktabs* or *madrashas*.[8] The *maktab* is a primary school often attached to a mosque, the chief business of which is to instruct boys in those portions of the *Koran* which a Muslim is expected to know by heart in order to perform his devotions and other religious functions. Sometimes instruction in reading, writing, and simple arithmetic (3 *R*'s) was also included in the curriculum. Primary education was also carried on in private houses. *Madrashas* were school for higher learning. They too were generally attached to mosques and monasteries. Some of them rise to the status of universities. The course included grammar, rhetoric, logic, theology, metaphysics, literature, jurisprudence, and science.

Certain subjects were more cultivated in some centres than others. The medium of instruction in these schools was Persian. But the study of Arabic was compulsory for Muslims.

According to A.L. Shrivastava,

> "There were no *maktabs* and *madrashas* for girls throughout our medieval Indian history. Perhaps it was not considered desirable and necessary to educate the female section of population. There were, however, arrangements for the education of girls of the well-to-do and royal families."[9]

Therefore, we find many scholar women in the royal families. Among the women some became successful rulers also, like Rajia Sultan, Chand Bibi, etc. Nurjahan was adviser-in-chief to her husband Jahangir, son of Akbar the great.

During the period between the invasion of Mohammed of Ghor and the advent of the British rule in India, the position of Indian women deteriorated. The menfolk being constantly engaged in warfare with the Muslims, it was considered safer to keep the women in seclusion. This was the beginning of the *purdah* system. As *purdah* prohibited the movement of women outside the house, it proved a positive impediment in the way of their education and also tended to make the women-folk more and more dependent on men for their affairs outside the homes. Ongoing political struggle made life invariably very uncertain and insecure. Protection of young and lonely girls became a problem for the parents and this gave rise to various social evils like, female-infanticide, child-marriage, *Sati,* etc. We may call this period as a dark period as far as Women's education is concerned.

Of course, the progress in the field of women's education was disgusting and disheartening, at the same time with the cultural synthesis point of view this period very notable. S.R. Sharma has rightly observed:

> "If the love between Baz Bahadur and Rupmati, celebrated in songs and paintings, belonged to the 'private sector' of sentimental romance, the confidence that the chaste *Rajputtni* Karnavati placed in the Turkish emperor Humayun, as '*rakhi*-brother to save her from the clutches of Bahdur Shah of Gujarat (who was then besieging Chittor), belongs to the high-souled realm of real chivalry. Both together were relieving features of an age of tensions yielding place to one of increasing harmony between the Hindus and the Muslims. Akbar with his wellknown flair for synthesis was a product of these tendencies. The spirit of *Din-e-Ilahi* and the cultural *milieu* which

inspired it are more important than any sectarian details incidental to its social formulation."[10]

His search for the synthesis was really commendable, particularly in the perspective when he was surrounded by the fundamentalists. Before his towering personality they have no voice; but after Akbar they raised their heads again during the reign of Jahangir onwards. The final out-burst of this fundamentalism came to the surface during the reign of Aurangzeb.

Akbar's importance lies in his sincere endeavours to work out on a very comprehensive scale the largest, most thoughtful and deliberate rapprochement ever attempted until then—to unify "the warring world of Hindustan" as Tennyson has expressed in his famous poem titled as "Akbar's Dream." He makes Akbar to say:

"I hate the rancour of their castes and creeds
I let them worship as they will, I reap
No revenue from the field of unbelief,
I cull from every faith and race the best
And harvest soul for counsellor and friends."

The elaborate discussion on the women's education under the Islamic system has been given in this book in a separate chapter.

After the Muslim period, the British Government assumed a position of domination in India. It was basically interested in establishing their colonial rule and as such refrained from interfering with their life-style of the local people. As a result, it did not pose any problem to existing practices in the country. The East India Company did not consider it necessary to educate the fair-sex, perhaps because lady clerks or officers were not required for administrative purposes. At the same time, a variety of odd superstitions held back girls' education. Nevertheless, some efforts were made during the colonial regime to create opportunities for elementary education for women. Gradually, the British Government became interested to end some of the evil and inhuman practices in India like *Sati*, child-marriage, etc. This led them to introduce women education. Actually the Christian missionaries, who followed the advent of the Britishers in India, worked for women education.

According to S.N. Mukerji,

"During the Company's rule, there were no separate state schools for girls, and hardly a few girls were attending boys' schools. Most of the girls' schools were run by missionaries and a few by private bodies. In 1851, the Protestant Missions were conducting 86 boarding schools for girls and 286 day schools for girls with an enrolment of 2,274 and 8,919 respectively. The Roman Catholic Missions were also active, but the figures for their schools are not available. A number of private schools were conducted by British officials in their private capacity. The most important institution of this type was Bethune School, which was founded by Mr. J.E.D. Bethune in 1849. Mr. Bethune was the Legal Member of the Supreme Council of the Government of India. This school gave an impetus to Indians to start similar institutions in the country."[11]

Initially the missionaries started schools for educating their Christian converts only. But at a later stage they opened schools for non-Christian girls also in Bengal, Mumbai and Chennai. This fact has been reported in Educational Records of Government of India (1927, p. 34). Because of the age-old prejudice against mixed classes, for boys and girls, the Mission started *zanana* schools staffed by lady teachers to which girls alone were admitted. The schools were availed of only by the higher-ups in the society. The mission schools had two definite aims in starting girl schools. Firstly, they hoped that the educated girls would in future establish schools for educating women, and secondly, it was their hope that many of those educated girls would become converts and would be a suitable means for spreading Christianity and the truth of the Gospel among their countrymen.

The despatch of 1854 (Charles Wood's Despatch) gave lot of encouragement to such efforts. The despatch stated, "No subject could have a stronger claim to have our attention than education. It is one of our sacred duties." On the other hand it also declared: "We must emphatically declare that the education which we desire to be extended in India is that which has for its object the diffusion (of useful knowledge and which India may, under providences, derive) of the improved Arts, Science, Philosophy and Literature of Europe; in short of European knowledge." The despatch fully endorsed the declaration of Governor-General of Bengal that for women education, the Government should extend an active cooperation and help. The directors of the Board of the Company were of the opinion that women education will give an impetus to the moral standard of the public. According to Wood's Despatch the total number of girls' schools was 256 in Chennai, 65 in Mumbai, 288 in Bengal and 17 in the Northeastern Provinces. In the Punjab, the traditional education of women had continued as an indigenous effort and the modern type of girl's schools had just begun to come into existence.

The Indian Education Commission of 1882, while examining the question of girls' education remarked, "Female education is still in an extremely backward condition and needs to be fostered in every legitimate way." It recommended that it should receive a larger share of public funds. As a result, state funds were spent more freely on girls' education. There was a sharp rise in private efforts also. Owing to these two factors, girls' education progressed. This was noticeable amongst Europeanised communities, *viz.*, the Brahmo Samaj, the Parsees and the Christians. In 1901-02, there were 12 colleges, 467 secondary schools, and 5,268 primary schools for girls, but the total girls' enrolment in all educational institutions was 447,470 only.

But very soon, the feeling of passive apathy was changed into active sympathy owing to sentimental and material causes. Parents were gradually realising that the education of their daughters was as much a part of their duty as the education of their sons. The demand for educated wives also developed. The Education Departments also took some active steps and devised new plans for spreading education, *viz.*, separate schools were started, arrangements of conveyance for taking girls to schools were made, inspectresses were appointed, liberal prizes were offered to girls and fees were remitted at times, many schools run by local bodies were transferred to government, favourable grants were given to private girls' schools. Teachers of boys' schools were rewarded for every girl whose attendance could be secured, steps were taken to attract ladies to the teaching profession, and provincial committees with a fair proportion of lady members were set up for discussing the problems of girls' education.

These steps gave a great encouragement to girls' education. In 1904, Mrs. Annie Besant established the Central Hindu Girls' School at Benaras with the object of imparting western education to girls quite separately from boys in a modernised school of Hinduism. In 1916, the first Medical College, Lady Hardinge College, Delhi, was established for the fair sex in the country. The Women's (SNDT) University was also established in the same year. In 1917, there were 12 arts colleges, four professional colleges and 166 secondary schools for girls. The enrolment also showed an increase; but the problem of retention persisted due to several socio-economic factors.

The British Government adopted a liberal policy for promoting girl education. A number of schemes were started. The period after 1921 was charged with national awakening among the people as a result of the steering of the struggle for freedom by the Indian leaders, who realised that women's participation was important for social progress. There were some notable leaders including Raja Ram Mohun Roy, Ishwar Chandra Vidyasagar, Annie Besant and Sir Syed Ahmed Khan who advocated education for women, removal of their social disabilities and restoration of their legal and social rights. Socio-economic movements like the Brahmo Samaj and Arya Samaj lent further support to these concepts. The reform movements brought a new awakening among the women-folk and they, specially from the middle classes, were imbibed with new ideas. As modern education became a torch light for them, they came out of the four wall of the homes and took active part in various social activities.

In 1931, the Karachi Session of the Indian National Congress passed a resolution laying down certain fundamental rights to the citizens. These promised rights contained a significant clause that there shall be no discrimination on the ground of sex. This marked the birth of a new era for Indian women.

The detailed discussion on this topic has been done in an independent chapter titled as 'Women Education under British Rule'.

REFERENCES

1. Radha Kamal Mukerji, *Ancient Indian Education*, pp. 1-2.
2. A.S. Altekar, *The Position of Women in Hindu Civilization*, p. 15.
3. *Mahabharata*, Arantak Parvan, pp. 33.77.
4. N.L. Gupta, *Education in Mahabharata*,pp. 81-83.
5. A.S. Altekar, *ibid.*, p. 13.
6. *Ibid.*, p. 17.
7. *Ibid.*, pp. 353-54.
8. F.E. Keay, *Education in India and Pakistan*, p. 108.
9. A.L. Shrivastava, *Medieval Indian Culture*, p. 67.
10. S.R. Sharma, *Soul of Indian History*, p. 155.
11. S.N. Mukerji, *Education in India : Today and Tomorrow*, p. 223.

3

SOCIO-CULTURAL STATUS
Through the Ages

I
HINDU LEGACY

> "So too the subjection of women, the propriety of man over the women, was once an axiom of social life and has only in recent times been effectively challenged. So strong was or had become the instinct of this domination in the male animal man, that even religion and philosophy have had to sanction it, very much in the formula in which Milton expressed the height of masculine egoism, 'he for God only, she for God in him'. This idea too is crumbling into the dust, though its remnants still ailing to life by many strong tentacle of old legislation, continued instinct, persistence of traditional ideas, the fiat has gone out against it in the claim of woman to be regarded, she too, is a free individual being." —*Aurobindo*[1]

Linton[2] refers the term "status" as the position of an individual in social structure, defined by his/her designated rights and obligations. These rights and obligations, to be justified, have to be made use of by the individual concerned—this is defined as the "role." Thus, the "role" that an individual will assume in a social set-up ultimately determines her "status;" the dynamic aspect of "status" is thus the "role" that the individual plays for a woman, which in a culture complex. A person can play more than one role at the same time, some more dominant than others. Broadly speaking a woman has three roles—that of a wife, mother and career woman. In a progressive and balanced society adjustment has to be made and a cohesive balance has to be struck between the three. There is no gainsaying the fact that it is the cultural pattern which determines the position and not legal rights or constitutional guarantees as the acceptability of the society is one of the prominent factors in deciding the position. Unless the role conforms with the prevailing scheme of values, it may not be acceptable and non-acceptability by the society entail a great struggle for a woman, which she has been facing throughout the ages, right from the epic period to the modern time.

Vedic Age

The *Vedas* also speak of the woman-feminine powers without whom the masculine are not effective for work and formation, for some of the Vedic rites the very presence of woman was very essential. In one of the greatest hymns, the twenty-second of the first *mandal*, he (Medhatithi) expressly mentions of the *Patnih Devanam*, the brides of the Strong Ones, who are to be called to extend protection, to breathe a mighty peace, to have their share in the joy of Soma Wine. In one of the hymns of *Atharva Veda*[3] the husband and wife are called as complementary to each other. The prayer is as below :

> "May the husband and wife be each other's
> complementary.
> The husband a song, the wife a verse,
> the husband a sky, wife the earth. It is in their
> union that offspring result Each emotionally fulfils
> the other to completion."

In one of the hymns of *Rigveda* Goddess of learning, Saraswati, is invoked in the following manner:

> O, Saraswati, Goddess of learning, symbol of purity and
> source of intellectual powers, with your wisdom, be our
> inspiration.
> Come and participate in our noble deeds.
> The whole cosmos is aflame under the impact of your
> wisdom, without which there will be darkness.
> All awakening in the world is only manifestation of your
> supreme intellectual power.
> You are the power behind all achievements of human
> genius.[4]

In Hindu scriptures we find two extreme types of description of a woman. On one side it is said that a woman does not deserve any freedom and as such she is protected in childhood, youth as well as in old-age by the parents, husband and children respectively. On the other hand she is described as inspirer, complementary to a man, energy supreme, an emblem of *Shakti,* etc. In the difference and divergence of such descriptions the angle and insight of the describer, poet or author counts a lot, as Aurobindo has rightly observed. According to him,

> "The women of Vyasa and Sophocles have all a family resemblance, all possess a quiet or commanding masculine strength of character which reveals their parentage. Other poets we see succeeding in a single feminine character, often repeating, but failing or not succeeding eminently in the rest. Otherwise women in poetry are generally painted very much from the outside. The poets who have had an instinctive insight into women, can literally be counted on the fingers of one's hand. Shakespeare in this as in other dramatic gifts is splendidly and unapproachably first, or at least only equalled in depth though not in range by Valmiki. Racine has the same gift within his limits and Kalidasa without limits. . . ."[5]

In *Ramayana*, the statement of Ravana himself indicates the attitude of *Rakshas* towards the women-folk. He persuaded Sita at Lanka to accept him as husband. Eloping the married or unmarried woman was common in demoniac culture when Ravana could not succeed to persuade Sita, he ordered demoniac guards to behave harshly with Sita so that she might be compelled to accept his proposal. On this Sita told the *Rakshasas* about the difference in life-style of Demons and Aryans. Refusing completely to accede to the demand of Ravana she said:

> "A girl of Manava creed cannot become the wife of a demon. You all may swallow me but I cannot accept Ravana's proposal. My husband may be weak or deprived of kingdom. He is my master, he is my instructor, I am always thirsty of his love and would ever remain so like a sunshine which remains the follower of the Sun."[6]

Besides this Sita enumerated the examples of other ladies like ladies Savitri, Rohini, Damayanti and Anusuya, etc., who remained true to their husbands even in miserable moments. On the other hand Shrupanakha the real widowed sister of Ravana approached Rama and Lakshman with the request to accept her as their wife.

While analysing the 'place of women' Subramania Bharti, an apostle of patriotism, writes thus with pointed force:

> "Nations are made at home. And so long as you do not have justice and equality fully practised at home, you cannot expect to see them practised in your public life. Because it is the home life that is the basis of public life. And a man who is a villain at home cannot find himself suddenly transformed into a saint the moment he gets to the councils or to courts of justice."[7]

Deteriorating Trend

Educational development of women as depicted in the *Mahabharata* reveals that women were not given adequate opportunities for the development of their personalities. While tracing the reasons of backwardness of women in education, we find that their overall social status was mainly responsible for this. Their field was mainly household. They were not supposed to earn the livelihood. In the prevailing social phenomena, they were not safe. There was every fear of atrocities by enemies or abduction by dacoits. Under such circumstances it was not considered wise to send girls to the hermitages located in far-flung forest areas. Therefore, as far as possible, their education was arranged at home only.

According to Altekar[8] education of women prevailed in the Vedic society. But by the time of the *Mahabharata* the tradition of study of the Vedas by the women folk was almost extinct. This very phenomena is indicative of the degeneration of the then civilization. It was mostly confirmed opinion of the people that the knowledge of scriptures was not essential for women.

Again security problem seems to be one of the reasons, as said above, for depriving women from the study of the *Vedas* and allied scriptures. However, in sptie of certain restrictions and lack of safety, some women used to study the *Vedas*. In the *Mahabharata* many women are said to have learnt by heart many hymns and prayers from the *Vedas*. Vinata blessed Garuda by reciting Vedic verses. While deserting "Karna" Kunti prayed[9] for his welfare and recited *Vedic mantras*.

Socio-Religious Status

In the *Rigveda*[10] it is mentioned that couple, who perform sacrifices and offer prayers with harmonious minds, always become happy. It was a common belief that the mental make-up and conduct of a child is influenced by his parentage. Therefore, the right of learning the *Vedas* and performing *Agnihotra* was given to women. They deserve initiation (*Maunji-Bandhan*) also, as *Nirnaya-Sindhu* puts it.[11]

Theoretically the *Mahabharata* holds that women have the right not only for learning but teaching also. There is good evidence to testify to this notion. There is a reference of Brahmin (female Brahmin) named "Ṣhiva"[12] who studies all the *Vedas* and having practised penances attained salvation.

Similarly there was a Brahmini Siddha[13] Who attained the heavenly abode by the virtue of her celebacy and *yogic* practices. In *Shanti Parva* there is a famous episode of *Sulbha*, who debates with Janaka on various subtle issues of spirituality and introduces herself to Janaka.[14]

Formal *vs.* Non-Formal Education

In general, girls used to have non-formal education from elder brothers, parents, learned guests, etc. King Drupad had appointed a learned Brahmin to teach statecraft to his son. His daughter (Draupadi) also learnt Brihaspathi-*Arthashastra* from a learned Brahmin at home.[15] Shakuni, the Prince of Gandhar and Gandhari (sister of Shakuni) was both well-versed in the *Arthashastra.*[16] Though the girls were not sent to hermitages, they were sent to stay with some female members used to live which included the Guru's wife, daughters, etc.[17]

Muni Durwasa, being pleased with the hospitability of Kunti, at her father's (Kuntibhoj) house, trained her in the effective use of the "Atharva-shiras" *mantra.*[18] By the virtue of this very *mantra*, it is said, Kunti pleased various gods and got three sons—Yudhishthir, Bhima and Arjuna. Madri followed the footsteps of Kunti and pleased the twingods (Ashwini) and got twin sons—Nakula and Sahdev.

From the above description, it is clear that though the girls were not sent to the hermitages, for princesses and womenfolk of hermitages such occasions were not rare when they received knowledge of the *Vedas* and other scriptures through learned fathers, brothers or other scholarly guests. They also used to develop their knowledge and understanding by listening to the discourses of sages and other scholars from time to time particularly on occasions of certain ceremonies including various sacrifices, etc. In ordinary families also traveller guests used to tell various interesting stories pertaining to the various places they had travelled through. In village "Ekchakra" where the Pandavas lived in disguise with their mother (Kunti), a Brahmin had narrated various interesting stories to Kunti.[19] Shakuntala living in the hermitage of Kanva came to know about her parentage by hearing a conversation between the sage Kanva and a traveller guest.

Women used to take keen interest in narrating and listening to stories. This was not only a source of entertainment for them but also a book of knowledge. Brihannala (name adopted by Arjuna in disguise in the kingdom of Virata) used to narrate various interesting stories and amuse the ladies in the inner apartment of King Virata.

Special Tutors

In affluent families or royal families special tutors were appointed to teach the girls. In the palace of Virata Brihannala was entrusted with the duties of training the females in the fine arts like dance, singing, music, etc.[20]

From this singular evidence available in the *Mahabharata* it appears that the appointment of male teacher for girls was not appreciated. This is why King Virata got the impotency of Brihannala ensured before assigning him the job. In the joint families the girls used to get practical lessons in various useful matters before their marriage from their father, mother and other elderly women available in the family. Kunti[21] and Gandhari[22] had educated their daughters and daughters-in-law in arts and crafts and also duties towards other members of the family.

The data available in the *Mahabharata* reveals that women's education was almost informal. There were no formal agencies of education for them. The attributive used for maid servants of Yudhishthir indicates that they were well-versed in all the 64 arts mentioned in *Kamasutra* and other treatises. They must have learnt these arts informally only. In such informal education, women used to learn all that was required for leading a happy married life, but at times, because of emotionality, they ignored their duties. Because of such informal education, they were generally found to be good at heart but they lacked rational temper at times. Being invoked with *Pativrit Dharma* Gandhari used to have her eyes entied with a piece of cloth (because her husband was blind). By doing so she neglected her duties as a mother. Had she not done so she could have reared her children in a proper manner and cultivated in them the desired social and spiritual values.

In his famous treatise, *Education in Ancient India,* Dr. A.S. Altekar rightly observed: "In the heyday of her glory education in India was broad-based." Women and ordinary people were allowed to derive the maximum benefits from it. Although it would not be fair to compare "the scanty remains of a bygone system" with the tremendous advance that the West has made in our times, it can be said that the education during the epic period "developed character and personality. It included civic virtues, introduced a high standard of culture and emphasised the necessity of self-imposed discipline and stern regard for duty."

Ambivalent Attitude

Though the early Indian mind, prone to exaggeration, perhaps over did the necessity of wifely obedience, her status was not without honour.

> "The wife is half the man,
> The best of friends,
> the root of the three ends of life,
> and of all that will help him in the other world.
>
> "With a wife a man does mighty deeds . . .
> With a wife a man finds courage.
> A wife is the safest refuge . . .
>
> "A man aflame with sorrow in his soul,
> or sick with disease, finds comfort in his wife,
> as a man parched with heat
> finds relief in water.
>
> "Even a man in the grip of rage
> will not be harsh to a woman,
> remembering that on her depend
> the joys of love, happiness, and virtue.
>
> "For woman is the everlasting field,
> in which the Self is born."[23]

Passages like these, showing the honour and esteem in which women were held, are quite as numerous as those which stress their subservience. Everywhere it is stated that a woman should be lovingly cherished, well fed and cared for, and provided with jewellery and luxuries to the limits of her husband's means. She should never be upbraided too severely, for the gods will not accept the sacrifice of the man who beats his wife. The ancient Indian attitude to women was in fact ambivalent. She was at once a Goddess and a slave, a saint and a strumpet.

The latter aspect of her character is frequently brought out in semi-religious and gnomic literature. Women's lust knows no bounds:

> "The fire has never too many logs.
> the ocean never too many rivers,
> death never too many living souls,
> and fair-eyed woman never too many men."[24]

As in Greece, the higher class hetaira was an educated woman. The authorities on erotics demand that, as well as in the art immediately essential to her profession, she should be thoroughly trained in "the sixty-four arts." These formed a stock list, which included not only music, dancing and singing, but also acting, the composition of poetry, impromptu and otherwise, flower-arrangement and garland-making, the preparation of perfumes and cosmetics, cooking, dress-making and embroidery, sorcery conjuring and sleight of hand, the composition of riddles, tongue-twisters and other puzzles, fencing with sword and staff, archery, gymnastics, carpentry and architecture, logic, chemistry and mineralogy, gardening, training in fighting cocks, partridges and rams, teaching parrots and mynahs to talk, writing in cipher, languages, making artificial flowers, and clay modelling.

It is hardly likely that the 'ganika' did in fact study all the arts of this rather bizarre list, but it shows what was expected of her. If she mastered those arts most suited to her profession a brilliant future awaited her. "A courtesan of a pleasant disposition, beautiful, and otherwise attractive, who has mastered the arts...has the right to a seat of honour among men. She will be honoured by the king and praised by the learned, and all will seek her favours and treat her with consideration."[25] The literature of the Middle Ages fully bears out this statement.

Ideal Women

Sita, the heroine of *Ramayana*, had a number of names, all derivatives. Sita, the principal one of these, came from a Sanskrit root meaning the "furrow left by the plough," in accordance with the Sanskrit grammatic *sutra* (or aphorism) "Sita Langala Padhathi" (*i.e.*, the way the edge of the plough goes is called 'Sita') and is based on a story connected with her origin on earth. Vaidehi, Maithili and Janaki, her other three names, were derived, respectively, from Videha, the name of the country to which she belonged, Mithila, its capital, and Janaka, her foster-father, She was an *avatar* (or incarnation) of Goddess Lakshmi, the spouse of Lord Vishnu.

Sita is one of the noblest of the feminine characters of the *Ramayana*.

Janaka, the King of Videha Desa (modern Dharbhanga changed present form of the original Sanskrit word, Dhanurbhanga District and adjoining territory in Bihar State) was an ideal monarch. His qualities were so pure that he was considered an ascetic among kings and actually used to be referred to very often as Janaka *Maharishi*. He was childless and was worried on that account. His advisers suggested his performing a *Yaga* (or sacrifice) to appease the gods, whereupon, pleased by his devotion and austerities, they were certain to bless him with progeny.

For the performance of a Vedic sacrifice the spot of ground whereupon it was to be performed, had to be carefully selected and ploughed so as to rid it of all extraneous impurities. A certain field was accordingly chosen for the purpose. Normally such preparation of the land through ploughing and the like operations was done by servants. This time, however, King Janaka decided to do all that work himself, so that the gods might be doubly propitiated and pleased.

The news that the King himself was going to plough the field had spread all over the country. Thousands of people were drawn to the site longing to witness the unique phenomenon of the Royal personage at the plough. They all felt, as if by a premonition, that something strange would happen that day. Their expectation was not to be belied. Hardly had the King's plough turned the soil into a few furrows, when much to the astonishment of the gathering and the King himself, the edge of the plough hit a hard substance. On examination it was seen to be box. When it was opened, there was found in it a newly-born baby girl of resplendent beauty.

Saying that the gods had been pleased even before the starting of the sacrifice, the king accepted the baby as his own and gave it to his queen. They named her Sita, because of her having been found in the furrow produced by a plough.

In course of time King Janaka's wife conceived in the normal manner and they had another daughter. This baby was named by them Urmila. Sita and Urmila got on in years and, as days passed by, bloomed into a pair of dazzling beauties.

Among King Janaka's collection of war weapons there was a giant bow which had come into his possession as a present and which had originally belonged to Lord Siva Himself (*i.e.*, Divinity as the destroyer of the Universe). It was hence referred to as the *Siva Dhanus*. People felt that it would be a mighty feat for anyone to lift and string that great weapon. One day when Sita, Urmila and their other companions were playing with a ball, it rolled under that terrible bow and got entangled. No one could extricate it from that position. Sita, however, nonchalantly lifted the bow with her left hand, put it in another position, as though it were just a piece of stick, and released the ball. Janaka had seen this smart performance on the part of the girl from a distance. The thought then occurred to him that he who would wed her and become her partner in life should also be one who could lift and string that bow.

Accordingly, when Sita came of marriageable age, Janaka sent out a proclamation throughout the length and breadth of the land to the effect that a day would be announced for Sita's *Swayamvara* (choice of her husband) when, from among those assembled for the purpose, whoever could lift and string the great *Siva Dhanus* in the armoury of weapons in his palace, would win the hand of the Princess.

The appointed day was soon to arrive. In the meantime, however, an incident had occurred which made that day synchronise with the performance of a sacrifice of victory by King Janaka. When Janaka made his intention widely known that Sita would be given in marriage only to one who could lift and string of the holy bow of Lord Siva. Sudhanva, the King of a neighbouring territory called Sankasyapuri, got annoyed, because he felt that Sita should become his spouse. That King, therefore, invaded Janaks's territory of Videha Desa. Before setting out with his forces to meet the invader, Janaka performed *Puja* (worship) to Lord Siva to propitiate that Divinity and secure His blessings. This was done, he marched with his men and joined issue with the aggressor. In a fierce battle that ensued the invading army was routed and put to flight. Sudhanva himself was killed in the fray and Janaka put his own cousin, Kusadhwaja, on the vacant throne of Sanksayapuri. Then and there King Janaka also renewed his proclamation regarding the test to be applied for the choice of husband for Sita. Simultaneously with this he also announced the performance of sacrifice to celebrate his recent victory in battle. This sacrifice and Sita's *Swayamvara* (choice of her husband) were fixed at about the same time.

All the kings of the various *desas* (countries) into which the continent of India was then divided (traditionally these were fifty-six in number) had, on invitation, gathered in the palace of Janaka in Mithila both to see the sacrifice and to try a hand at the contest for winning Sita's hand in marriage. The *Rakshasa* (or Demon) King of Lanka (the present day Ceylon, now Sri Lanka), Ravana, had also arrived. In a corner of the audience were also present two young lads, who had just reached their teens and who were the two sons of King Dasaratha of Ayodhya, the capital of *Kosala Desa*. These were the Princes Rama and Lakshmana. They had been taken there by the sage Viswamitra to whom they had rendered yeoman service in protecting the latter's sacrifice from the misdeeds of the *Rakshasas* (or Demons) of the forest.

The sacrifice of victory duly completed, King Janaka had the mighty bow of Siva brought before the assembled audience of royal personages and others. Formally announcing to the audience once again his decision regarding Sita as the stake to be won at the ensuring contest. King Janaka invited them to come forward and participate in the test. The very sight of the august weapon terrified most of the assembled kings. They started excusing themselves on some pretext or other and the scene produced a comic interlude. One of them said that he did not wish to invite the wrath of Lord Siva on his head by tampering with that Divine bow. Another backed out saying that the one wife he already had was enough for him and that there would only be trouble if another wife was added to the household. Some of the princes, who managed somehow to muster sufficient courage to make an attempt, quailed on actually approaching the bow. A few who tried to handle the weapon miserably failed, being not even able to lift the bow, not to mention stringing it. Even the great Ravana proved an ignominious failure and ran away in utter shame and discomfiture. King Janaka was getting worried at seeing that there was not one among that vast assembly who could perform the task set before them successfully. Just then, the sage, Viswamitra, asked Janaka's permission to let Rama, the elder of the two Princes from Kosala whom he had brought there, to try a hand, explaining to the King at the same time who they were and in what circumstances they had got themselves associated with the sage. Janaka readily agreed, feeling inwardly elated at the thought that, if the young Prince succeeded and became his son-in-law, nothing could give him greater pleasure than getting thereby united in matrimonial alliance with the great King Dasaratha of the Ikshvaku line.

Young Rama went near the bow, lifted it and not only stringed it but also broke it into two pieces in the attempt. With him it was just veni vidi vici, and that too within the twinkling of an eye. Sita's hand had thus at last been won. There was great natural rejoicing everywhere over the happy event. Even the gods in heaven showered flowers on the young conquering hero.

Sequal to the evil council of Manthara and unbecoming attitude of Kaikayee, Rama was exiled for 14 years. In spite of resistance from Rama, Sita resolved to accompany him. She firmly declared, "To go with you wherever you go—this is my only course." She further assured Rama that she can and she will bear forest life and she will not be a source of trouble at all to him. She shall eat fruits and roots like him and shall not lag behind as they (Rama and Lakshmana) walk. She shall endure the Sun, rain, wind, hunger, etc. without any complaint. Thus, she talked at the height of an ideal of an Indian woman, quite befitting to her royal race and her own sublimed character.

During exile once Sita saw a stag with wondrous beauty having skin shining like gold. Sita being enchanted by unique beauty of the stag requested Rama to catch it for her. Though Rama knew that it was a trick being played by *Rakshasas*, he, on insistence by Sita, had to set out in pursuit of the deer. It was actually Mareech, in the disguise of the deer, who soon changed back to the original form with a shot of Rama's arrow and cried "Ah Lakshmana, Ah Sita." Taking this as Rama's cry Sita forced Lakshmana to set out in search of her husband. Lakshmana obeyed her, but quite unwillingly. Meanwhile Ravana, in the disguise of an ascetic, abducted Sita. On the way Jatayu, an old bird, tried to save Sita; but in vain. The gallant bird could not save Sita and laid his life fighting with mighty Ravana. Ravana carried Sita and kept her in 'Ashoka Vatika'.

Rama,in alliance with Sugreeva, a close friend and devotee, could trace out the whereabouts of Sita. Sampati, beloved brother of Jatayu, informed Angad that he had seen Ravana carrying Sita to Lanka, a city built by Maya, father of Mandodari. Being inspired by Jambuvan, Hanuman approached the coast of Lanka, met Sita in 'Ashoka Vatika' and consoled her conveying the message of Rama. He also gave Rama's signet ring to Sita. Sita was consoled but also pained by the thought that Rama had not forgotten her, but was thinking of her, grieving and searching for her. This shows her love and dedication towards Rama.

Sita was endowed with a practical wisdom in state-craft worth to her royal race. When Hanuman proposed to carry her on his back, she flatly refused the proposal saying: "If you snatch me away stealthily from *Rakshasas* it would be no credit to the valour of my Lord. The honour of the Kshatriya race demands that he should come and fight and vanquish Ravana and redeem me as prize of victory."

After abducting Sita, Ravana adopted various ways to compel Sita to surrender. But she was quite firm and never yielded to him. Sita's joy was beyond words when Ravana was killed by Rama. Sita was taken respectfully to the Rama's camp in a palanquin. Seeing Rama Sita's face beamed with joy, but seeing her Rama was not happy, he spoke, "I have slain my enemy and have recovered you now. I have done my duty as a Kshatriya. But you have lived for a year in a stranger's house. It is not proper that I should take you back now." Thus, Sita had to prove her untainted virtue by throwing herself into a lighted pyre and then coming out of it uninjured. At length Rama accepted Sita. They returned to Ayodhya and ascended the throne. But the suspicions of the subject fell on Sita. They doubted her untainted character. For fear of the people Rama had to send Sita to exile, when she was in family way.

Valmiki received her at Chitrakuta, and there her two sons, Lava and Kusha, were born. Valmiki composed the poem of the Ramayana and taught them to repeat and thus years were passed.

After some years, through Lava and Kusha, Rama got united with Sita before he performed *Ashvamedha* sacrifice. But Sita's tragedy did not end here. When Sita reached Ayodhya, people again started to criticise Rama since their suspicion could not be allayed. Rama could not put up with this embarrassing situation. Seeing the pitiable condition of Rama, the earth, which had given birth to Sita, yawned and received its long suffering child.

Some scholars take Sita as a mythological feature; but for millions of Hindu Sita is a real human character, a pattern of female virtue and female self-abnegation. She is regarded as the noblest creation of human imagination. Sita's gentleness, virtues, uncomplaining and unconditional devotion and unconquerable love for her Lord, were more than human, her sufferings and woes too were more than usually fall to the lot of woman. Even to this day for Hindu woman, Sita is a model of character, she would like to emulate and to strive after. Thus, Sita was one of the shinning gems amongst the Princess of Ancient India.

Tara, wife of Baali, was a wise and brave lady. She had foresight regarding Rama's divinity and saw Vishnu in him. That is why she tried her best to restrain Baali from taking dual with Sugreeva for second time. Her council to Baali on this occasion was as following:

> "I am afraid there is a deep game. Your brother was defeated and disgraced and ran for dear life and concealed himself for safety. Now he has returned and raises his noise. Your brother is not such a fool as to challenge you again so soon after the punishment you inflicted on him unless he was assured of help and protection from an invincible ally of tried prowess. Did you not observe that his very roar of challenge had a new note of confidence in it? I shall tell you what I heard from Angada who had it from our scouts who range the forests. Two Princes of unrivalled valour, Rama and Lakshmana, have come from Ayodhya and Sugreeva has secured the promise of their assistance. After all, my lord, your brother is virtuous and brave. Why should you hate him? Who in the world is closer to us than he? He will be your devoted servant and strong ally. It is best to forget the past and make it up with Sugreeva. My dear Lord, listen to my words."

This is an indicative of her virtue and foresightedness. But Baali did not give any heed to her advice. He lost this reason because of excessive wrath and fell in the trap of death. At length, he was killed by Rama. After the death of the King (Baali) there was panic and chaos in Kishkindha. Tara, seeing all this, set aside her own lamentation and put courage in her husband's subjects saying "Till this day you walked before the King to battle! Why then do you flee in fear now. There is no danger for you. Rama killed Baali only to make Sugreeva King. Your lives are in no danger; you will only have a different ruler; that is all. You need not fly or fear." This shows her wit and presence of mind. She was a queen of a hero in real sense. When Rama approached to console her, she said to Rama without any sign of malice on her face—"With the weapon with which, O Warrior, you killed my husband, kill me too and enable me to join him. Even in heaven, he will not be happy without me. Do not fear that it would be a sin. It will be a meritorious act to unite husband and wife. This will cleanse your sin, your treacherous slaying of my husband.

Kaikeyee was the youngest queen of Dasharatha and mother of Bharata. Basically she was very noble and kindhearted lady. She was well-versed in theoretical knowledge of warcraft. Once Dasharatha, on Indra's request, went to his help when the latter waged war against powerful demon-king Shambara. In battle when Dasharatha got wounded and lose consciousness she drove his chariot skilfully out of battlefield, carefully removed the darts from his body and revived him. Thus, saving the life of her husband she proved her worth as a queen of gallant Dasharatha. She loved Bharata; but she equally loved Rama and other sons of Kaushalya and Sumitra.

When Manthara, her pet maid-servant, informed her about coronation of Rama, she was overwhelmed with joy,like the rest of the household. She aptly awarded also Manthara for communicating such a good news. Manthara went on poisoning her mind but she did not allow her advances. She said "Manthara, have you not known and rejoiced in Rama's truthfulness, right conduct and humility? He is elder prince and he gets kingdom. Bharata will get it one day after. What is wrong with all this? Here Manthara caught the point to trap her net. Very crookedly she pointed out that after Rama's succession there will be no chance for Bharata because eldest son succeeds eldest son and not the younger brother as per the rule of succession. She also said that Rama's succession may cause a danger to Bharata's life. Now fear entered in the mind of Kaikeyee. She used for two fatal boons—coronation of Bharata instead of Rama and 14 years' exile of Rama. Rama, in order to keep the promise of his father and keep intact the glory of *Raghukula*, accepted both the boons in the befitting manner without showing any resistance or sign of disappointment. But these boons proved to be very fatal for the King Dasharatha. He could not bear the shock of the separation of his most beloved son, Rama. Soon after his departure alongwith Lakshmana and Sita, to the forest, Dasharatha breathed his last.

When Bharata came to know the crookedness and treachery of her mother he totally disapproved her course of action and showed utter hatred to his mother. Seeing the real face of Bharata Kaikeyee also repented upon her meanness. She also accompanied Bharata to the forest-side to get back Rama; but of on avail. Ultimately Bharata came back and ruled Ayodhya on behalf of Rama. Being at Nandigram he led a life of an ascetic and carried out all royal business with excellent sense of detachment.

Savari, disciple of the sage Matanga, living in a hermitage situated on the bank of Pampa lake. After the death of her Guru Matanga, Savari waited in the hermitage being blessed by him with the boon that she will be able to have *darshan* of Rama over there only. She welcomed them (Rama, Lakshmana and Sita) and offered water to wash their feet. She then presented the berry fruits, which she had gathered specially for them.

She was a staunch devotee of Rama. She told him that she wished to depart from that life long ago; but the *Rishis* told her that she was destined to have attained the Supreme bliss she kindled a fire and, entering into it, ascended to heaven.

When Vanaras set out in search of Sita, in a secluded cave they saw an aged ascetic lady (*Sanyasini*) practising penances. She was Swayamprabha, a close friend of Hema, a daughter of Vishwakarma who was an architect divine. Being inducted by Lord Vishnu Swayamprabha was practising severe penances for *darshana* of Rama. At length her desire was fulfilled and she was blessed by Rama and instructed to go to *Badarikashram*, where being engaged in penances she attained salvation. During her stay in the cave she helped Vanaras to reach sea-shore and further their great mission.

Polyandry and Polygamy

Polyandry means to have more than one husband and polygamy means to have more than one wife. Both of these customs have been prevailing in Hindu society from very ancient time. In the *Mahabharata*, great epic of India, we find a single example of Draupadi, which was not well-received by the then society and thus subject to criticism. Opposing this custom Drupada, father of Draupadi says: In scriptures, of course, we have heard of many wives of a king, but there is no provision of many husbands of one wife. Even the *Vedas* do not enjoin for this and it is against the tradition and convention. O Yudhishthir! a religious man like you should not indulge in such an unrighteous act."[26] Dhrishtdyumna, son of Drupada, had also objected to it.[27] On this Yudhishthir put-forth the following arguments:

1. When Pandavas were in exile of 12 years, once all the five Pandavas alongwith Draupadi came to the house and while knocking the door one of them said, "Mother, what a nice thing we have brought! Without knowing about the reality of the thing Kunti said, "All of you enjoy it together." Yudhishthir wanted that the words of his mother (Kunti) should not be proved to be false. Hence they shared Draupadi.
2. Keeping in view the great attraction of the Pandavas Yudhishthir thought such marriage necessary.
3. Thirdly, Yudhishthir said to Drupada, "The very nature of religion is very mysterious. We cannot understand it. Whatever our ancestors have done, we are doing the same. In this context he narrated the story of one *Kutila Gautami*, who got married with seven sages. Thus Yudhishthir concluded that polyandry was not unrighteous at all.[28]

Some of the law-givers have clearly opposed the custom of polyandry. The *Tantravartika* goes to the extent of denying it, asking us to take it only figuratively as five persons marrying one Rajyalakshmi or royal glory. The custom prevailed among the Kshatriya tribes. Tantrika writers, among others, protested against it. According to Dr. Radhakrishnan, "Even in Malabar communities, where it has survived, it is passing out of fashion."[29]

According to Dr. D.N. Mazumdar,

> "Girls in Jaunsar-Bawar enjoy an inordinate latitude in their sexual preferences. As soon as they marry, they are regarded as people's concern, that of their husbands' family, and the parents do not like to meddle in the affairs of their married daughters, nor are they anxious to exercise their parental rights. The parents can secure the services of their married daughters by conforming to a *laissez faire* or neutral attitude to them and thus a kind of freedom has become

the right of *dhyantis* (daughters) of Jaunsar-Bawar. The misuse to which such neutral relations or indifference can be put has been demonstrated to the parents by their daughters, particularly in the lower caste families, but there has not been any searching of the heart on this count. Parents defend their attitude by mentioning the life of sweat and toil that await a woman in her husband's house, and consider it a duty to see that she gets a sweet deal at her parents' house. In some cases, such relations in the parents' house have secured loyalty of daughters to the latter, and several women are known to have remained with their parents for the major period of their life, occasionally visiting the husbands' house."[30]

As a matter of fact, monogamy has been the ideal and there is no double standard of morality. The examples of Shiva and Parvati, Rama and Sita, Nala and Damayanti, Satyavan and Savitri were impressed on the minds of the Indian people. As in other early societies, polygamy was the privilege of princes and noblemen. Common people were ordinarily monogamous. But the *Shastras* allow a husband to contract a second marriage with the consent of his wife. It is justified also, where the first wife is found to be imbecile or suffering from an incurable disease, or barren or adulterous. Though polygamy is becoming rarer in Hindu society, it is still practised.

The unfairness to women in Manu comes out when he requires a good wife to adore a bad husband.[31] This is a sort of slavery to the husband. By such exaggerated teaching he attempts to extol the duty of devotion to the husband. Of course, husbands who are unfaithful to their wives come in for severe censure. Apastamba requires them to wear donkey's skin and beg for food. The practice has, however, been unkind to women. There is also a difference in the treatment of widowers and widows. Men obtain permission to marry after the wife dies by the device that they cannot discharge their religious duties except by marrying a second time, though the presence of the wife is not indispensable for the performance of religious duties. The *Aitareya Brahmana* states that a widower can continue his Vedic sacrifices, even if he has no wife.

Thus, we see that in spite of fixed social hierarchy social and ethical honour was enjoyed by women-folk of ancient India. About civic rights of women Shri Aurobindo has aptly remarked:

"It may be noted too that in Law and Theory atleast women in ancient India, contrary to the sentiment of other peoples, were not denied civic rights, although in practice this equality was rendered nugatory for all but a few by their social subordination to the male and their domestic preoccupation, instances have not yet survived in the existing records of women figuring, not only as queens and administrators and even in the battlefield, a common enough incident in Indian history, but as elected representatives on civic bodies."[32]

REFERENCES

1. Sri Aurobindo and Mother, *On Women*, p. 21.
2. R. Linton, *The Study of Man*, New York, 1936.
3. अमोऽहमस्मि सा त्वं, सामाहम्
   अरस्यृक् त्वं, द्यौरहं पृथिवी त्वं
   ताविह सं भवाव, प्रजामा जनयावहै।

   —*Atharva* 14.2.71

   Compare—
   यो भर्ता वासितातुष्टो भर्तुस्तुष्टा च वासिता।
   यस्मिन्नैव कुले सर्व कल्याणं तत्र वर्तते।।

   —*Mahabharata* 13.122.17

   दम्पत्योः समशीलत्वं धर्मः स्याद्गृहमेधिनः।

   —*Mahabharata* 13.141.43
4. अहो अर्णः सरस्वती, प्रचेतयति केतुना।
   धियो विश्वा वि राजति।।

   —*Rigveda* 1.3.12

   पाव्का नः सरस्वती वाजेभिर्वाजिनीवती।
   यज्ञं वष्दु धियावसुः।।

   —*Rigveda* 1.3.10.
5. Sri Aurobindo and the Mother, *On Women*, p. 15.
6. न मानुषी राक्षसस्य भार्या भवितुमर्हति।
   कामं खादत मां सर्वा न करिष्यामि वो वचः।।
   दीनो वा राज्यहीनो वा यो मे भर्ता स मे गुरूः।
   तं नित्यमनुरक्तास्मि यथा सुर्य सुवर्चला।।

   —*Ramayana*
7. Quoted in "Subramania Bharti" compiled by Prema Nand Kumar, p. 122.
8. Dr. A.S. Altekar, *Position of Women in Ancient India*, p. 10.
9. स्वस्ति तेऽस्त्यन्तरिक्षेभ्यश्च पार्थिवेभ्यश्च पुत्रक।
   दिवेभ्यश्च भूतेभ्यस्तथा तोयचराश्च ये।।

   —*Mahabharata*, Aranyak 292.10.14
10. या दम्पती मुमनसा सुनुत आच धावतः।
    देवाःसो नित्ययाडशिरा।।

    —*Rigveda* 8.31.51
11. पुराकल्पे तु नारीणां भैज्जीबन्धनमिष्यते।
    अध्यापनं च वेदानां सावित्रीवाचनं तथा।।

    —*Nirnay Sindhu*

12. अत्र सिद्धा शिवा नाम ब्राह्मणी वेदपारगा।
अधीत्य सकलान् वेदान लेभेऽसन्देहमक्षयम्।।
—*Mbh., Udyog.* 190.8
13. *Mahabharata*, Shalya Parvan, 54.6.
14. प्रधानो नाम राजर्षिर्व्यक्त ते श्रोत्रमागतः।
कुले तस्य समुत्पन्नां सुलभां नाम विद्धि माम्।।
साहं तस्य कुले जाता भर्तर्यसति मद्विधे।
विनीता मोक्षधर्मेषु चराम्येका मुनिव्रतम्।।
—*Shanti Parvan* 320.82
("I am Sulbha, born in the noble family of the king named Pradhan. Since I could not get a suitable match, I learnt the *Vedas* and other sacred scriptures from learned scholars and now I follow *Moksha* and other sacred vows.")
15. *Aranyak*, 33.57.
16. जज्ञातेऽर्थविदावुभौ।
—*Adi Parvan* 57.94
17. स वसतस्तत्रोपाध्यायस्त्रीभिराहूयोक्तः।
उपाध्यायिनी ते ऋतुमती। उपाध्यायश्च प्रोषितः।।
—*Adi Parvan* 3.89
18. *Aranyak* 289.20.
19. *Adi*, 253.6.
20. *Virat*, 2.54.
21. *Aranyak* 122.32.
22. *Ashramvasik* 44.55.
23. *Adi.*, 68.40-44.
24. *Udyog*, 30.6.
25. *Kam Sutra* 1.3.
26. एकस्य बह्व्यो विपिता महिष्यः कुरूनन्दन।
नैकस्या बहवः पुंसो विधीयन्ते कदाचन।।
लोकवेदविरुद्धं त्वं नाधर्मं धार्मिकः शुचिः।
कतुमर्हसि कौन्तेय कस्मात्ते बुद्धिरीदृशी।।
—*Mahabharata, Adi Parvan* 187.26-27
27. *Ibid.*, 188.10-12.
28. सूक्ष्मो धर्मो महाराज नास्य विद्मो वयं गतिम्।
पूर्वेषामानुपूर्व्येण यातं वर्त्मानुयामहे।।
—*Adi Parvan*, 187.19
(Yudhishthir told Drupad, father of Draupadi: "O great King! the contents of the religion are full of secrets. We do not know it. We are doing nothing anew. We are just following the path paved by the fore-runners.)
29. Dr. S. Radhakrishnan, *Religion and Society*, p. 174.
30. D.N. Mazumdar, *Races and Cultures of India*, p. 197.
31. *Manu Smriti*, V.154.
32. Sri Aurobindo, *The Foundations of Indian Culture* (VII impression,1992). pp. 348-49.

4

SOCIO-CULTURAL STATUS
Through the Ages

II

CUSTOMS AND PROBLEMS

In the Ancient Indian literature we find very contradictory statements. On the one hand great concerns have been showed towards honour, safety and security of women. Manu, a noted law-giver of ancient India, goes on saving: "Gods enjoy that place where women are worshipped."[1] The *Mahabharata* enjoins that "A husband, who becomes unfaithful to wife commits a sin for which there is no adequate penance."[2] Such statements reveal that in all climes and times men have laid down a much higher standard of sexual morality for women than what they were themselves prepared to accept.

Varahmihir, the author of the *Brihata Samhita* observes:

> There are no greater jewels created by God than the jewel that is woman, that is capable of giving delight to man by sight, by hearing, by speech . . . Women are superior to men in their capacity for virtue, men are pure in their feet, the cow on her back, the goat and the dog in the mouth, but women are pure in the whole body. Women are incomparably pure, they are never defiled . . . Man's sex desire is not abated even when he is hundred years old . . . whereas in women it is controlled. Man is born of woman, O ungrateful ones slander women suffers to whom you owe your very existence, how can you ever be happy?"[3]

In conformity with high tradition of nice ideas about women Dr. A.S. Altekar has rightly remarked:

> Hindu society has sought to show its concern for the woman in a

variety of ways. On crowded streets way was to be made for her. If she was in difficulties in her journey, it was the duty of every cultured person to help her in overcoming them. She was to be exempted from the ferry tax. If she had no proper guardians, the state was to look after her interest and property. To accept a bride-price was a great sin. The marriage expenses of a daughter were a charge on her father's property, and brothers were expected to meet them, even if there were no ancestral assets. For the same offence law courts were usually to impose a lighter punishment upon women than upon men (*Arthashastra*, iv, 12). Merit was to be always honoured, whether it was found in men or women.[4]

The above statements undoubtedly express fine and chivalrous ideas about the women. On the other hand, there are number of passages decrying women. To quote a few:

1. *Rigveda* declares that "women are fickle-minded."[5] Of course this is the statement of a disappointed husband (Pururva) whose beloved (Urvashi) has left him.
2. Women are falsehood incarnate.[6] This has been said in the context of women having shady characters.
3. In *Ramayana* Lakshman observes that women are cruel and malicious by nature.[7] This was said when Sita rebuked him quite unjustly.
4. In *Ramayana* itself Kaikeyee has been said as wicked and selfish (II.12.99) because of her unbecoming gestures at the nick of the time when the eldest son Rama was going to be enthroned very justfully and as per the tradition.
5. In the great epic, *Ramacharitamanas*, the *Bible* of the Hindi speaking Hindus, in one context the author and saint-poet Tulsidas has compared with an animal, who understand the language of beating only.[8]

The contexts clearly show that many of the passages cited above, where women have been decried, merely the views of men in throes of bitter disappointment. According to Altekar "The exigencies of the situation are often responsible for such opinions and they ought not to be taken at their face-value." But with the passage of time, particularly in later medieval period society began to change its attitudes towards women. Various ascetic schools also became hostile owing to several socio-cultural reasons.

The discriminate attitude towards women can be well traced from *Vedic* times, though the scriptures have laid down that the religious duties should be performed only in association with wife. Varahmihir, referring to the cases of misogamy, has produced a critical and searching analysis. Thus, defending the fair-sex he says:

> "All the defects that have been attributed to women exist in men as well. Women, however, try to remove them, while men are supremely indifferent in the matter. Marriage vows are equally binding on the couple. Men treat them lightly, while women act up to them. Who suffers more from the sex-urge, men who marry even in their old age or women who lead a chaste life, even if widowed in the prime of their youth? Men, no doubt, go on talking of their love to their wives while they are alive, but contact second marriages soon after their death; women, on the other hand, feel grateful to their husbands and decide to follow them on funeral pyre, urged by the promptings of their conjugal love. Who then is more sincere in his love man or woman? For men to say that women are fickle, and faithless is the height of imprudence and ingratitude; it reminds one of the audacity of clever theives who first send away their loot and then challenge innocent persons demanding from them the stolen articles."[9]

Thus, we see that in the male-dominated society women have been becoming the victims of numerous social hazards and evils from the time immemorial. The violent acts against women—rapes, assaults, battering, incest, etc. that we read in newspapers project just one aspect of the vulnerability of women. Unfortunate and unimaginable incidents hitting majority of Indian women remains unreported. Many a woman out of sheer fright of being turned out of the husband's house bears the gross injustice inflicted and sheds silent tears as a mark of silent protest.

During modern period remarkable changes have been made in the country; but unfortunately less or no changes have come to majority of our women. The age-old attitude towards women still prevails considering them to be the second class citizens with no rights of their own. Women's social isolation and marginalisation from decision-making process, limited employment opportunities, inequality of wages, lack of access to reduction and above all foeticide projects the disability suffered by Indian women. The gamut of phenomena nothing but reveal the most isolation from their legitimate rights.

We may confess it or not; but it is felt that besides many objects and ideas, plannings and programmes, for liberation of women what needed most is the change in the attitude of all the persons concerned with the theme. We have to part with the age-old feminist idea and assess their abilities and calibre in the realistic sense. Dr. R.P. Sharma has rightly observed:

> "A genuine programme of women's liberation will have to break-down the fictionalized images of feminity. Those fighting for women's rights to freedom and equality will have to define and establish feminity afresh. They will have to create and project the correct image of the authentic women biased on scientific evidence and honest insight. No false theory of women's nature, no ideology of the so called proper roles of women, no artificial gender norms must be allowed to characterize and determine the new woman. The female has to develop into the human. Every woman must be assured of equality of education, opportunity, income and status on a par with a respectable man."[10]

The present society of ours is facing many burning problems like child marriage, dowry deaths, problems of unwed mothers, problems of widows, and so on. In spite of the fact that the Acts like Hindu Succession Act, 1956; Sati Prevention Act, 1929; Dowry Prohibition Act, 1961; etc. are passed; but in fact these Acts have little or no effect in reality. Here we will discuss some of such problems of women.

Unwed Mothers

Contraceptions, conceptions and abortions annually humiliate, hurt or kill hundreds of thousands of women in our country, a vast majority of whom are Hindus. Immaterial it is whether such deeds or misdeeds are marital or extra-marital, legal or illegal. Do educated Hindu males realise that abortions and contraceptions by far outnumber live births? Do they realise that incidents like contraceptions, abortions and live births are anti-women, even though they are carried out by men and for women? Why do such incidents take place at all? Is there any reason to identify contraceptions and abortions with freedom for women? Does the question 'freedom for what?' ever prick the conscience of men who persuade or force women to avoid or to get rid of unwanted conceptions?

Conceptions outside marriage may be (or often are) horrifying experiences for the victims of male sexuality. Stories of children born out of wedlock are legion in Hindu history and yet the unwed mother remains an offence to public opinion. Children born out of non-marital unions live and grow to be baffling anomalies and shameful reminders to the custodians of marital sanctity, apart from turning the helpless mothers into a community of outcasts. Even within marriage a conception or a child birth acquires various implications for women. It may be for one a cherishable experience, an act of self-fulfilment; for another it may be an act of temporary inconvenience or even a symbol of pollution, while for the third it may be a permanent handicap.

As an experience, maternity is unique to woman and as such it is only proper that in matters like conception, contraception and abortion the woman has thelast word. Men cannot and must not impose on women their notions of maternity or femininity. It is, therefore, obligatory for a society to ensure that there is no coercion of a women into a sex act so that there is no coercion later on for contraception or abortion. Any sex act which is not based on the emotional involvement of the women, whether wife or non-wife, must be declared an incidence of rape by law. Husbands, Hindu husbands in particular, should be compelled to realise that any sexual act without the consent of the wife is an act of rape and therefore, punishable under the law.

Not many years ago, a Japanese District Court sentenced a twenty-six year old husband to two years' imprisonment on the charge of raping his wife (*Hindu* 18 Dec., 1986). If Hindu husbands were to be brought to court on charges of marital rape, millions of them would find themselves behind the bars almost every day of the year. The sexual exploitation of the wife by the husband is so common in our society that one does not need to invoke statistics to prove that husbands are guilty of numerous rapes. Havelock Ellis rightly holds that many more rapes are committed within marriage than outside (of Beauvoir 1953: 162). A Hindu writer says that husbands in general tend to use their wives just as sex objects with no regard to their mood or health (of Kapor 1974: 34-35). Unless men develop a healthier attitude to heterosexual relationships and recognise women's autonomy in matters like maternity, incidents like unwanted conceptions, contraceptions and abortions will continue to plague the generality of women.

Child Marriage

The ancient Hindu institution of what is known as 'child marriage' points to the age-old masculinist philosophy of exploiting and limiting women on all levels. Most authorities on ancient India agree that the ideal age of marriage for girls in those days varied from seven to ten years (Basham 1967: 167, Shastri 1969: 87-88 & Chakladar 1976: 125-

126). The general view in ancient times was that the ideal marriage was a marriage in which the bride was one-third of the age of the groom—so that a man of twenty-four could marry a girl of eight and a man of thirty could marry a girl of ten. A verse in the *Mahabharata* explicitly states: "A thirty year old man should marry a girl of ten years called *Nagnika*. Or, a twenty-one year old man should get a girl of seven years" (Banerji 1976: 12:29). The *Vishnu Purana* recommends: "One should marry a girl whose age is one-third of one's own" (cited in Chakladar 1976: 124). Vatsayana suggests that the bride should be three to seven years younger than the groom but he also insists that the bride must be a *Nagnika* (*ibid*., pp. 125-26). The law books warn that if a father does not give his daughter in marriage before her first menstruation, he incurs a sin worse than murder (Basham 1967: 167). Manu's code, for example, lays down that a father "who gives in marriage a girl of eight goes to heaven, the giver of a girl of nine to *Vaikuntha*; one who gives his daughter in marriage before she obtains the age of ten attains the heaven of Brahma. But the father of a girl married after puberty goes to hell" (Thomas 1964: 225). One of the most notorious statements in favour of child-marriage occurs in the *Bhagavata Purana:* "an unmarried girl who menstruates, living in her father's or mother's house, should be regarded as a degraded woman; a man commits no sin by carrying her away from the custody of her guardian" (Baig 1976: 118).

Shakuntala Rao Shastri is not correct in her assertion that child-wives are mentioned for the first time in the *Chhandogya Upanishada*. Perhaps with the single exception of widow-burning (*sati*), almost all Hindu customs, practices and views may be traced back to the *Vedas*. Of course, the *Vedas* do not insist on child marriage as the only form of marriage for girls; there are mentioned adult wives as well. It is probable that Vedic Aryans recommended child marriage for girls even though they tolerated adult marriage. *Ghosha* is described as an adult-wife While *Romasha* is spoken of as a child-wife in the *Rig Veda* itself (Chakladar 1976: 126). It is, however, interesting to note that child-husbands, even boy-husbands, are not mentioned in ancient Hindu texts. The hero of the *Ramayana* may be solitary example of a boy-husband. Ravana meets Sita to abduct her but he engages her in a pleasant conversation by introducing himself as a mendicant and in the hope that he might as well win her over. It is during this conversation that Sita informs him that at the time of her marriage she was only six years of age while Rama was just thirteen (III: IXX, p. 390).

The rigidity of the scriptural demand that girls must be married at the earliest possible age, in any case before the first menstruation, should be viewed as a concrete example of what might be called *sadistic paedophilia.* We may bear in mind that while the marriage age prescribed for girls varies from seven to ten, that for men varies from twenty-one to thirty. Even the latest Marriage Act prescribes twenty-one as the age for men to marry. As regards men, the ancient law makers were so generous and forward-looking. They were obnoxious only with regard to women, whether it was marriage or maternity.

The doctrinisation of such disparity between Hindu males and females in respect of their desirable age for marriage finds its parallels also in Greece. The Athenian in Plato's Laws declares that the marriage age for girls "shall be sixteen to twenty years and for a man from thirty to thirty-five years" (p. 785). The main reason for prescribing an earlier age for women than for men to marry was the same as that among ancient Hindus. The necessity that the bride be "a virgin, coupled with the ancient belief that the young girls were lustful, made early marriage (in Greece) desirable" (Pomeroy 1975: 64). As for the Hindus, Basham observes: "A woman was thought to be naturally libidinous; an unmarried girl attaining puberty would proceed to find a lover, however, strictly her parents guarded her" (1967: 168). Imaginary apprehensions like these motivated the custodians of communal morality to make laws that could catch girls young so that they could not defile the family or defame the community. Child marriage was, therefore, made compulsory for all girls. Such were the views of daughters and sisters held by their noble and enlightened guardians in the golden age of Hindu civilisation.

Pointing to the inevitable consequences of child marriage, a scholar has this to say: "Condemned to domestic drudgery, ignorance and premature motherhood, developing in most cases, physical infirmities or deformities, the married woman in respectable households was not fit company for a normal healthy man, and this was in no small measure responsible for the extraordinary high position prostitutes gain in later India and for the hold they obtained even in temples and places of pilgrimages" (Thomas 1964: 228). Also, as frequent pregnancies and child births rendered these young women, sick, ugly and uncouth, men hated and tortured their wives to spit out the deeprooted frustrations of their conjugal hopes. The modern Hindu starts gasping for breath when he finds such condemned, helpless and hopeless women glorified both in holy texts and literary masterpieces.

Centuries have come and gone but we are still stayput with our obsolete Law Books. As we Hindus have always steadfastly held on to our 'glorious' past, we have religiously refused to change with the times. The world goes ahead, but we refuse to move forward because, by heredity and nature, we are a backward-looking crab like people. Because we always look back to our illustrious ancestors to illumine our minds and direct our conduct about everything in life, we fail to criticise our heritage. We are probably the only community on earth who can fish out millions and millions from our depleted bank accounts and near-empty purses to watch on portable black-and-white TV sets the antique tales of men and monkeys as picturised. It is no wonder, therefore, that we still have hundreds of millions of childwives and child mothers in our midst. The Sharda Act of 1929 had decreed that girls before sixteen could not be married off without their parents risking the rigorous of the law and yet a study conducted by Lucknow University in 1971 revealed that in Uttar Pradesh alone 52 per cent of girls were married by the age of fifteen (Mehta 1970: 20 and Sahai 1985: XVII). The Marriage Act of 1978 allows a girl to be married only when she is eighteen years of age but a study conducted by the Family Planning Foundation 1987 showed that 33 per cent girls in Orissa, 38 per cent girls in Uttar Pradesh, 48 per cent in Karnataka and 58 per cent girls in Madhya Pradesh had become married mothers before they were eighteen years of age. These under eighteen mothers raised the national average of infant mortality rate in India to 105 a thousand, thereby making it one of the highest in the world (*Indian Express*, 28 Dec., 1987).

Plight of Widows

Close on the heels of the notorious custom of child-marriage comes the heinous Hindu practice of widow-burning (*sati*). In a way, widow-burning and child-marriage are the two sides of the same coin. Motivated by the view of femininity, widow-burning has to be analysed in terms of the same scale of values as child-marriage. A girl is to be bound in early childhood to an adult male as her husband, otherwise she will give up her originity and defile the family. Likewise, a widow must be disposed of alongwith her dead husband as she has already lost her virginity. As a wife, a woman has to surrender her virginity only to her husband and, having done that, she must remain totally tied down to him for ever, that is, both here and hereafter. Only the husband is authorised by Law Books to monopolise his wife's body and soul. A woman not monopolised thus by her husband is impure and sinful. Any Hindu female who has extra-marital sex relations, whether by choice or under compulsion, is a public woman. No other system on earth maintains such a rigid separation between the wife and the prostitute as orthodox Hinduism does. A woman, in its view, is either 'private' or 'public' property. There is no third category. Every woman has to be either a wife or a prostitute for life; the system does not visualise spinsterhood as a possible choice for a woman. But even in the binary division between private and public roles, a woman does not have any option. Whether a girl is going to be a wife or a prostitute is decreed by the male majority. Once decreed to be a wife, a woman must live for the husband and die with the husband because her survival after the husband's death is fraught with hazardous implications. This, in brief, seems to be the crux of the Hindu rationale for burning the dead man's wife on his pyre.

Many ancient people like the Chaldees, Celts, Gauls, Goths, Scythians, Slavs and Thracians buried or burnt a man's widows, slaves, hearses and other cherished possessions with his corpse in order that he might have all that he loved and needed, in the other world (Basham 1967: 188, Sengupta 1974: 97 & Baig 1976: 19).

It is possible that ancient Hindus borrowed this custom from some of these peoples. But there is a basic difference between Hindu widow-burning on the one hand and widow-burning in these peoples on the other. Widow-burning (*Sati*) for most of them was part of their pre-history whereas for Hindus it was part of their post-Vedic history. Vedic Hindus probably did not kill their widows. Then the widow used to be persuaded to marry her husband's younger brother or cousin. This custom was known as 'levirate marriage' (De 1969: 4-5). It was a common practice that the dead man's younger brother or cousin came to his bereaved widow and proposed: "Rise woman and come to the world of living beings. Come, this man near whom thou sleepiest is lifeless, thou has enjoyed the state of being the wife of thy husband, the suitor who took thee by the hand. Come, thou hast now entered upon the wifehood of this the Lord who takes thy hand to be the husband and woos thee" (Shastri 1969: 20-21). Levirate marriage remained in vogue for quite sometime. The *Arthashastra* mentions widow-marriage as prevalent among various castes (Thomas 1964: 73-74). That widows were allowed to survive is evident from the *Kamasutra*, although by this time they have ceased to enjoy the privilege of remarriage. Widow-burning (*Sati*) may have started sometime in the fourth century BC. The earliest datable notice of the immolation of widows occurs in "Greek accounts of Alexander's invasion" (Basham 1967: 189). Together with child-marriage, it appears to have been firmly established on a large scale during the post *Smriti* period. The prohibition of widow-marriage by the Sacred Law was logically followed up by the caste Hindu immolation of widows. Manu represents the consensus of his contemporaries when he declares: "Nowhere is a second husband permitted to respectable women" (V: 162). He clearly lays down that a man may marry after the death of his wife but a wife can never think of another man after the death of her husband (V: 157 & 168).His advice to a surviving widow is: "Until her death let her be patient (of her hardship), self-controlled, and chaste, and strive to fulfil that most excellent duty which (is prescribed) for wives who have one husband only" (V: 158).

According to the Law Books, the highest religious duty of a wife was to see in her husband, alive or dead, her God and her ultimate salvation. Widow-burning followed as a natural corollary of such prescriptions, and in course of time reached menacing proportions. A thirteenth century inscriptions, for instance, reads: "those who do not bind her (*i.e.*, the widow) and throw her into the fire and kill her would get the sin of prostituting their own wives" (Thomas 1964: 235). Six centuries later, Raja Ram Mohun Roy and his associated claimed in their representation against widow-burning that they had been eyewitnesses to widows having been "forced upon the pile, and they are bound with ropes and pressed with green bamboos, were kept until consumed by the flames" and that those who tried to run away from the flames were "carried back by their relations and burnt to death" (*Ibid.*, pp. 295-96). The worst part of this atrocious ritual was that the widow's son (or nearest kin in the absence of son) had to set fire to his living mother tied to his dead father on the funeral pyre (Sengupta 1974: 70).

Historically speaking, the custom of widow-burning appears to have been practised on a selective basis for a fairly long time from Vyasa to Vatsyayana. The *Mahabharata*, for example, shows that some widows were immolated and some were not. Madri was immolated on Pandu's funeral pyre but Kunti was not. Devaki, Bhadra, Rohini and Madira were burnt with Vasudeva's corpse but his other wives were not. Similarly, Rukmini and seven other queens of Krishna were consigned to the flames alongwith their dead husband (Krishna) but Satyabhama and the other queens were not (Lal 1980: 84, 352-53 & 385). As time drew on, immolation of widows became increasingly rigid and regular. It was, however, during the Perso-Arabic period that it acquired the status of a ritual with all the sanctions of the hoary tradition. To prevent her escape from the raging flames, the widow was usually surrounded by men armed with sticks who goaded her to her destination by physical force. Describing his decision to abolish *sati* by law, William Bentick wrote: "To consent to the consignment, year after year, of husbands of innocent victims to a cruel and untimely death, when the power exists of preventing it, is a predicament which no conscientious man can contemplate without horror . . . I should be guilty of little sort of the crime of multiplied murder if I could hesitate in the performance of this solemn obligation" (Thomas 1964: 263). *Sati* was not totally abolished immediately after Lord Bentick's Edict, proclaimed on 5 December 1829. Writing in 1911, Edward Thomson points out: "The number of women burned alive at his funeral had in many states been the criterion of a Prince's success in life. Eighty-four women died with Raja Budh Singh of Bundi, sixty-four with Raja Ajit Singh of Jodhpur, and numbers in the neighbourhood of twenty were usual" (Baig 1976: 20).

To think about *sati* is to be filled with horror and shame, astonishment and indignation. *Sati* was, in most cases, the cold blooded and brutal public murder of a lone and helpless widow by the males of the family and locality. All religious or doctrinal rationalisations of this custom are hideous and barbaric. Most Hindu texts contain motivated interpolations and distortions but no distortion is so disastrous and demoralising as the one which converts a marriage ritual into a death warrant. The *Rig Vedic* instructions for the widow originally read: "Let the woman advance to the altar first" (*i.e., Arohantu janayo yonim agre*). This line refers to the *Vedic* custom in accordance with which the widow had to ascend the funeral pyre of her husband only to be led away by his younger brother or cousin for her marriage with him. The post-Vedic Brahmanas replaced the last but one letter of the line (*i.e*., 'r' with 'n' so that 'agre' became 'agne') and it read: "Let the woman advance to the womb of fire" (*i.e., Arohantu janayo yonim agne* of. Mangalwadi 1987). The replacement of 'r' with 'n' turned 'to the altar' into 'to the fire' which converted 'widow-marriage' into 'widow-burning'. Max Mueller rightly describes this vicious replacement as "the most flagrant instance of what can be done by an unscrupulous priesthood" (*ibid.*).

It was a rare moment in Hindu history that a crusader like Raja Ram Mohun Roy vowed to fight against this most sinful custom. Started in 1818, his campaign achieved historic success on 5 December 1829 when Lord Bentick passed his Edict banning widow-burning (*Sati*) throughout British India. By 1862 *sati* was banned throughout India, including the native states. In spite of this, stray incidents of widow burning continued to occur from time to time. Roop Kanwar's consignment to flame on 4 September 1987 at Deorala in Rajasthan is the most recent public incidence of widow-burning. In spite of incidents like these and a great deal of obscurantism around (*Indian Express*,

13 April 1988), it would not be wrong to say that widow-burning stopped (almost totally) by 1862 itself.

Once a widow-burning was abolished, the number of widows suddenly shot up. In a few decades the population of widows, including a large number of child-widows, ran into millions. The Widow-Marriage Act of 1856 and the Hindu Code Bill of 1954 have not achieved any tangible results. Besides, obscurantist slogans like 'once a widow, always a widow', further add to the ever increasing widow-population. Looking back over a century and a half, we clearly realise that the legal abolition of widow-burning was one thing, while the legal amelioration of widowhood is quite another. The death of the husband even today means for an average Hindu wife a further worsening of her position in the family.

For a Hindu wife widowhood traditionally means one of three things: immediate death (whether murder or suicide), life long condemnation to segregation and drudgery, and subjection to clandestine sexual exploitation by the males of the family and/or locality. It is probable that in days of old widows at times themselves preferred a painful death to a dreary life of 'hunger, scorn and domestic servitude' (Basham-1969: 190). Forced to refrain from all that was good, healthy and auspicious in life, the widow had to have her head clean shaven as a punishment for her past sins causing the death of her husband in her next life. Presumably large chunks of Hindus believed in the cathartic efficacy of the endless persecution and torture of widows. Always watched by the parents and relatives of her dead Lord, lest she broke her vows and imperilled the dead man's spiritual welfare, and shunned as unlucky even by women and servants of the family, the life of the widow was (and is) miserable in the extreme. In the wake of the public uproar against the Deorala outrage, a woman social worker from Rajasthan told a journalist:

> "At the very moment a dead man's body is removed from the house for cremation, a black sheet is drawn around the widow. For a year she is not to be seen by males or married women. She sits on the floor within this black sheet cubicle, with knees pulled to the chest and the head touching the knees. For ablutions and bath she leaves the cubicle at night. Saltless food is brought to her. Before a meal, she must cry because food is the basis of life, and as a widow she is deemed to have lost her moral right to life after her husband's death. She must cry before eating, also to express her guilt" (Singh 1987). Sitting on knees twelve hours a day, forced to live on insipid and

scanty food, shunned by people and surrounded by so much condemnation, the widow soon loses her will to live, takes ill and succumbs to death in a few months or years.

The Hindu widow, on the one hand, is ostracised and required to observe a vow of continence and chastity, while on the other, she is often seduced or subjected to sexual exploitation by starving males around. The widow, like the unwed woman, is forced to contraception and abortion. In case she bears children, they are illegitimate and they make her more scornful but not less vulnerable. It is astonishing that the sexual abuse of widows is sometimes recommended or appreciated. The *Kamasutra* describes a widow as a sexual object. As there is no regular marriage for the widow, she is exhorted to ally herself to a seeker after pleasure (*bhogin*) and make the best of her life. Vatsyayana's term for such a widow is *punarbhu*, that is, 'a woman allied to a man for a second time'. He places the *punarbhu* between a maiden (*kanya*) and a prostitute (*Veshya*). She is just a mistress. She is allowed a degree of freedom unknown to the wife but she is also denied the privileges of wifehood (De 1969: 97-98 and Chakaldar 1976: 181-82). How unfortunate it is that most widows are still shunned and sought for wrong reasons and yet they cannot enjoy even the kind of 'acceptability' that was available to Vatsyayana and his contemporaries.

Benevolent Ideas and Institutions in Renaissance

Some organisations came into existence during the last two decades of the 19th century and early 20th century. Sometimes women teachers' conference was held and sometimes at the venue of the Indian National Congress women used to meet separately. But the early organisations and conferences were very limited in their scope and programme and without any definite shape. However, they worked for the general welfare of the women and their importance lies in their beginning of the women's movement in India.

Under the auspices of the Brahmo Samaj the Ladies Association was founded at Calcutta in 1886 by Swarn Kumari Devi with the object of promoting friendly relation and spirit of service among the Indian women. It also provided for the training of poor girls to become teachers. Pandita Ramabai Sarswati founded *Sharda Sadan* at Poona in 1892 to provide education and employment for women. After some time the field of social service was extended and relief was given to the orphans, the destitutes and victims of famine. Like buds opening their petals, the girls began to expand learning to appreciate the cult of service and sacrifice which Ramabai inculcated. In the same year Shri Mahipatram Rupram *Anathashram* was founded at Ahmedabad to help the poor women and the widows. It also gave shelter to the illegitimate children and pregnant women.

Shri Zorostrian Mandal was started at Bombay in 1903 to help the women in general and the Parsi women in particular. It inspired women to become economically independent. It distributed food, milk and medicine among poor Parsi families and also made provision for their education. In 1908 the *Gujarati Hindu Stree Mandal* was started by Shri B.N. Motiwala, one of the impprtant social workers of Mumbai. Its objects were to promote contact among Gujarati women to provide them with appropriate education and to raise their status in different fields. The Mandal organised classes in sewing, embroidery, painting, leather work and for training teachers. It taught Gujarati, Hindi, Sanskrit, English and Music. It had also library for women and children. It also started a young girls' association and published a monthly bulletin.

Ramabai Ranade started *Seva Sadan* at Poona in 1909. It imparted education to the women and gave training in industry, teaching, nursing and midwifery. It also established a hostel. In 1917 it became an independent rgistered organisation. The names of Ramabai Ranade and Seva Sadan became gradually synonymous.

Mahila Samitis (Women's Institutions) were organised by Saroj Nalini in Bengal in many districts, towns or villages, with a view to imparting education to women. They adopted measures against *purdah*, early marriage and inspired widow remarriage. They enlightened the public on health and sanitation and pleaded for the equal rights of women in franchise and education.

Chiman Bai Maternity and Child Welfare League was established in Baroda in 1914 to take care of the health of women. Maharani Chiman Bai Udyogalaya was also started to train middle and working class women in some crafts and industries. An organisation was also founded for the sale of manufactured goods on a cooperative basis.

Bhagini Samaj was started at Poona in 1916 to serve the society in general and women and children in particular. Its programme for the welfare of women was very comprehensive. It covered education, social service, propaganda and legal work.

But women felt the necessity of an organisation of an all-India character. An humble beginning was made towards the end in 1910 when various women's groups came together and formed Bharat Stri

Mahamandal. It was an attempt to weld the women of the different provinces of India into one association. But the conditions not being ripe enough for this, it did not take deep root. But three women's organisations which came into existence later on became very important. Women's India Association (WIA) 1917, National Council of Women in India (NCWI) 1925 and All India Women's Conference (AIWC) 1926.

Women's Indian Association 1917-37

Origin: An association was started on the 8th May, 1917 at Adyar, Chennai by Mrs. Dorothy Jinarajadasa, wife of the President of Theosophical Society of Chennai and a notable social worker of her time. She was very sincerely assisted by an Irish lady Mrs. M. Cousins. Another Irish lady Dr. Annie Besant was chosen its first President and she remained on the post continuously for about 17 years till she passed away in 1933, Mrs. Jinarajadasa got the privilege of being its first Secretary. The Association was named as Women's Indian Association. It could have been named as Indian Women's Association also but this title was not chosen because it carried narrow meaning. The title Women's Indian Association was preferred as it was wide in meaning and scope. It had a wider outlook, a larger purpose and a deeper understanding. . . . It was a right ideal not only for all womanhood but for all humanity. The Women's Indian Association was the first organisation whose aim was to be All Indian in scope, to include as members all types of women who were residents in India and to band them together for mutual service and the good of the country.

Aims and Objectives

The aims and objects of this Association were the following:

1. To present to women their responsibilities as daughter's of India.
2. To secure for every girl and boy the right of education through schemes of compulsory primary education, including the teaching of religion.
3. To secure the abolition of child marriages and other social evils.
4. To secure for women the Vote for Municipal and Legislative Councils on the same terms as it was or might be granted to men.

5. To secure adequate representation of women in Municipalities, Taluks, Local Boards, Legislative Councils and Assemblies.
6. To establish equality of rights and opportunities between men and women.
7. To help women to realise that the future of India lies largely in their hands, for as wives and mothers they had the task of training, guiding and forming the character of the future rulers of India.
8. To band women into groups for the purpose of self-development and education and for the definite service of others.

The Association began to grow from the very day of its inception. The time was ripe for such an organisation. Within the first year of its existence 33 branches were formed in many towns. The Association has a good record of achievements to its credit within the two decades (1917-37) of its existence. We have to remain satisfied with a brief review of them.

The most important and fundamental work of the Association was in the sphere of education. But very soon it began to take interest in political sphere also. In 1917, the year which saw the birth of the Association. Women's interest in the Home Rule Movement was deeply stirred by the internment of Dr. Annie Besant who belonged to their own sex. The various branches of the Association took an active part to secure her release.

Home Rule was the talk of the day and this implied extension of franchise. Women's Indian Association was the first organisation in India to make a demand for women's franchise and it succeeded in its mission. It organised a deputation of 14 women to wait upon Mr. Montague, the then Secretary of State for India. He visited India in December, 1917 and the Deputation waited upon him on the 18th December at Chennai. Since then the Association, identified itself with the cause of women's franchise and the removal of sex disqualification for election to all the deliberative bodies. It did not rest until its demand was fulfilled. The franchise committee had denied extension of franchise to women. But the claim was pressed by the Women's Indian Association and its allies and the provincial councils were empowered under the Electoral Rules to consider the matter. By 1930 women got franchise in all the provinces of British India. After the attainment of women's franchise the Association began the movement for their representation in the legislative councils. We should also remember that the Association throughout protested against communal representation and reservation.

Three members of the Association were elected to the Corporation and one was unanimously elected as an Elder Woman.

The official organ of the Association was Stridharma which was started as a quarterly publication but became full fledged journal within a few years. It was published in more than one language English, Tamil and Telugu. For about a year (1935-36) Mrs. Cousins was its Editor. It carried the authentic news of the progress of the Indian Women's Movement in India and round the world. There were readers of this magazine in several countries of the world.

By 1923-24, the Association had 51 branches and 1500 membership. They gradually continued to increase. By 1926-27, there were 80 branches and over 4000 members. These branches spread from Cape Camorin in the South to Kashmir in the North. The Association did a lot of useful work in political, social and educational spheres. It took up the cause of moral and social hygiene. It took interest in child welfare work. It expressed satisfaction at the passing of the Child Marriage Restraint Act. During 1931-32 a Sarda Sub-Committee was formed to see the enforcement of the Sarda Act against Child Marriage. It facilitated their entry into legislatures and public offices. Many women were appointed as Honorary Magistrates and many became members of the local bodies. It took interest in the spread of girl education and guiding. It emphasised the introduction of compulsory primary education for girls. It was responsible for the *abolition of Devadasi system* and suppression of immoral traffic in women.

The Association with its branches were active in time of epidemics and distress. They rendered useful service to the needy. The members took an active part in social gatherings, parties, picnics and other cultural programmes.

The Association also took interest in Adult Education, village uplift and Harijan welfare work. The Association gave a number of scholarships to deserving girls including Harijans. On visit to Chennai, Gandhiji was presented a purse for Harijan work. It started and maintained Rescue Homes. An orphanage was started at Mylapore called Avai Home. It was started in 1930 with 10 girls. But during 1931-32, this Home had grown into a multipurpose centre with many sections, catering to more than 800 beneficiaries and had spread its activities on 1 acre land in beautiful suburb of Adyar. The underlying principle of the various activities of the Avai Home Orphanage was to protect all women especially young girls and children not only from the evils of poverty and destitution but also from undesirable associations and surroundings and to educate and to train them to a useful and independent profession.

The Children Aid Society and the Juvenile Court were also established.

Mrs. Sarojini Naidu presided over the 17th Annual function of the Association. Gandhiji visited Chennai in December, 1933 and the Association had the privilege of organising the only public meeting of women. In 1933 Dr. Annie Besant died and now Dr. (Mrs.) S. Muthulakshmi Reddi was elected as its President. She continued on this post for a long time even after the end of the period under review.

Women's Indian Association became the parent of All India Women's Conference which was born in early 1927. It became the vehicle for the expression of the united voice of the Indian womanhood. This was the great pioneering work of the Association.

International Outlook

The Association also developed international outlook and maintained links with various international organisations for some financial help or the other. It sent delegates to attend international conference and also invited outsiders at their own sessions.

The activities of the Women's Indian Association were many and they were expanding each year. Its achievements embraced social, educational and political fields. It was the largest Women's Association in India that had a unitary and all-round programme of work, social, educational and political. It had 72 branches, 23 centres and nearly 4000 members. It has rightly been called the mother of women's organisations in India. By 1937 with the growth of feminine organisations in the country it began to confine its activities to Chennai Presidency.

The National Council of Women in India

The National Council of Women in India was formed in 1925 and in the same year it was affiliated to the International Council of Women which was founded in 1888. As a matter of fact it originated as a branch of the latter organisation.

The aims and objectives of the National Council of Women in India were, briefly, to:

1. Promote sympathy of thought and unity of purpose among women in India.

2. Work for the removal of disabilities of woman, whether legal, economic or social, and for the promotion of the social, civil and educational welfare of women and children, ensuring opportunities for their full and free development and advancement.
3. Organise, develop and coordinate the work of its existing Councils and Branches and such other councils as may hereafter be formed under its auspices or may be accepted by it.
4. Co-ordinate the activities of other National Organisations in India, whose aims are in conformity with it.
5. And form a link with National Councils in other countries through the International Council of Women.

It had been working along these lines and had also tried to live up to its Motto *Do unto others As ye would That they should Do Unto you.* In short, it aimed to raise the status of Indian women in all possible ways at home and abroad.

Activities

As one of the pioneering all-India organisations, the National Council of Women in India had played a significant role in raising the status of women by working for the removal of various legal and social disabilities from which women suffered for centuries. By mobilising public opinion through seminars, conferences and meetings, the National Council focused attention on many existing problems and those which arose with the march of time, and changed conditions.

The National Council was one of the pioneers in turning the attention of women social workers to village welfare and city labour problems and sponsored a labour conference as early as 1933. It contributed substantially to the passing of the Prostitution Act in Mumbai and conducted intensive propaganda in favour of the Sarda Act.

The National Council played an important part in the women's suffrage movement. Jointly with other women's organisations the National Council took a firm stand in favour of unqualified adult franchise for both men and women and opposed reservation of seats on the ground of sex.

Since its inception the National Council has spread education and advocated increase in women's wages and women's inheritance rights, maternity benefits, provision of better facilities for nurses, reforms in women's wards in jails, women police, slum clearance, etc. After the first ten years of work, the Council began to expand into new fields of activity.

Council's Affiliated Branches

The National Council of Women in India was composed of Councils and Branches in almost all the states in India. These were engaged in field activities which included running school libraries, literacy and handicraft classes, child welfare, health hobby and recreation centres, rescue homes, orphanage, clinics, hospitals and hostels.

The National Council holds Triennial Elections and its headquarters rotate with the Presidents. The official organ of the Council is an English language Journal entitled *NCWI Bulletin*. It has been published from the date of the inception of the Council in 1925. It gave news concerning women both at National and International levels. Its members mostly belonged to official and aristocratic classes and they had received English Education.

Thus, we see that the principles of gender equality have been basic to Indian thinking. Indian women were accorded a very high status in the Vedic era. We have examples of Maitreya and Gargi, the two females who were well-versed in Vedantic philosophy. The Vedic period extended over 2200-2000 B.C. We also have the glorious example of Rani Laxmibai, a woman who was widowed in her teens, providing leadership to the first liberation movement in India.

The Indian National Congress, the party which led the national liberation struggle for almost six decades adopted gender equality as its guiding principle in its fundamental rights resolution as early as in 1931. Mahatma Gandhi, the Father of Indian Nation, was a champion of women's rights. He always emphasised that 'subjugation and exploitation of women was a product of men's vested teachings and women's acceptance of the same." Under his leadership, many women in India stepped out of their homes perhaps for the first time, and took very active part in Freedom Movement of India.

Reforms and the Reformers

> "In this Indian Renaissance in its many-sided aspects, social, political and economic, revolutionary and constitutional, woman of this country walked hand in hand with men and their part in our freedom struggle is one of the gloriest chapters of not only Indian history,

but the history of the whole world. The emancipation of women has been a very important programme of social reform in India for the last hundred and fifty years and all the Indian reformers of this period have emphasised the great significance of the status of women in society. This approach to women and her status was in line with the best traditions of our ancient culture."[11]

The Indian Renaissance affected men as well as women. Nationally, the political struggle led by Mahatma Gandhi gave an impetus to eradicate the social evils prevailing in the society during the period under the review.

Raja Ram Mohun Roy (1774-1833) was the first Indian in modern time to initiate social reform movement and champion the cause of women. To him women did not belong to a weaker sex and she was not inferior to man morally and intellectually.[12] He advocated equality between the two. The practice of infanticide had already been declared illegal.[13] So first of all his attention was drawn towards the cruel practice of *Sati*. He had seen with his own eyes the malpractices associated with this evil custom. His brother's wife, when widowed, was a victim to *Sati*. So he was determined to put an end to this custom at any cost. Since 1818 he began to propagate by his writings and speeches against it. He also tried to persuade people not to indulge in inhuman custom. He boldly declared that scriptures did not support it. It also did not appeal to reason. To him *Sati* was nothing less than the sin of a female murder. With his cooperation Lord William Bentick declared the practice of *Sati* as illegal and punishable offence in November 1829.[14] The progressive Hindus thanked the Governor-General for his humanitarian work. But the orthodox Hindus made an appeal to the Privy Council against the measure. Raja Ram Mohun Roy who had gone to England made every effort to get the appeal rejected and he succeeded in the task.

He protested against evils like early marriage, polygamy, *kulinism*. He supported female education, widow and inter-caste marriage. He wanted that women should enjoy the right of inheritance and property. In 1822 he prepared and published a pamphlet—*Brief Remarks Regarding Modern Encroachments on the Ancient Rights of Women*. By upholding the cause of women and denouncing the rigours of caste system he showed. His ideals of womanhood inspired by the golden past, were far advanced of his time.[15] In 1928 he founded the Brahmo Samaj with a view to carry on the reform activities on a solid basis.

Devendranath Tagore (1817-1905) joined the Brahmo Samaj in 1843 and made it more active. In 1854 he inspired the establishment of the society of friends for organising social uplift and he remained its president for a long time. It aimed at female education, remarriage of Hindu widows, prevention of early marriage and polygamy. Leading public men were associated with this organisation. Tagore also submitted a memorandum to the Legislative Council for the removal of the legal disabilities of married widow and establishment of girls' schools in every quarter of the suburbs of Calcutta.[16]

Keshav Chandra Sen (1838-84) joined the Samaj in 1857. But by 1865 the Samaj was divided into two groups—the conservatives under Devendranath and the progressives under Keshav. The former group took more interest in religious reform than social reform. The latter group had programme of advanced social reforms like widow marriage, intercaste marriage, promotion of female education abolition of *purdah* and early marriage.[17] The Samaj under Keshava's leadership became a very powerful all-India movement. It seemed the period of reformation begun by Ram Mohun Roy was over and a revolution was now in progress.[18]

Keshav took great interest in the welfare of women. He started several girls' schools to promote female education. In 1863 he established the society of Theistic Friends in order to encourage, among other things, the habit of study among women confined to the *Zenana*. Provision was made for the annual examination and distribution of prizes among successful ladies. A magazine, the first monthly for women, *Bambodhini* was also started.[19] In 1865 he also started a prayer meeting called *Brahmika Samaj* meant exclusively for women.[20]

> "Keshava's zeal for social reform carried him far beyond the moderate position taken by Devendranath. When the two finally parted in 1865 over the wearing of the sacred thread. Keshav set up an independent organization named *Brahmo Samaj of India*. From this point on, his faith in inspiration as the guide to action grew more pronounced. In 1878 another and more fatal fission took place within his own movement. Despite his prolonged advocacy of a minimum age for the Brahmo marriage, and his opposition to idolatry he was persuaded to marry his thirteen-year-old daughter to a Hindu prince, feeling that such was the will of God. Scandalized by this betrayal of his previous principles, most of his followers abandoned him and set up a third group, the *Sadharan* (general) Brahmo Samaj."[21]

Ishwar Chandra Vidyasagar (1820-91), a great Sanskrit scholar, was also a great social reformer. He possessed rational outlook and broad vision. He was keenly conscious of the social evils from which the society was suffering. He attacked the system of early marriage and polygamy. He was the great advocate of women's education. To promote female education he also took the help of Bethune. Both succeeded in founding the first school—*Hindu Balika Vidyalaya* for the girls of high caste families in May 1849, which was later on called Bethune School which later on rose to the status of a famous college. Thus, Vidyasagar succeeded to a great extent in removing the prejudices against female education in the country. The crowning achievement of Vidyasagar was the legislation in favour of widow-marriage. He waged crusade against ban on widow marriage and with vast learning at his command he proved that scriptures did not sanction any ban on widow-marriage. There was no ban on males' marriage. So he, day in and day out propagated in favour of widow marriage. In 1855 several petitions were sent to the Government of India for regularising widow marriage and giving property rights to the widows. On the 26th of July 1856 Widow-Remarriage Act (Act XV of 1856) was passed. It proved a great boon for the Hindu widows as it opened the gate of new bright life for them. The first Hindu remarriage took place at Calcutta on 7th December 1856 under the guidance of Vidyasagar himself.

Shasipada Banerji of Barnagar was also interested in the cause of widows. His own widowed niece was remarried on 28th November 1868. His house became refuge for widows and about 40 widow marriages took place under its roof. The Widow Remarriage Act solved the problem of those young widows who were willing to remarry. But the problem of those widows who did not remarry was to be solved. For such widows Shasipada Banerji established a Widows' Home near Calcutta where they could receive education and training in small industries. Jotiba Phule, Karsondas Mulji, Vishnushastri Pandit, Hari Deshmukh, M.G. Ranade and so on strengthened the widow-remarriage movement in Maharashtra.

B.M. Malabari, a Parsi social reformer, vehemently opposed early marriage and enforced widowhood. He published a book with two notes—*Infant Marriage and Enforced Widowhood in India* to acquaint the people with these two evils. He also started a journal—the *Indian Spectator* through which he expressed his views on social reforms in forceful language. Once he argued how child marriage was weaking the Hindu race.[22] He tried his best to create favourable atmosphere of social legislation in both India and England. He had gone to England where he had issued an appeal on behalf of the daughters of India in 1890. It was undoubtedly the result of his efforts that the age of Consent Act was passed in 1891 raising the age of consummation from 10 to 12. The orthodox Hindus took it as 'an infringement of the Queen's Proclamation of 1858. But their opposition was to Government'.

Later on this issue was taken up by many reformers including Mahatma Gandhi since it was felt by one and all of the progressive lot that the custom of early marriage is the main stumbling block for the education of girls. Gandhiji wanted it to be raised to 14. He also tried his best to make the public opinion in his favour for this purpose. The National Committee, in its report, has rightly observed:

> "A very significant development of the period was the considerable rise in the age of marriage, especially in the urban areas and among the upper classes of society. This was due mainly to the pressure of changing social and economic circumstances. To begin with, the age of marriage was raised for men because now they began to refuse to get married until their education was completed and they were able to secure a job. A great disparity between the ages of husband and wife is not favoured and the age of marriage for girls also was, therefore, automatically raised. Another social factor which contributed to the same end was the gradual break-up of the old system of joint families. Child marriages could exist largely because of the joint family system, which could easily accommodate the child wife, but they were unsuitable to the modern small family where the wife was expected to shoulder the responsibilities of managing the household immediately on her marriage. This rise in the age of marriage naturally increased the educational opportunities for girls and their continuance in secondary schools and even colleges became possible for the first time. This trend was further increased by the demand of the educated men themselves to have educated wives and preferably those who had been to secondary schools and colleges. . . .[23]

Thus the names of Vidyasagar and Malabari stand foremost in connection with uplift of Indian women. Their hearts were touched by the miseries of women, and they carried on a life-long campaign to better their lot.[24]

Mahadev Govind Ranade (1842-1901) besides being a high-ranking government, he was also a social reformer. He joined the *Prarthana*

Samaj when he was 28 years old. He was also a member of *Sarvajanik Sabha* through which the government was acquainted with the public opinion on social matters. He was in contact with other social organizations also which were established at Poona. He fixed some guidelines for the reformers. It goes to his credit after two years of the establishment of Indian National Congress in 1885 the Indian National Social Conference was established. This was the first social organisation at the national level. Ranade staunchly supported the cause of widows and joined the Widow Marriage Association founded by Vishnu Shastri. He did not like early and arranged marriages and desired freedom to women in the choice of their life-partners.[25] To him the improvement in the status of women was not by innovation but a restoration of the position enjoyed in the past golden age.

Swami Dayanand Saraswati (1824-83)[26] was a great scholar of Sanskrit and Hindu scriptures. He opposed the evil practices of child marriage and enforced widowhood. He did not find any sanction for these social evils in the *Vedas*. He favoured the study of scriptures by the women. He also supported liberal education for them and asked them to follow the Vedic women. He wanted to abolish early marriage, *purdah*, dowry, ban on widows' marriage and on women's education. He also pleaded for women's right of divorce and widows' right in property.[27] He attracted the attention of the thoughtful Hindus to the pitiable lot of child widows. He did his best to encourage their remarriage Dayananda's stand against these two evil practices of Hindu society went a long way in generating reformist spirit among the Arya Samajists. It was equally a powerful influence in creating consciousness among the women of India.[28]

The Sharda Bill (prohibiting child marriages), sponsored by H.B. Sharda, an eminent Arya Samajist of Ajmer, was inspired by the teachings of Swami Dayananda.

Swami Vivekanand (1863-1906) was a great nationalist and propounder of spiritual nationalism in India. He was also well aware of the social evils and tried his best to remove them. In 1881 he met Ramkrishna Paramhans (1834-86) at Dakshineshwar and felt great relief in his presence. In 1893 he attended a parliament of religions at Chicago, where he earned high reputation due to his towering personality, spirited speeches on Hindu religion and Indian culture. On his return he started Ram Krishna Mission in 1897.

Vivekanand was a great advocate of the uplift of women. He was opposed to all sorts of superstitions, illiteracy, *purdah*, and early marriage.

He believed that education was essential for women and that education would be able to solve their problems.[29] He exhorted the women to be strong, hopeful, and unashamed.[30] Pointing to the Indians once he said:

> "All nations have attained greatness by paying proper respect to women. That country and nation which do not respect women have never become great, not will ever be in future. The principal reason why your race is so much degraded is that you had no respect for these living images of *Shakti.*"[31]

Thus, he warned the people that if the status of their women was not raised, they could not hope to rise and make any progress.[32] He used to say that there is no hope to rise for that family or country where there is no estimation of women, where they live in sadness. For this reason, they have to be raised first; and an ideal Math has to be started for them.

Gopal Krishna Gokhale (1866-1915) opposed the seclusion of women and was deeply interested in the promotion and spread of their education. The women were more religious-minded and combination of ignorance with religion made them the willing victims of customs, unjust and harmful in the highest degree and also the most formidable because they became the most effective opponents of all attempts at change or innovation.[33] So he wanted a wide diffusion of education in all its branches and with all its solvent influences among the women of India. He was quite convinced that education was the only means of emancipating their minds from the degrading thraldom to ideas inherited through a long past.

He was also quite sure that such emancipation would restore the women to the honoured position which they at one time in India and also facilitate the assimilation of essential elements of western civilization without which all thoughts of India's regeneration were mere idle dreams.

Dhondo Keshav Karve, a Professor of Mathematics at Fergusson College, Poona made a notable contribution for the liberation of women in India through various ways and means. Karve founded the Hindu Widows Home Association on the 14th June 1896, and remained the secretary for 20 years. He also established three institutions for the welfare of Hindu women—Anath Balikashram (Widows' Home), Mahila Vidyalaya (Girls' School), and Nishkam Karm Math (Selfless Work Mission). His great contribution was in the field of fmale education and the greatest achievement in this sphere was the foundation of Women's University on the 3rd June 1916.

In December 1914 Rai Bahadur Ganga Ram (1851-1927) a retired engineer, started a widow Remarriage Association in the Punjab. When Widows' Home established by Sasipada Banerji ceased to function, the Dev Samaj at Firozepur and Bhatinda, the Arya Samaj at Jullundar, and Digamber Jain at Mumbai had established Widows' Homes. Between 1906 and 1912 several Widows' Homes were founded. The most important being the Widows' Home in Mysore (1907), The Mahila Shilpashram in Calcutta (1907), the Widows' Home in Bangalore (1910), Widow's Home in Dacca and the Brahmin Widows' Hostel in Chennai (1912).

Establishment of Indian Ladies Samaj

To prevent minor girls from undesirable association and guardianship, to educate and train them for an independent and honourable profession, under the initiation of Dr. S. Muthulakshmi Reddi, Indian Ladies Samaj was established in 1923-23 and Lady Sivaswami Iyer who headed many a social reforms in Chennai was the first President. They formed an association with Lady Sadasiva Iyer as the head to reclaim young girls from the pernicious customs of society and provide facilities for their bringing up and education. With the abolition of Devadasi system in Chennai, the temples freed a number of families from compulsory service. The girls of such families were to be trained in various kinds of profession. The *samaj* collected funds from the public and arranged for these girls who were trained as nurses, doctors and teachers most of them were married and began to lead a normal life. Such service was rendered till 1937 and after that there was no need for giving help to these girls and they became used to a new life of respectability and got merged in the general society.

Establishment of Rescue Home

Dr. Muthulakshmi Reddi was instrumental in abolishing the immoral traffic on women and under her able guidance the Women Indian Association started a home in 1930. The "Avvai Home" was started in Mylapore with ten girls. The main aim of the home was to protect all women especially young girls and children not only from the evils of poverty and destitution but also from the undesirable association and surroundings and to educate and train them to an useful profession. The institution depended on public support and the government grant was a meagre one. With determined efforts of Dr. Reddi, the home had grown into a multipurpose centre with many sections catering to more than eight hundred beneficiaries and had spread its activities on the one acre of land in the beautiful suburb of Adayar, Chennai, "The Avvai Home" treated all the girls on equal footing without any caste distinctions. Dr. Reddi one of the founders of the home, spent her whole life for the development of this home, which trained girls for useful occupations such as midwives, nurses, teachers and her sincere service was appreciated by all the social reformers including Mahatma Gandhi.

The Madras Sevasadan

The Women Indian Association started in 1923 started "Women's home of service" at Udayanavanam, Royapettah High Road, Chennai with the object of promoting adult education among women and making them self-reliant and self-supporting and thus enabling them to earn an honourable living. Dr. Muthulakshmi Reddi, one of the founders of the Home took unmitigated interest in the development of this Home. The Home gave scholarships to the students from the fund collected from the public and from the numbers of Women Indian Association. The students were taught lessons in vernacular and English. But the course were most vocational, such as lace making, embroidery, weaving and spinning.

The Home had a "Baby Welcome" attached to it and give medical help to ninety babies a day, Expectant mothers were attended by the nurses of the Home. The Home was managed by the members of the Women Indian Association.

As the Deputy Speaker of the Chennai Council Dr. Reddi requested the government to start at least ten times to meet the demand of women to be saved. In the women's home girls were trained as nurses and as vocational teachers and music teachers. Inspired by the activities of Sevasadan, a similar home was started at Trinplicant, Chennai. Fr. Reddi pleaded with the government to sanction a special grant for the rescue home. But the minister did not accept her request on the ground that the government should not help any institution mainly because it was started with a good intention. But Sevasadan was able to get a grant from the Industrial Department of Government of Chennai from 1929 onwards.

Dr. Reddi put forth enormous labour for getting the sanctions. But she was successful in her efforts to provide a safe shelter to women who were thrown out by their own family members and helped them to earn their own living with confidence.

Madras Vigilance Association

Another association which provided a helping hand to the victims of immoral life was the Vigilance Association started by Women Indian Association, Chennai. This Association associated itself with the "Moral Welfare Work" and served not only the Chennai city but also the whole of the province. Miss V.T. Lakshmi, a noted welfare worker of Chennai was closely associated with the working of the Association.

The moral work undertaken by the Association consisted of three aspects: (1) rescue and reclamation; (2) moral reformation; and (3) rehabilitation.

The Association brought about a change in the attitude of public towards the rescue and reclamation work which was looked down upon with disdain and fear in early days. The members sympathetically proceeded with the work and the public began to extend help more and more in that direction.

As far as the reformation work, the Rescue and Training home in Chennai had provided all facilities to he unfortunate girls. They were given all-round training. Girls from other districts were also given chances to reform themselves. 'Stri Sadana' a Higher Elementary. Arts and Crafts School was attached to this house. While speaking on the moral welfare work in Chennai, at the sixteenth Session of All-India Women's Conference, Kakinada 1941. Miss V.T. Lakshmi said, "As far as the rehabilitation work is concerned we require moral sympathy and cooperation from the public as well as from the government. Several ladies who are graduates of the universities have come forward to do honorary work. But it is not possible for all of us to do honorary work for a long time, however, selfless one may be it should be placed on par with other services of the society." The Association members took greater interest in rehabilitating the unfortunate girls. Even during the troubled days of war time the shelter remained in Chennai.

Remand House of Delinquents

The Children Act passed in 1929 in Chennai made provision for the treatment of young delinquents by establishing Reformatory Schools. But their operations has been proved to be very meagre and insufficient. Moreover, the main drawback in the act was that it was operated only in the Chennai city and its immediate suburbs. There was no provision to safeguard the juvenile offenders in the districts and they were treated as Adult criminals.

The Women Indian Association pressed for the amendment of Children's Act of 1920 for making provision for separate Remand Houses for children during the pendency of their cases and separate children's court with women Magistrates. The All India Women's' Conference at Chennai passed resolutions in favour of amending the Children Act of 1920 in the case of girls also as there was no Act to look after the girls committing crimes. The Women Indian Association went on a deputation to the member incharge of the department and urged that it would be made applicable to the case of girls as well. After which women Honorary Magistrates were established. Mrs. Radha Bai Subbarayan in appreciating the work done by Madras Presidency in dealing with Juvenile Delinquents remarked, "it would stand a good comparison with such kind of work done in any western country."

Dr. (Mrs.) Reddi as the Deputy President of the Madras Legislative Council fought for these provisions inside the Council and the members of Women Indian Association outside the Council.

Saradha Ladies Union (Hindu Widows Home)

The educated women took up the responsibility of widows, who had a parasitic living on the family without any status of their own. In 1912, Smt. Sister Subbalakshmi Ammal, a child widow herself took up the cause of Hindu widows and etablished a widows Home at Chennai in the fact of much opposition from the orthodox people. As an Educationist, Sister Subbalakshmi devoted her whole life for the educational attainment of Hindu widows and thereby brought a new light of hope in their life. In the beginning orthodox Hindus were reluctant to send their widowed daughters outside their houses because of the fear of social criticisms. But sister Subbalakshmi's successful career itself showed them that a widow's life need not be a culmination of activities. Dr. (Mrs.) Muthulakshmi Reddi pleaded with the government and tried to take up the building for a college hostel. She was instrumental in getting scholarships for widows in all the educational institutions. The Seva Sadan opened a branch at Chennai and trained Hindu widows as teachers and mid-wives. Dr. (Mrs.) Reddi appealed to the government on several occasions for liberal grants to associations trying to help the widows to earn a honourable means.

Vidhava Vivah Sahiya Sabha

To encourage widow remarriages the Vidhava Vivah Sahiya Sabha was established in Chennai in 1921 against much opposition from orthodoxy especially Brahmins who regarded the remarriage of a widow as the most sinful act. Moreover, Hindu widow who were uneducated or ill educated opposed the very idea of remarriage on the firm belief that because of their own "*Karma*" they had been destained to suffer as widows.

But during 1921-37 the gradual spread of education and culture loosened the bonds of castes and widened and liberalised the outlook of young people. Gradually Hindu women also came forward to receive western education and these educated women became conscious of their inferior positions and began to assert their rights. The Women Indian Association and All India Women's Conference succeeded in getting various legislations relating to inheritance rights of widows and remarriage. Moreover, some of the educated and progressive sections of young men came forward to rebel against superstition and remarriage widows.

In 1924 under the auspices of the Sabha six widow remarriages took place in Chennai. In 1929 it performed nine such marriages. In early 1930 a huge meeting was held at Triplicane. Chennai, under the auspices of the Sabha in which several persons spoke in favour of widow remarriage and particularly the marriage of young widow.

Shri Virashlingam, a social reformer did a memorable service in performing the widow remarriage. The Reformist Association of the presidency did valuable propaganda in the encouragement of widow remarriage. Sister Subbalakshmi, a virgin Brahmin widow, and an educationist devoted her life for the cause of virgin widows.

REFERENCES

1. यत्र नार्यस्तु पूज्यन्ते तत्र रमन्ते देवताः।

   —Manu.

2. एवं भार्यास्त्यजतां नराणां नास्ति निष्कृतिः।।

   —Mbh. XIII, 58.13.

3. Varahmihir, *Brihata Samhita*, p. 280.
4. Dr. A.S. Altekar, *The Position of Women in Hindu Civilization*, pp. 317-18.
5. न वे स्त्रैणानि सख्यानि सन्ति सालावृकाणां हृदयान्येता।

   —*Rig*. X.95.15.

6. अनृतं स्त्री अनृतं वैषा करोति या
   पत्युः क्रीता सति अथान्यैश्चरति।।

   —M.S. I.10, 11.

7. स्वभावस्त्वेष नारीणां लोकेषु दृश्यत।
   विमुक्तधर्माश्चपलास्तीक्ष्णा भेदकराः स्त्रियः।।28।।
   स्त्रीत्वं दुष्टं स्वभावेन गुरुवाक्ये व्यवस्थितं।।31।।

   —*Ramayana*, III.45.

8. ढोर गंवार शूद्र पशुनारी।
ये सब ताड़न के अधिकारी।।

—रामचरितमानस

9. Dr. Altekar, *ibid.*, pp. 321-22.
10. Dr. R.P. Sharma, *Woman in Hindu Literature*, p. 246.
11. Report of the *National Committee on Women Education*, p. 10.
12. Please see his treatise on *Sati.*
13. Regulation XXI of 1795, VI of 1802.
14. Regulation XVII of 1829.
15. R.C. Majumdar, *An Advanced History of India*, p. 813.
16. Sishir Kumar Mitra, *Resurgent India*, p. 89.
17. C.Y. Chintamani, *Social Reform*, Vol. IV, p. 261.
18. R.C. Majumdar, *op. cit.*, p. 879.
19. Shishir Kumar Mitra, *op. cit.*, p. 119.
20. *Ibid.*
21. *Sources of Indian Tradition*, Vol. II, p. 45.
22. B.M. Malabari, "Editorial Note," *Indian Spectator*, 1st March, 1891.
23. National Committee Report, (1958-59), p. 24.
24. R.C. Majumdar, *op. cit.*, p. 887.
25. M.G. Ranade, *Religious and Social Reforms: A Collection of Essays and Speeches*, p. 107.
26. Report of the *Ninth National Social Conference*, Poona, 1895.
27. Lala Lajpat Rai, *The Arya Samaj*, 1915, pp. 144-45.
28. For the details of the ideas of Swami Dayananda his Monumental work *Satyartha Prakash*, Delhi may be referred.
29. Swami Vivekananda, *Our Women*, p. 39.
30. *Ibid.*, p. 58.
31. *Ibid.*, p. 29.
32. *Ibid.*, p. 53.
33. *Speeches of Gopal Krishna Gokhale*, 3rd ed., 1920, p. 882.

5

WOMEN EDUCATION UNDER JAIN-BOUDDHA SYSTEM

> "The nuns (*Bhikkhunis*) formed a distinct community in the Buddhist Church. They had their own *Saṁgha*, which was guided by the same rules and regulations as that of the monks. The Bhikkhuni *Saṁgha* was, however, for all practical purposes, subordinated to the Bhikkhu *Saṁgha*. The ordination of a new Bhikkhuni, although carried on in the Bhikkhuni *Saṁgha* in exactly the same way as that of Bhikkhu in the Bhikkhu *Saṁgha*, had to be confirmed by the latter. The general tendency of the Buddhist canon law was to assign a distinctly inferior position to the Bhikkhunis, as the great Buddha was of opinion that their admission into the Buddhist Church was calculated to destroy its purity. Many safeguards were devised to avert the evil, but the essential principles guiding the corporation of monks were equally applicable in the case of the nuns."[1]

During the last phase of his life, on the insistence of his pet disciple, Anand, agreed to admit nuns (*Bhikkhunis*) in the Buddhist Church (*Sangha*). He did so very reluctantly saying that "the religion that merited its longevity for five thousand years, may now be short-lived for five hundred years or so."

Males and females differed in social rights and duties but as far as religious rights were concerned, according to some Buddhist scriptures, there was no difference. In Jainism, whatever small or big vows (*Anuvritas* or *Mahavritas*) were applicable for both males and females. According to *Thanga Sutra*[2] Jain monastic life is open to all, irrespective of caste, status and sex. However, to maintain a high moral standard and for practical reasons, certain qualifications and restrictions were imposed at a later date. Twenty categories of persons such as following are debarred from monastic life: a child under eight years, an old person, a eunuch, a sick person, one devoid of limbs, a timid person, a mad or an imbecile person. Robbers, traitors, enemies of the state, slaves, servants, and persons in debt are debarred for purely social reasons. Similarly, in Digambar sect of Jainism females were not allowed, most probably due to its nudistic character, but in Swetambar sect they were allowed.

Because of the propaganda that asceticism (*Samnyasa*) is essential for liberation, alike males, many females (nuns) were also attracted toward ascetism, but according to Mahayanist ideal penance in its various forms leads to sorrow only. Ashwaghosh in his *Buddhacharita*, included among Mahayana literature, make the future Buddha, during his period of spiritual apprenticeship, to exhorts as following:

> Penance in its various forms is essentially sorrowful;
> And, at best, the reward of penance is heaven.
> Yet all the worlds are liable to change,
> So the efforts of the hermitages are of little use.
>
> Those who forsake the kin they love and their pleasures
> To perform pleasures and win a place in heaven
> Must leave it in the end
> And go to greater bondage.
>
> The man who pains his body and calls it penance
> In the hope of continuing to satisfy desire
> Does not perceive the evils of rebirth
> And through much sorrow goes to further sorrow.[3]

As a matter of fact Buddha, during his last phase of apprenticeship, realized that the life is like a lyre, whose strings are to be tightened balancingly. Otherwise, it will not work. If they are loose it would not sound, and if tightened too much they are sure to be broken down. Therefore, ultimately he propounded the doctrine of 'Mean' (*Maddhyam Pratipada*).

In Jainism *Tapas* (penance) forms an important part not only of the life of a Jain monk but of all Jain devotees. So great is the stress laid on *tapas* that it is added to the *triratnas* (three jewels) to form the fourth pillar of Jainism. It is the most important means of rapid elimination of already accumulated *karmas* (*nirjara*). There are in all twelve forms of *tapas*. The six external austerities are fasting, observing rules regarding food, begging, control of palate, mortification of flesh, and living on solitude. We have seen that in Mahayan sect of Buddhism mortification of body has been denounced, whereas in Jainism it has been cited as one of the six external *tapas*. Again six internal austerities are—repentance, humility, service to the monks, study, meditation, and indifference towards the body. The last one indirectly hints to the severe penance without caring for the physique. Thus, six external and six internal austerities have a number of sub-varieties described in *Uttaraddyayan Sutra.*[4]

The position of nuns in Buddhism as well as Jainism was far inferior to the monks. Both placed nuns under a more rigorous discipline than monks. Some of the restrictions placed upon the nuns were no doubt seasonal ones, thus it was laid down that they should not stay alone without the protection of monks; that they should avoid the company of men of doubtful character, that only monks of unquestioned purity and integrity should be allowed to preach before nuns; that they should always live together in groups of twos and threes, etc. Some other rules, however, betray a lack of confidence in the character and judgement of women. Thus, the admission of new nun was to be sanctioned by a joint meeting of nuns; new monks, however, could be admitted without consulting nuns at all. Nuns were to go out to beg only when led by an experienced matron. The climax is, however, reached by the rule which lays down that a nun, though 100 years old, must stand in reverence before a monk, though he may have been just initiated.[5]

The founders of Jainism and its four branches, *viz.*, monks, nuns men lay-devotees, and women lay-devotees are twenty-four Tirthankaras, the first and the last of being Rishabha and Mahavir respectively. All these prophets were monks and except Malli, who was a women, all were men. Only the two, *viz.*, Parshva and Mahavir, are historical. Parshva was born 250 years before Mahavira, and his order was prevalent when the latter was born. Parshva preached a four-fold religion consisting of non-violence, truth, non-stealing, and non-possessiveness (*aparigriha*) and allowed monks to wear clothes.

Jainism as practised today is largely based upon the teachings of Mahavira who died in 527 BC at the age of 72. He was succeeded as the head of the order by Gautama and Sudharma successively. Eight schisms occurred in Jainism, two during the life-time of Mahavira himself. The final division into Digambara and Shvetambar sects occurred most probably at the end of the first century AD. During the twelve years long famine in North and West India, a portion of the community migrated to South India. Years later when the leaders met it was found that irreconcilable differences in their modes of living and conduct had developed between them.

Eligibility

Jain monastic life is open to all, irrespective of caste, status and sex. However, to maintain a high moral standard and for practical reasons, certain qualifications and restrictions were imposed at a later date. Twenty categories of persons such as the following are debarred from monastic life: a child under eight years, an old person, a eunuch, a sick person, one devoid of limbs, a timid person, a mad or imbecile person, robbers, traitors, enemies of the state, slaves, servants, and person in debt are debarred for social reasons. The majority of people renounce due to disgust for the world and a desire for liberation. Sometimes a woman may renounce when her husband or her son becomes a monk.[6]

Some embrace the monastic life after being impressed by the teaching of Mahavira. Besides these, the Jain scriptures cite many worthy and unworthy causes such as anger, poverty, enlightenment in dream, illness, humiliation, which may lead one to become a monk.[7]

Subordination of Nuns

Unlike Buddhism, the Jain order of nuns has been a distinct feature of their church from the very beginning. Mahavira had in his congregation greater number of nuns (nearly 36,000) than monks, and this state prevails even in the modern time. Like men, women also renounce for various reasons. Cases of child widows becoming nuns are not wanting. Generally, the permission of the guardian must be obtained. Even women must do *kesh-lunchan* (plucking hairs).

Nuns are organized under their officers *ganini, pravartini, theri* and *bhikkhuni* are the offices in the descending order of importance and seniority. A young nun not yet confirmed is called *kshullika.* All the offices of nuns are subordinate to the offices of monks. This subordinations supreme that a monk of three years' standing could become the *upadhyaya* of a nun of thirty years' standing.

Like monks, nuns too lead a wandering life and their rules and regulations are similar to those of monks. A spotless life and practice of rigorous discipline are expected, and punishments for transgressions are severe. Monks and nuns are not allowed to stay under the same shelter except during calamities or under unforeseen circumstances. There are some special rules which help to maintain pure and unharassed life of nuns in the society. There are approximately eight thousand Jain monks and nuns in India today belonging to some twenty-five different sects.

Buddhistic Monastic System

Monastic system was an important feature of Buddhist education. It as based on the concept of a well-ordered organization. The monks (*bhikshus*) who lived in the monasteries (*viharas*) were required to lead a well-regulated life in keeping with the dignity of these institutions. The monasteries, which were educational-cum-religious centres in which the monks led a corporate life, were built in many parts of India. In many respects they were like the medieval monasteries in Europe. Many of these medieval monasteries were also centres of learning and religious training. In Europe, monasticism grew up as a movement designed to counteract and correct wickedness and corruption in Roman society. It also grew in response to the desire of those faithful people within the church, who were interested in deeper religious life.

On joining the monasteries, the Buddhist monks became pupils (*saddhiviharikas*) and came under the direction and supervision of their preceptors (*upajjhayas*). In this connection, it is interesting to note although the Buddhist system of education was non-selective, making room for all, it did not encourage mass teaching. These monasteries were situated in rural areas, "far from the madding crowd's ignoble strife." Their peaceful surroundings provided a stimulus for study and meditation. Their atmosphere was conducive to the growth of an intimate pupil-teacher relationship which was one of the greatest achievements of Ancient Indian Education. Buddhist educational ideals and practices, which did not differ very much from Vedic and Upnishadic ideals of education. The religious and philosophical background was also an integral part of Buddhist education.

The well-known Chinese travellers like Fahien, Hsuantsang, etc. came to India with the thirst of religious knowledge, visited various monasteries and gave a vivid picture of the working of the monastery at Pataliputra, Nalanda, etc. for admission to the 'Sangha' of monks certain rules were prescribed. The young pupil had to obtain the permission of his parents, he had to be free from certain types of diseases, etc. The ceremony of admission which is described in details in *Vinaya Pitaka*. Amongst other things he had to take an oath of allegiance to Buddha saying the following:

"I take my refuge to the Buddha;
I take my refuge to the Dhamma;
I take my refuge in the Sangha."

The ceremony performed at the time of initial admission (*pabajja*) was a significant event. The candidate was made conscious of his responsibilities and duties as a novice. The ceremony for full admission (*upsampada*) had also its significance. In Jain system a candidate having accepted the monastic life is put on probation after a preliminary *Diksha* call *samyaka-charitra*. This involves vows to avoid sins and to practise equanimity. Such a probationer is called *seha, samanera* or *antevasi*. The use of the term 'antevasi' is quite in vogue for *Shishya* (disciple), whose initiation (*upnayan*) has been completed. Literally means "the one who stays near his preceptor (*guru*). This closeness or proximity between disciple and preceptor was the redeeming feature of ancient system of education. Nietzsche had rightly said, "An academic system without personal influence of teachers upon pupils is an arctic winter." In Buddhism and Jainism there is an identical word, *i.e.*, *upsampada*.

After initial admission he had to prove himself worthy of monastic life and must show implicit obedience to seniors. After a variable period of seven days to six months, he is confirmed (*upsampada*) and given the final vows (*mahavritas* in Jainism). In Buddhism, similarly the candidate had to accept a few strict rules of chastity, poverty and abstinence from worldly pleasures. Begging for food was permitted; it was the usual mode of subsistence. Very often wealthy householders invited monks to feed, and even allowed them to take food to the monasteries on occasions. In addition to begging for food from house to house, novices had to perform manual duties. These ranged from cleaning and sweeping the cells to repairing the roofs and walls of the monasteries.

In *Mahabharata* we find that many teachers (*acharyas*) put their disciples to very hard trials. Acharya Dhaumya had three disciples— Upmanyu, Aruni, and Ved, who were from Panchal and were ideal students in term of devotion to their Guru. Dhaumya had tested the devotion of his disciples. All the three disciples of Dhaumya stood the test administered by their preceptor successfully and were blessed by him. In the name of *guru-seva* (service to the teacher) some teachers used to compel the students for hard manual work and harass them. Dhaumya used to put *Veda* even under the plough in lieu of an ox. Many a student were very grieved because of this type of vexing behaviour at the hermitage.[8]

In Jain or Buddhist viharas we do not find any such example of cruel and vexing treatment towards the inmate of the community (*sangha*).

Those who had crossed the initial stage and had gained seniority by virtue of their work in the monasteries had to devote themselves to meditation and to the study of the doctrines of Buddhism. It is interesting to note that these monastic institutions did not inculcate a cloistered outlook. The monks as well as nuns often travelled extensively spreading their doctrines. Their extramural activities were designed to confer educational and spiritual benefits on the world at large. It was only during the monsoon that they had to carry out an intensive programme of work in the monasteries.

Buddhism envisaged the democratisation of education, according to its doctrines, was not just meant for the selective few but for all those who had the will and the desire to be benefited by it. In other words, the broad-based liberal outlook on education and learning, which was one of the essential features of Buddhism, anticipates, in many ways, the present-day attitude of educational thinkers. It is widely believed today that universalisation of primary education would not only strengthen the moral and intellectual fibres of a nation but would also build its back-bone and help it to fight the battle of life.

Teacher-Taught Relationship

In the Jain-Buddhist system of education the teacher-taught relationship was very cordial and smooth. Duties were laid down for students and teachers in a variety of ways. They had to rise in their presence; and obey them without demur. They had also to minister daily needs and comforts. It was obligatory on them to listen to their discourses rapt in contemplation. Teacher in their turn, were enjoined to protect their students physically. Their intellectual and moral achievements were held up as their models were praised in public. One of their primary duties was to foster in their students a genuine desire for learning. If their teaching was not forceful and lacked inspiration and spontaneity, their reputation, it was pointed out, would decline, and the knowledge which they would impart would be dull, lifeless and insipid. Therefore, they were expected to impress upon their students. They were told that it was incumbent on them to acquire proficiency in their ancestral arts and crafts. The heritage had to be perpetuated.

Education in Morals and Ethics

Morals and Ethics of any system are regulated and monitored by its tenets or postulates to its culture, most of which are enshrined in its religion. In the following statement of T.H. Huxley we find the main tenets of Buddhism:

"Buddhism is a system which knows no God in the western sense, which denies a soul to man, which counts the belief in immorality a blunder, which refuses any efficacy to prayer and sacrifice, which bids men look to nothing but their own efforts for salvation, which in its original purity know nothing of vows of obedience and never sought the aid of secular arm; yet spread over a considerable moiety of the world with marvellous rapidity—and is still the dominant creed of a large fraction of mankind."

Out of these tenets the most important, practical and inspiring is—"Men should look to nothing but their own effort for salvation." In *Dhammapada* it is said, "Man is the master of his own destiny, if he controls himself or exercise self-restraint he can achieve supreme bliss, *i.e.*, salvation."[9] Similar thoughts are expressed in *Kammasuttam*.[10] During the time of Buddha there were many *acharyas* who believed in determinism', and because of their negative influence people were becoming inactive losing faith in themselves. Therefore, in the *Nakhatta Jatak*,[11] it is said that a man should not depend on planets and stars; but try to exert himself to achieve his goal. Those who believe in stars and planets only they do not succeed in their actions. In *Mahabharata*[12] it is rightly said, "Without adequate efforts destiny does not work. As for the movement of a chariot two wheels are required, in the same way for success both—effort and destiny—are necessary.

To the ordinary householder whose highest happiness consists in being wealthy here and going to heaven hereafter, Buddha inculcated a simple code of morality. The student of Buddhism abstains from destroying life, he is modest and full of compassion. He is kind to all living beings. Thus, the value of non-violence is the arch value in Jainism and Buddhism both; but in the former the rules of Non-violence are very strict whereas in the latter it is not so. Such type of rigidity and restrictions of Jainism was one of the causes of its non-spread beyond the boundaries of the country. Contrary to this because of the flexible and accommodative character of Buddhism it could have its dominance all over the world, particularly in South-East Asia.

The First Message

Giving his first message to his disciples, Buddha said:

"Open ye your ears, O Bhikkhus, deliverance from death is found. I teach you, I preach the Law. If ye walk according to my teaching, ye shall be partakers in a short time of that for which sons of noble families leave their homes and go to homelessness—the highest end of religious effort; we shall even in this present life apprehend the truth itself and see it face to face." Further the exalted Buddha spoke, "There are two extremes, O Bhikkhus, which the truth-seekers ought are not to follow; the one a life of sensualism which is low, ignoble, vulgar, unworthy and unprofitable; the other the pessimistic life of extreme asceticism, which is unworthy, and unprofitable. There is a Middle Path, discovered by the Tathagata, the Messiah—a path which opens the eyes and bestows understanding, which leads to peace of mind, to the higher wisdom, to full enlightenment, to eternal peace. This *Middle Path (Maddhyam Pratitada)*, which the Tathagata has discovered is the noble Eight-fold Path, *viz*., Right Knowledge—the perception of the Law of Cause and Effect, Right Thinking, Right Speech, Right Action, Right Profession, Right Exertion, Right Mindfulness, Right Contemplation. This the Middle Path which the Tathagata has discovered, and it is the path which opens the eyes, bestows understanding which leads to peace of mind, to the higher wisdom, to perfect enlightenment, to eternal peace."

The essence of the vast teachings of the Buddha is:

The entire obliteration of all that is evil,
The perfect consummation of all that is good and pure,
The complete purification of mind.

The wisdom of the ages embodied in the three *Pitakas*—the Sutta, Vinaya, Abhidhamma comprising 84,000 discourses delivered by Buddha during his ministry of forty-five years.

King Asoka, the great, inscribed his famous edicts on rocks and pillars. These inscriptions, which were in the vernacular of the day, proclaimed the ethical supremacy of duty (*dhamma*). The publicity given to these edicts indicated that popular education at this time was fairly wide-based. However, a mere knowledge of reading and writing was not considered enough. Moral instruction was not neglected as could be gathered from the didactic tone of the edicts on rocks and pillars. To quote a few:

* True conquest consists, of the conquest of men's hearts by the Law of Duty or Piety.

* Even upon the forest rock in his dominions, His Sacred Majesty looks kindly, and he seeks to make them think aright, for, if he did not, repentance would come upon his Sacred Majesty. For His Sacred Majesty desires that all animate beings should have security, self-control, peace of mind and joyousness.
* All sects deserve reverence for one reason or another. By thus acting, a man exalts his own sect and at the same time does service to the sects of other people.[13]

"Asoka's efforts for propagating the teachings of the great Master not only in India but abroad also has been very tremendous. He not only taught the tenets of Dhamma but also translated them into actions through various tools and techniques. In the words of H.G. Wells, "His reign for eight-and-twenty years was one of the brightest interludes in the troubled history of mankind. He organized a great digging of wells in India and the planting of trees for shade. He founded hospitals and public gardens and gardens for the growing of medical herbs. He created a ministry for the care of aborigines and subject races of India. He made provisions for the *education of women.* He made vast benefactions to the Buddhist teaching orders, and tried to stimulate them to a better and more energetic criticism of their own accumulated literature. For corruption and superstitions accretions had accumulated very speedily upon the pure and simple teaching of the great Indian Master. Missionaries went from Asoka to Kashmir, to Persia, to Ceylon, and Alexandria."[14]

Thus, we see that, among other things Asoka was the instrumental in the development of women's education. He sent his son and daughter (Mahendra and Sanghamitra) as missionaries to ceylon. Besides this famous example there were many nuns who worked as missionary in the country and abroad as well. No doubt, Buddhist monasteries were active centres of learning, in which secular and spiritual instruction was imparted as systematically, methodically and efficiently well-conducted and properly organised educational institutions in our own times. Many Buddhist nunneries also contributed in this direction to certain extent. Many Buddhist nuns became famous teachers, and their intellectual attainments were of a very high order. Unfortunately, there is no evidence to show that Buddhist nunneries were as active centres of learning as Buddhist monasteries were. Buddhist nunneries, it seems, made very little effort to spread educational amongst women.

It will not be out of place to give here brief life sketches and the contribution of the famous Buddhist nuns who made a mark in the history of the development of Buddhism in India and abroad by their subtle contribution. Amongst these are—Gopa (*Yashodhara*), Gautami (*mahaprajapati*), Supriya, Patachara, Ambpali, Sanghamitra, and Kisa Gotami.

Famous Buddhist Nuns

Gopa (Yashodhara)

Amongst the Buddhist nuns Gopa occupies a paramount place. When the prince Siddhartha, with the desire to attain enlightenment in the midnight left the palace, Gopa was asleep with her son Rahul. But on this, she neither repented nor displayed any mark of anguish against her husband, though she was very much aggrieved. She could realize the greatness and compassion of his heart, who used to be worried about the sorrows of the mankind. Even being in the luxurious palace she adopted the life-style of an ascetic.

The joy and mirth of the public of Kapilvastu knew no bounds when they saw the Prince Siddhartha in the attire of a monk after having achieved enlightenment. The mind of Gopa was so much vibrating with the sublime thoughts of Buddha that at the spur of the moment she decided to be disciple of Buddha and thus became a nun. Not only she became nun; but she sacrificed her only son also to Buddha, who was initiated by Anand at the instance of the Lord Buddha. This was a great sacrifice on the part of Gopa. In the word of Vivekananda: "The greatest disciple of Buddha was his wife, Gopa, who got the credit of infusing the spirit of Buddhism among the women."

Gautami (Mahaprajapati)

There was a younger sister of Buddha's mother (Mayadevi) named Gautami, who was also married to Shuddhodhan. Just after seven days of the birth of Siddhartha his mother, Mayadevi expired. On her death Gautami became very much aggrieved. Meanwhile Gautami gave a birth to a son; but she was very much worried about the up-bringing of Siddhartha. Ultimately she took a very harsh decision of giving her own child to the care of the foster mother and accepted the responsibility of Siddhartha whole heartedly and with all sincerity Siddhartha also loved her like her own mother. She succeeded in her mission and inculcated such high and sublime values in the child (Siddhartha) that enabled him to attain enlightenment and become Buddha in future. Gautami was immensely influenced by Buddha. Later on under her guidance about

500 women of Shakya dynasty were initiated to Buddhism. In the area of spiritual development she attained a great height and devoted her entire life for the spread of Buddhism.

Supriya

Supriya was the only daughter of a very rich feudal of Shravasti. She was brought in a very affectionate, luxurious and affluent way. She was a very learned lady. Mahaprajapati Gautami, aunt and his foster mother, had initiated Supriya, at the tender age of seven years, to the Buddhism. She was very famous for her scholarship and sharpness. She was not only a great scholar; but also an excellent social worker also. She lost no opportunity to serve the sick and needy persons, the poor and destitutes. An incident of her childhood indicates the height of her character, confidence and altruist nature.

Once upon a time there was a fatal famine in an affluent city of Shravasti. For want of minimum basic needs people were starving and suffering with several types of ailments and many of them died too. There were many well-to-do people also in Shravasti, who could help needy and the starving people; but they did not do so because of their selfish attitude and other personal reasons.

One day a boy in a very pitiable condition appeared at the door of the monastery where Gautam Buddha was staying. On seeing him, Ananda, pet disciple of Gautam Buddha, became very compassionate. For listening to the discourses of Buddha many people had come to the monastery including the rich persons of the city. Buddha asked them to observe charity and help the starving people and save their lives. All of them refused the appeal of the Buddha on one pretext or the other. On this occasion, Buddha's pet disciple, Anathpinda was not present over there. Buddha looked around and exclaimed: "Is there nobody who could save these brethren from this severe famine?" After the silence for some moments, one girl child stood up and said very confidently and fearlessly: "O Lord! this *Dasi* (Supriya) is prepared to carry out your orders. It is great fortune to be able to serve the people. For this purpose even if we have to sacrifice our lives, we will do so." It is needless to say that this girl child was none other than Supriya. Buddha asked her "How will you be able to feed such a great number of people?" On this Supriya said very confidently," O Lord! with your grace, my begging bowl will never be empty. It will provide food to the hungry and life to the dying; and the famine of Shravasti will disappear in no time."

Appreciating his bold but moral gesture Ananda said, "O Mother, in the form of a child, Lord Buddha may fulfil your desire." Buddha also blessed her and the gathering was dispersed.

Patachara

Patachara was born in the family of business man. On attaining the youth her parents searched a good and handsome bridegroom for her; but she refused to marry with him and married a young man of her choice. On this her parents got annoyed and she left the city and went elsewhere with her husband. She spent a happy married life and gave birth to two sons. After a gap of many years she became anxious to see her parents; and for this purpose she proceeded to Shravasti alongwith her husband and two sons. But to her bad luck, on the way her husband died of snake-bite. Even being very much upset, she continued her journey. When she was sleeping under the tree alongwith her sons, a wild animal carried away her younger son. But this was not the end of her journey, while crossing a small river, her elder son was carried away by a speedy stream. Thus on the sad demise of all her family members she was very aggrieved. Somehow she reached Shravasti, where she became totally disgusted and disappointed after having learnt that her parents also expired due to the roof-falling of the house.

At that time Buddha was staying at Shravasti. She took refuge in Buddha and his Dhamma and, in course of time she became a great nun of the monastery, and devoted her life for the propagation of Buddhism. She was a good orator. In Buddhist scriptures it is reported that once in the assembly of 500 women she gave such an extraordinary speech that being influenced by her speech the audience was so much impressed that all the 500 women got themselves converted as nuns in the Buddhist order. This is a glorious example of such a nun who could rise to such a height of spiritual vigour from an ordinary worldly life. It also proves that the words achieve power and grace from one's noble deeds and internal purity of heart. Moreover, nature of intention and will also make the words most powerful. These elements are lacking very much in our modern leaders and as such their words have almost lost the charishmatic power.

Amrapali

In Shravasti there was a prostitute (Ganika) named Amrapali who was very rich and among her properties a garden name as 'Amravan' or

'Amra-kunj' very famous. Once Buddha and his disciples passed by this way and they decided to stay in that very garden. Getting the news of Buddha's arrival Amrapali came to the garden for his '*Darshan*'. She was very famous for her beauty, etiquette and manners. After saluting the Buddha she sat by the side of Buddha in a very calm and quiet posture. Realizing the deep sense of reverence and faith in him Buddha sermonized her. Amrapali invited him to her house. Buddha gave a silent consent to her invitation. Soon after many princes came to Amrakunj to invite Buddha; but he could not or did not accept any other invitation except that of Amrapali's.

As per the promise Buddha went to Amrapali's house alongwith his disciples. Her house was none the less than any king's grand palace. For Buddha's welcome both the building and the campus were extraordinarily decorated. After the great Buddha had taken his meal, Amrapali came to him and requested him with folded hands: "O Lord! I wish to dedicate all my properties including my buildings, garden, jwellery and every thing to your lotus-feet. Kindly accept this little gift and fulfil my desire." Buddha accepted the gifts of Amrapali and made his disciple by initiating her. After some days Buddha went to Vaishali; but Amrapali stayed back at Shravasti for the service of the people. She devoted her entire life to the service of the poor and destitutes. She tried her best to purify herself by rendering selfless service to the needy and the poor. This is a glorious example to prove the divinity and dignity of a man. Once who had been prostitute, now left no stone unturned to sanctify herself by following the noble path shown by the Lord Buddha.

Sanghamitra

Sanghamitra was a daughter of the emperor, Asoka, the great. Though the foreign scholars differ on it for want of the evidence. After adopting Buddhism (After Kalinga war) Asoka devoted his entire life for the spread of Buddhism. In the eighth edict the great emperor says:

> "I have also appointed ministers of religion in order that they may exert themselves among all sects, monks as well as worldly men. I have also had in view the interest of clergy, of Brahmins, of religious mendicants, of religious Nirganthas and of various sects among whom my officers work. The ministers exert themselves, each in his corporation and the ministers of religion work generally among all sects. In this way acts of religion are promoted in the world as well as the practice of religion, *viz*., mercy and charity, truth and purity,

kindness and goodness. The progress of religion among men is secured in two ways: by positive rules and by religious sentiments. Of these two methods that of positive rules is of poor value. It is the inspiration in the heart which best prevails. It is solely by a change in the sentiments of the hearts that religion makes a real advance in inspiring a respect for life, and in the anxiety not to kill beings."

Thus, Asoka laid more and more emphasis on the second method, *i.e.*, by a change in the sentiments of heart. To achieve this noble aim he sent missionaries to all parts of world. In this process Prince Mahendra and princess Sanghamitra, 20 and 18 years of age respectively, were initiated into Buddhist Sangha. While Asoka was thinking to have coronation of his son as his apparent heir, one monk came to him and advised, "you are the real friend of religion who can induce his children to this noble cause of spreading religion." The said advice seemed to be pertinent and he asked his son and daughter very affectionately by saying these touching words: "My dear children, are you prepared to live in poverty, purity and in the service of the world till your life?" Their joy knew no bounds when they listened these words of their beloved father, since they themselves were aspiring for such type of devoted life. Enthusiastically they replied:

"We will take it as our great fortune, if you kindly permit us to spread the message of universal love and peace of the Lord Buddha. If your lordship permits us we will enter into the Sangha and devote our lives and thus will be able to contribute to attain the real aim of life by disseminating knowledge among the people."

Hearing these words of the children Asoka was overwhelmed and sent the message to the Sangha that he has dedicated both of his children to the service of Lord Buddha. The news spread like fire in Pataliputra as well as in Magadha and the people of the kingdom took the sacrifice of Asoka in a very high esteem. After their entry into the Buddhist order Mahendra and Sanghamitra were adorned with new names, *i.e.*, Dharmpal and Ayupali respectively. Both of them were ordinated in the Sangha and they started their missionary work very zealously.

At the age of 32 Prince went to Ceylon (Sri Lanka) as a missionary of Asoka for the propagation of Buddhism. Tistha, the then King of Sri Lanka was very much impressed by the charming personality and spiritual vigour of Mahendra and extended a very warm welcome to him. After sometime Anula, the princess of Sri Lanka, her 500 girl friends decided to enter into the Sangha as nuns leaving their relatives and families. There was an acute need of training in Buddhist scriptures for the nuns recently ordained. Mahendra thought that for their difficult task his sister Sanghamitra will be the most befitting one and after getting a written consent from his father Asoka, he called his sister Sanghamitra for this important task. When she reached Ceylon the islanders were almost wonder-struck to see the unique personality with modesty, simplicity, peace and piety and holy spiritual vigour on her bright face. She established Bikkhuni Sangha. With the sustained efforts of Mahendra and Sanghamitra entire Lanka became the follower of Buddhism. At the centre of the Island a township called Anuradhapur was established. This was a great event in the history of Buddhism. During her stay in the island she did many religious works for the propagation of Buddhism. The credit goes to Sanghamitra for establishing Bikkhuni Sangha of a very high order, who became very famous not only their own country but abroad also.

Once Chinese nuns were eager to get their Higher Ordination before both Bikkhunis and Bikkhus at the first available opportunity as their aim was to conform to the full *Vinay* procedure prescribed at a time when both orders were functioning under the Buddha. The *Vinaya* rules are silent as to how the Higher Ordination on Samaneris should be given at a time or a country where senior Bikkhunis are not available. The Chinese nuns came to know that in Sri Lanka after Fa-Hien returned to China from India after a sojourn at Abhayagiri Vihara, Anuradhapur. Shortly after that the Indian missionary monk Gunvardhan also arrived in China after visiting Lanka and Jawa. He too confirmed the availability of Bikkhunis at Anuradhapur.

It was when the Chinese Buddhists received government support and when sea-route from Sri Lanka to China became open to sea-faring vessels that it became possible for Bikkhunis to be brought down from Sri Lanka to China. Thus on a request made by the Chinese Emperor to the Sihalese King Sri Meghavarna a delegation of nuns was sent to China in 429 A.D. It was headed by Devasara. Four years later when the first batch of Sinhalese Bikkhunis gained proficiency in the Chinese language, a second delegation of nuns was brought down. Thus, they performed the Senior Ordination (*Upsampada*) of Chinese nuns in the full *Vinaya* Tradition. Since then the Chinese Bikkhunis Order has existed in China and Taiwan in unbroken pupillary succession observing the *Vinaya* requirements laid down in Patimokha which is common to the *Therevad Vinaya* and the Dharmagupta version of the *Vinaya* observed by the monks and nuns of China.

Kisa Gotami

Kisa Gotami, a young woman, had an only child who died. Overpowered by grief, she was not able to convince herself that her child was dead. Her friends and relatives advised her to go to Buddha, who alone, they thought, could give her spiritual help and guidance. When she went to Buddha, he told her to bring him a handful of mustard seeds from the house of a person in which there was not a single death. The woman, at first thought that it was a simple remedy. Whenever she went she mentioned the condition and asked for the seeds. But everywhere she was told by the householders that the dead exceeded the living. She then realised that she was not the only grief-stricken person in the world and that death was universal.

This story discloses on of the fundamental principles of Buddha's philosophy. Death, said Buddha, must be realistically accepted. Had there been Christ in place of Buddha, he might have brought the child to life by the virtue of his usual miracle. Mahavir and Buddha were against such miracles. This parable, contained in *Their Gatha* highlights these principles of Buddhist philosophy—(1) All things great and small whether conscious or unconscious, animate or inanimate, are subject to decay and death, (2) Everything is transient, nothing is permanent, (3) In the highest sense, there is no such thing as self.

In Jain Viharas of nuns the population was more than monks. In *Antakriddasha*, a Jain scripture (VIII volume out of 12 volumes) where the details of those nuns and monks are given who attained salvation (*Nibban*); we find the names of 33 nuns (*shravikas*), who attained the salvation in their lifetime itself. They are: 1. Padmavati, 2. Gauri, 3. Gandhari, 4. Lakshmana, 5. Suseema, 6. Jambvati, 7. Satyabhama, 8. Rukmini, 9. Mulshree, 10. Muldutta, 11. Nanda, 12. Nandvati, 13. Nandottara, 14. Nandisenika, 15. Maruta, 16. Sumaruta, 17. Mahamaruta, 18. Marudeva, 19. Bhadra, 20. Subhadra, 21. Sujata, 22. Sumana, 23. Bhootdutta, 24. Kali, 25. Sukali, 26. Mahakali, 27. Krishna, 28. Sukrishna, 29. Mahakrishna, 30. Virkrishna, 31. Ramakrishna, 32. Pitrakrishna, and 33. Mahasen Krishna.

In *Prameya-ratna-manjusha*, we find the list of 64 arts and crafts is given, which is, of course, different from the list of 64 arts given in the *Kamasutra*. For the common women-folk the education was confined to reading, writing and arithmetic (Three R's); but in the affluent families expert teachers used to impart training in different arts to the girls of these families. Kusumavali was well-versed in drawing and painting. Damayanti had got training in different arts.

In Jataka tales refer to many learned women. Sariputta was one of the main disciples of Buddha. Once, in Shrawasti four women challenged Sariputta for *Shstrartha* (debate).[15] No doubt, in Jain and Buddha system of education there were some learned women. But the number of such women was very meagre.

REFERENCES

1. R.C. Majumdar, *Corporate Life in Ancient India*, p. 297.
2. Thanang Sutra, Commentary by Abhayadev, quoted by S.B. Dev in "History of Jain Monachism" in '*Anga Suttani*', p. 140.
3. Ashvaghosh, *Buddhacharita*, VII. 20-22.
4. *Uttaraddhyayan Sutra*, Chapter, XXX.
5. *Vinaya Chullavagga*, X.1.4.
6. Dev, S.B., *op. cit*., p. 140.
7. Thanag Sutra, *op. cit*., X. 15.
8. For details please see '*Education in the Mahabharata*' by the author, pp. 153-54.
9. अत्ता हि अत्तनो नाथो को हि नाथो परो सिया।
   अत्तना व सुदन्तेन नाथं लभति दुल्स्नभम्।।
   —*Dhammapad* 160
10. जह रागेण कडाण कम्माणं, पावगो फल विवागो।
    जह य परिहीणकम्मा, सिद्धा सिद्धालयमुवें ति।।
    —*Kamma Sutta*
11. नक्खत्तं पतिमानेन्तं अत्थो बालं उपच्चगा।
    अन्धो अन्धस्स नक्खत्तं किं करिस्सन्ति तारक।।
    —*Nakkhatt Jataka*
12. यथा हि चक्रेणैकेन रथस्य गतिर्न विद्यते।
    पुरुषकारेण विना दैवं न सिध्यति।।
    —*Mahabharata*
13. J.L. Nehru, *Discovery of India*, p. 134.
14. H.G. Wells, *Short History of the World*, p. 115.
15. Natthoolal Gupta, '*Jain-Buddha Shikshan Paddhati*', p. 107.

6

WOMEN EDUCATION UNDER ISLAMIC SYSTEM

The Muslim rulers in India took a keen interest in education, and many of them founded schools, colleges and libraries in various places in their dominions. The examples of the rulers was followed by many of their influential subjects, scholars, poets and other literary men were often encouraged by the patronage of the court or of private individuals. Stipends and scholarships were often given to pupils and in many places orphanages were established. The permanent settlements of Muslims in India, and the conversion of some of the inhabitants to Islam, meant the establishment of mosques, especially in towns, was a centre of instruction and of literary activity. Muslim educational institutions are distinguished as *maktabs* and *madrasahs*.[1] The *maktab* is a primary school often attached to a mosque, whereas, *madrasah* was a school for higher learning. *Madrasahs* were schools attached to mosques and monasteries. Some of them might rise to the status of universities. The course included grammar rhetoric, logic, theology, metaphysics, literature, jurisprudence and science. Certain subjects were more cultivated in some centres than others. The medium of instruction in these schools was Persian; but the study of Arabic was compulsory for Muslims.

In Moghul times, the royalty and the aristocracy did not neglect the education of their womenfolk. Gulbadan Begum, Humayun's sister, wrote *Humayun Nama*, which is of great historical value. She has recounted the story of Humayun's marriage with Hamida Banu Begum, daughter of nobleman, who was an educated woman with strong character. She says that when Humayun offered to marry her, she refused to consider his proposal, as he had much too elevated a status for her. She said, "I would rather marry a man, whose collar I can hold than one whose skirt I cannot reach. (*Humayun Nama*) Salima, Sultan, Maham Angah, Nur Jahan, Chand Bibi, Sultana and Mumtaj Mahal were all educated women. Jahanara Begum, daughter of Shahjahan, had a genius for poetry. She wrote her own epitaph which is still to be found on her grave in Delhi and which reads:

> Let not anyone scatter over my tomb
> anything other than grass, for it is
> enough for the grave of the poor.

Zebunnisa, daughter of Aurangzeb, was a highly intellectual person who was interested in the advancement of knowledge. She established a literary academy and a library for the use of scholars. It was at her instance that Mullah Saifuddin translated Imam Razi's *Tafsire Kabir* into Persian and named it *Zebut Tafsir*, after the name of his patron. A contemporary historian has recorded that Zebunnisa was a sedulous collector of books and had a large library. (*Ma'asire Alamgiri*). She also wrote a poetry of a high order.

Besides royalty and the nobility, even among the middle classes the education of girls was quite common. There were *Maktabs* for imparting religious education to girls in private houses where the elderly ladies taught the *Quran, Gulistan, Bustan* and books on morals. It was customary that when a girl started a new book, her parents entertain the teacher and offered her presents. Even the widows of middle class families conducted private schools in their houses for the benefit of the daughters of poor people who lived in their quarters. This was considered as an act of piety.

In almost all the cities and towns of medieval India there were *Madrasahs* to mosques and mausoleums. Everywhere there were *Maktabs* in which reading, writing and arithmetic were taught to the children of all classes without any distinction of caste or creed.

The girls or women from royalty and aristocracy had the privilege to enjoy higher education also; but for their commoners there was little or no scope for this. Dr. A.L. Shrivastava writes:

> "There were no *maktabs* and *madrasahs* for girls throughout our medieval Indian history. Perhaps it was not considered desirable and necessary to educate the female section of population. There were, however, arrangements for the education of girls of the well-to-do and royal families. We know that during the early years of the Sultanate of Delhi, Sultana Razia, daughter of Iltutmish, was given good education which included not only reading and writing, but also riding and the use of arms. This shows that private coaching of

a high order was given to the daughters of rulers and nobles. Some of the wives and mothers of the Sultans of Delhi played an important role in the politics of their time. Obviously they must not only have possessed native intelligence but also some kind of literary ability imparted by well-grounded education. During the Mughal age many royal ladies, notably Gulbadan Begum, were well-read scholars and authors in Persian. She tells in the *Humayunnama* that Akbar's mother Hamida Banu Begum, when a girl, was an educated women of strong character. Maham Anaga, Salima Sultana Begum, Nur Jahan, Chand Sultana and Mumtaz Mahal were well-educated women and took intelligent interest in political and cultural matters. As Monserrate writes, Akbar bestowed "great care and attention to the education of the princesses, who are kept rigorously secluded from the sight of men. They are taught to read and write, and are trained in other ways by matrons." It can be presumed that this type of education of the inmates of the *harem* continued throughout the Mughal age. Shah Jahan's daughter Jahanara Begum was a talented poet and so was Zebunnisa, Aurangzeb's daughter. She founded a literary academy and a library. She was also a patron of scholars. We are told that she was a bibliophile and possessed a large library. It may be presumed that girls and ladies belonging to noble families were also given some kind of religious and literary education."[2]

Babar was the founding father of Mughal rule in India. Though Babar ruled over India for four years (1526-29 A.D.) only; but during this short period he made genuine attempt to spread and organize education in accordance with the liberal tradition of Islamic thought and culture. Although the exodus of many Hindu artists, craftsmen and scholars from the north to the south created a cultural hiatus, he tried very hard to bridge the gap by importing new Islamic ideas and impulses; but they were not strong enough to bring about a synthesis with the ancient Indian culture.

Humayun loved the company of learned men and often discussed literary subjects with them. Consistent with his cultural background and liberal outlook, he should have taken radical steps to coalesce Hindu-Muslim culture. But being a zealous advocate of the old Islamic tradition, he thought it best to follow a conservative policy in educational matters. He lacked the cultural vision of Akbar.

Akbar was a big synthesizer of the two cultures and lover of knowledge. He adopted and implemented a progressive educational policy. He built a library and made ample provisions for its management and maintenance. The hundreds of volumes which it contained were classified under two broad heads—sciences and histories. This step was the forerunner of subsequent developments which culminated in the emergence of the present-day scientific technique of administering libraries. It needs mention here that Akbar was not merely bibliophile. Consistent with his zeal for knowledge and mental receptivity, he spent a good deal of time in getting a number of books from his own library read and interpreted to him. It is said that he was not literate; but his innate intellectual resiliency enabled him to grasp and appreciate Hindu as well as Muslim learning. We may reasonably infer that he was eager to synthesize the old Hindu culture with the new Mulsim learning, he ordered the translation of a large number of Sanskrit books, as well as books in other languages into Persian and Hindi. This farsighted step was taken obviously with the intention of bringing about a cultural and national integration.

In the famous house of discourses (*Ibadat Khana*) numerous debates were held on philosophical and religious subjects. Preachers, lawyers, Brahmins, Jews, Jains, Buddhists, Zoroastrians and learned men professing other religions were invited to "this great meeting room" and were encouraged to express their views freely and fearlessly. Here it will not be out of place to write a few lines from 'Akbar's Dream' by Tennyson:

> "My noble friend, my faithful counsellor,
> Sit by my side. While thou art one with me,
> I seem no longer like a lonely man
> In the king's garden gathering here and there
> From each fair plant, the blossom choicest grown,
> To wreathe a crown not only for the king
> But in due time for every Mussalman,
> Brahmin and Buddhist, Christian and Parsee
> Through all the warring worlds of Hindustan."

★ ★ ★

> In our free Hall where each philosophy
> And mood of faith may hold its own, they blurt
> Their furious formalisms, I but hear
> The clash of tides that meet in narrow Seas—
> Not the great voice, not the true Deep.

After Akbar there was no foreign ruler that could reach the height of Akbar's vision as far as synthesis of two cultures is concerned. It is interesting to note that Akbar shared some of the views of present-day educational psychologies. He believed that intelligent memorisation was more effective and abiding than mechanical memorisation. Then again, his conviction that education should recognise the claims of science, on the one hand, and morality and theology, on the other, anticipated modern trends in education.

Neither Jahangir, Akbar's son, nor Shah Jahan, his grandson, could rise to Akbarian heights. The former belonged to the orthodox school of thinkers and as such he followed the old tradition of Islamic thought. Personally, he was a great lover of arts and literature. He wrote his memoirs with the help of two well-known historians of his days—Muhammad Hadi and Mutamad Khan. He had great respect for Hindu learning. But he lacked the courage as well as the vision of implementing with vigour the liberal educational policy of his father.

Shah Jahan was a patron of music, painting and fine arts. The Moghuls were great builders but Shah Jahan was the greatest of them all. His love of display, which abundantly manifested itself in the Taj Mahal, the Red Fort, the Jama Masjid and the Moti Masjid, far surpassed his desire to establish schools and colleges. In fact, he was caught in the clutches of the fundamentalists. Fundamental tendencies, actually, started soon after Akbar; but these became apparent during the time of Shah Jahan, who had the discredit of demolishing a number of Hindu temples, though he had many Hindu officers occupying high positions.

Prince Dara, Shah Jahan's son, was a great scholar and was very much interested in Hindu philosophy. He translated a number of Sanskrit works into Persian. He also translated the *Upnishads* into Persian with the help of a few learned Pundits from Benaras. As a devout Muslim, he had read many books on Sufi-ism. Nevertheless he found that "pantheism was nowhere more satisfactorily taught than in the *Vedas*, and especially in the *Upnishads*."

The desolate condition of many buildings, where higher education was imparted, throws an interesting and convincing side-light on the prevalent state of affairs. A few monarchs in their individual capacities, did give an incentive to learning, in those days. Akbar's nurse, Maham Anaga, was one of the benevolent individuals who founded a college at Delhi.

Aurangzeb was an orthodox Muslim. But he spent lavishly on Muslim education. In 1669 he ordered "the demolition of Hindu temples on an extensive scale and also banned the teaching of Ancient Indian philosophy and culture at Benaras and other places. But he was very eager" to foster the education of Muhammedan youths and diffuse learning in his dominions. "He also appointed learned professors in the different parts of his empire for educating Muslim youths." On account of his narrow outlook and fundamentalist approach he was not able to frame an enlightened educational policy. According to S.M. Jaffar, "Muslim Education helped to break down caste barriers, as Muslim schools were open to all and promoted the cultural unity of India."

As far as cultural unity of India and the remarkable progress in the field of art and architecture is concerned the remarks of Annie Besant are noteworthy:

> "Islam, in the days of its power, rejoiced to establish itself as Indian on Indian soil. The architectural works of Moghul emperors are full of enthusiasm for the Indian past, for the Indo-Saracenic style owes as much to Rajputana as to Mecca and constantinople. Asiatic among Asiatics—there was no wide gap between Mussalman conquerors and Hindu conquered: no gap in taste, or morals, or style of thought and education. The new-comer settled down as a child of the land, in his own home. His children were first Indian, and only in the second place members of Mohammedan confraternity. Today, under the necessity of a secular expression, there is nothing whatever to prevent him from projecting himself upon the cause of his own people, both Hindu and Mohammedan, and working for them with that same power with which his fathers once made the deserts of Arabia ring. For the Hindu, the point should be still more obvious. His *Avatars* have lived always for humanity. They have appeared in the hour of the national need. They have been followed by waves of popular and political rejuvenance. Neither Hinduism nor Mohammedanism has been weak in putting forward the claims of soil. The sacred text go so far as to say that he who dies for his country at once attains the Beatific vision. With regard to their fundamental duties, both faith stand like converging artillery in the world of motive, ready to shoot forth individuals upon the great common task of remarking the motherland."[3]

Teacher and Taught

After a boy or girl has finished the reading of the *Koran* from end to end, a propitious day is fixed, according to the system used in selecting names, for the purpose of making gifts to the tutor and exhibiting the child's skill in reading. The friends are invited, and the boy now able to read the *Koran*, dressed in his best, is seated in the men's hall with the *Koran* in his hands. A robe of honour (*khil'at*) and other gifts are set out for the tutor, and the boy is made to read the first, part of the second, the thirty-sixth, and the fifty-fifth chapters. The tutor then recites the *Fatiha* over the food in the name of the Prophet—the Blessing!—and makes the boy breathe on it. After the blessing he says 'I for give all the trouble I have undergone in teaching the sacred *Koran*, and I freely bestow on thee the knowledge which I have taught thee!' Then the food which has become sacred by having the whole contents of the *Koran* blown upon it is distributed, and the gifts are given to the tutor.

Besides this ceremony, at every feast, marriage, or dinner the tutor receives his dues. He is honoured, says Ja'far Sharif, as a father, because a man is said to have four fathers; his natural father, his tutor, his father-in-law, and his Murshid or spiritual guide. Besides this, the Prophet has assured us that if any person in his daily prayers says the *Dua-i-ma'sur*, or prayer for the remission of sins, for his parents and his tutor, the Almighty will hear and answer. For children who go to school the master usually writes the *Idi* or 'feast verse', or a blessing on the child, on paper sprinkled with gold dust (*zar-i-fishan*), and desires him to read it to his parents, who send an *Idi*, or feast gift, in return. Such presents are made at four festivals, the *Akiri-char-shamba*, the *Shab-i-barat*, the *Ramazan*, and the *Baqar Id*. In Mussalman schools in North India the pupils on the eve of the Friday holiday bring lamp-money (*charaghi, chiraghi*) for the teacher, a term also used for money spent in lighting a lamp on a Saint's tomb, or the percentage taken by the owner of a gambling-house.

There are thirty sections (*juz, sipara*) in the *Koran*, and at the beginning and end of each of these it is usual to give a present to the tutor, this gift being known as *Hadiya*. Of these there are four principal occasions: at the end of a quarter, half, three quarters, or the whole *Koran*, of which the last is most important. Besides this, when a boy begins a new book it is usual to give a present, sweetmeats, betel, and money. The tutor recites the *Fatiha* over these, rubs sandal-wood on the boy's neck and sometimes on his own, or taking them in his hand smells them, repeats the *Durud* or blessing, hears the lessons and then gives a half-holiday. If the number of boys be great, and so it would be necessary to give a half-holiday for each, he puts off the *Fatiha* till a Thursday, the usual half-holiday, and deals with the gifts of two or more boys at the same time.

In short, every opportunity is taken to compliment the tutor, for a blessing from his auspicious lips is as good as the reading of a hundred books, and if his curse rests on any one the reading of a hundred books will be of little profit; nay, he is equal to, if not greater than one's father or mother, inasmuch as he teaches the Law and the writings of God and His Messenger, and explains the doctrines of the Faith. While his natural parents nourish the body of their son with temporal food, he provides that which is spiritual.

Centres of Learning

In most towns where the Muslim power was established a *madrasah* or college was founded. At some places one or even many. These towns included places like Delhi, Agra, Lahore, Allahabad, and many others. Colleges were also established in some villages, such for instances Sahali[4] and Balgram[5] not far from Lucknow. Gopamau and Khairabad in Audh were at one time famous places of learning.[6] These colleges, no doubt, varied in their status and fame not only from place to place but from time to time. Much depended upon the ability and reputation of the *maulvis* who were teaching there.

The place in India which was the most famous in its days Muslim places of learning was Jaunpur.[7] It was compared to Shiraz of India. It came into prominence during the reign of Ibrahim Sharki (1402-1440) and although Sikandar Lodi destroyed its colleges when he conquered Jaunpur, it regained its position as an educational centre, scholars from far and wide came to study here. Amongst the students one, at least was Sher Shah,[8] who afterwards became the paramount Muslim sovereign of India. Having quarrelled with his father who was ruling in Bengal he went to Jaunpur, and his father wrote demanding his return, he replied that Jaunpur was the better place of education than Sasaram. The subjects which he studied were—History, Poetry, and Philosophy, and he learnt by heart the Persian poems of Sa'di. He also learnt Arabic. In the time of Ibrahim Shakri, it is said that Jaunpur accommodated hundreds of colleges and mosques, and up to the time of Emperor Shah Jahan (1627-1658) it was still in a flourishing condition. Afterwards it declined in influence, though it still continued as a place of learning well into the eighteenth century.

In the Muslim colleges for advanced learning, there were recognised grades of teachers and India had during the period of the Muslim power, when Muslim education at its zenith, many famous teachers. Specialization[9] was frequent and certain places were famous as centres for special subjects. For example, the Punjab for Astronomy and Mathematics, Delhi for the traditions of Islam, Rampur for Logic and

Medicine, and Lucknow for Theology. The higher teaching was carried on in Arabic, which was for Islam what Sanskrit was for Hinduism.

Among the many Muslim colleges which rose to prominence from time to time it is difficult to make a selection for special description. But it is difficult to make a choice for special description. But as an example of such we may mention Bidar[10] in the Bahmani kingdom. This college was founded by a private patron named Mahmud Gawan who lived in the latter part of the fifteenth century. He was an author and mathematician. His great wealth enabled him to give liberal benefactions for the advancement of learning. His college at Bidar was housed in a splendid building which he erected. It took about three years to build and cost a very large sum of money. Even in its ruined state it has been described as one of the best of the ancient buildings of India. When Aurangzeb capture Bidar the building was captured by his troops, and one part was used as a powder magazine. An accidental explosion unfortunately ruined a great part of the magnificent edifice. Attached to the college was a mosque, around which was a row of rooms for the teachers and students. There is no evidence that any girl student was admitted over there. The fame of this great historical institution could not stand with the ravages of time for a long period.

REFERENCES

1. S.M. Jaffar, *Education in Muslim India*, pp. 17-20.
2. A.L. Shrivastava, *Medieval Indian Culture*, pp. 87-88.
3. Annie Besant, *The Web of Indian Life*, pp. 96-97.
4. S.K. Das, *The Education System of Ancient Hindus*, pp. 381-83; H.D. Sankalia. University of Nalanda, p. 189.
5. Maulvi Abul Hasnat Nadvi, *Hindustan ki Qodim Islami*, pp. 36-38.
6. S.M. Jaffar, *ibid.*, p. 17.
7. Nadvi, *ibid.*, pp. 40-42.
8. Narendranath Law, *Ibid.*, p. 138.
9. Nadvi, *ibid.*, p. 104.
10. S.M. Jaffar, *ibid.*, pp. 121-26.

7

WOMEN EDUCATION UNDER BRITISH RULE

"The advancement of women is the most significant fact in modern India" wrote Mr. K. Natrajan, "a person who died a hundred years ago came to life today, the first most important change that would strike him is the revolution in the position of women." A century ago, girls' education had open enemies in India, but it is now a *sine qua non* of India's social and national development. It had to face many peculiar difficulties; the systems of *purdah* and child marriage, indifference of parents to the education of their daughters, distrust in western system of girls' education, financial pressure on the middle classes, lack of suitable curricula for girls, the absence of women teachers and girls, schools, and allied problems.

> "During the last fifty (eighty) years, however, girls' education has passed from the stage of ridicule and indifference to that of eager activity. The girl in India is no longer a step child of nature nor a Cinderella of fate. She considers herself a powerful element in national life."[1]

> "A census-taking, index-making age conceives that without literacy there is no education, as if to read the *Strand Magazine* were greater than to be the mother Shakespeare. With such an age it is difficult to argue regarding the existing education of a Hindu woman. Yet if a thorough training in a national mode of living—and extremely complicated—be an education, she has something; for the ordinary wife can act in any capacity, from that of cook or diary-mistress to that of chief of commissariat and general administrator for a hundred or more persons. If a knowledge of a language, poetry and folk-lore, with all thereby connoted of logical and imaginative development, form an education she has this, sometimes to the extent of

understanding and reciting works in Sanskrit. More: poor women who may not be able to read and write are deeply, and even passionately, possessed of the spirit of the ancient culture."[2]

Apathetic Attitude

The East India Company was first compelled to accept responsibility for the education of the Indian people under the Charter Act of 1813. But in working out this directive of the Parliament, the conservative officials of the company restricted their educational activities to men and refused to take any direct action for the education of women. They argued that the policy of the Company was one of strict social and religious neutrality; that the strong prejudices against the education of women which prevailed among the people were so deeply rooted in their social and religious life that any attempt to educate women was sure to create a very great commotion; and that the first attempts of the Company should be restricted to the education of men who would themselves, at a later date, undertake the education of their women-folk. They also refused to grant any financial assistance to special private schools established for girls. At this time, Indian private effort was almost exclusively meant for boys and most of the private educational institutions for girls were conducted by missionaries. The officials of the company felt that the encouragement of these institutions through a grant-in-aid might be regarded by the "suspicious and ill-disposed" Indian people as "subservient, in some degree, to the views of proselytism." They even refused to issue general instructions to the officers of Government to the effect that they should assist and encourage the establishment of special schools for girls under private effort on the ground that such action on the part of Government officers would be tantamount to a "compulsory order" and would be resented by the people.

A good deal of spade work had to be done by non-official effort, both Indian and, in some cases, even European, to change this attitude of apathy, or even indirect hostility, which the officials of this period showed towards the education of women. The void created by the utter absence of state effort was partially filled and the newly created desire to educate girls was first met to some extent by the missionaries who played the role of pioneers in this field also. The earliest modern schools for girls were, therefore, started under the auspices of missions for the instruction of the children of Christian converts only; but encouraged by the success of their attempts in this direction the missionaries set up institutions for the education of non-Christian girls also.

As a rule, Indians were unwilling to send their daughters to educational institutions conducted by the missionaries and it soon became evident that missionary effort, by its very nature, could not be an effective agency for the spread of education among Indian women.

A splendid lead was given at this juncture by liberal Englishmen who realised that the education of women in India could not be developed properly unless it was placed on a firmly secular basis and organised by the Indian people themselves. Among them may be mentioned David Hare who established a school for girls in Calcutta and conducted it at his own expense (1820), of Professor Patton of the Elphinstone College, Mumbai, who was responsible for the establishment in 1848, of the Students Literary and Scientific Society which organised a number of girls' schools in the city, and of J.E.D. Bethune, a member of the Council of the Governor-General and the president of the Council of Education in Bengal, who established a girls' school at Calcutta and maintained it from his own funds till his death in 1851. It was then taken over by Lord Dalhousie who also paid for its maintenance from his private purse for nearly five years.

As may be easily imagined, several great Indians, touched by the pioneer work that was being done in this field by missionaries and philanthropic Englishmen, began to lend their support to the organisation of special schools for girls and to break down the traditional popular resistances against the education of women. Among these, mention may be made of Raja Ram Mohun Roy who played an important role in the abolition of *Sati* in educating women's right to property and in emphasizing the need for their education. Another great worker in the cause was Pandit Ishwarchandra Vidyasagar who was responsible for the establishment of a number of girls' school in Bengal. It is not possible to describe here the work of the other Indian pioneers who worked in this field at this early stage and it would be enough to state that by 1854, when the Educational Despatch from the Court of Directors arrived, private Indian effort was well under way in the field of the education of women. Indians were conducting a number of special schools for girls for which liberal donations were being given by the people, and organising propaganda (through books, periodicals and lectures) to persuade the people to give education to their daughters.

By 1850, therefore, the stage had been set for a change in the State policy towards the education of women. The lead in this matter was taken by Lord Dalhousie who was then the Governor-General of India. He issued orders which observed that "no single change in the habits of the people is likely to lead to more important and beneficial consequences than the introduction of education for their female children," that a great work had been done for the "successful introduction of Native female education in India on a sound and solid foundation" and that a stage had been reached when Government should give its "frank and cordial support" to the education of Indian women. These orders were later on confirmed by the Court of Directors and by the Educational Despatch of 1854.

The Despatch of 1854 found that non-official effort had nursed the new-born education of women satisfactorily in spite of lack of support from the State. In Madras, the existence of 256 girls' schools with a total enrolment of about 8,000 of whom 1,110 were in boarding schools was reported. Most of this activity, however, was under the auspices of the missions. In Bombay, the Despatch found 65 girls' schools with an enrolment of about 6,500 pupils. In Bengal, it recorded the existence of 288 schools for girls with an enrolment of 6,869 pupils. In the North-Western Provinces and Oudh, the Despatch found only 17 girls' schools with 383 pupils, all conducted by missions. In the Punjab, the traditional education of women had continued as indigenous effort and the modern type of girls' schools had just begun to come into existence. This is not a bright picture by any means. But it is a great contrast to the conditions that existed at the opening of the nineteenth century.

The Second Phase (1854-82)—with the Despatch of 1854, the education of women enters a new phase. The primary responsibility for its development still lay upon non-official effort of missionary of India. But the State was no longer indifferent; it promised financial assistance and even direct action, if necessary.

Unfortunately, the enthusiasm with which the Despatch of 1854 accorded its support to the education of women was greatly undermined by the disturbances of 1857 which were followed by an emphatic declaration of the policy of social and religious neutrality by Her Majesty the Queen, and Lord Stanley's Despatch of 1859 sounded a more cautious note when it observed that "both the difficulties and the importance of female education are adequately appreciated by the officers of the Department of Education," and invited the views of the Governor-General-in-Council as to "the nature and degree of the influence which may safely and properly be exerted by the officers of the Department of Education to promote the extension of schools for females." The official effort in support of the education of women was, therefore, slow to expand and not much was achieved till about 1870.

The establishment of municipalities and the levy of the local fund cess were major events in the history of primary education; and they gave a great fillip to the development of the education of women also. The municipalities were local bodies and included the representatives of the Indian people. Unlike the British Government, therefore, they had no hesitation in expending money for the establishment and maintenance of girls' schools. The same could be said of the Local Fund Committees or Boards which were established for rural areas. It is true that the zeal of these local bodies for the cause of women's education was not uniform and that some of them were very progressive and liberal while others were miserly and conservative. But even after making allowance for these variations, it has to be admitted that the local bodies did a good service to the education of women by establishing special primary schools for girls, wherever necessary and possible. In consequence, a large expansion of the education of girls was brought about between 1870-71 and 1881-82.

An event of very great significance which occurred at this period was the visit of the great English social reformer, Miss Mary Carpenter, to India. Her interest in India had been greatly stimulated by her meeting with Raja Ram Mohun Roy in England and, between 1865 and 1870, she paid more than one visit to this country and gave a new lead to the education of women. Her great contribution in this field was to suggest that training colleges for women teachers should be established and that trained primary teachers should be employed in girls' schools in order to increase their utility and effectiveness. Her reputation as a social reformer and her direct access to the highest officers in the country made it possible to give immediate effect to her proposals and the first training college for women primary teachers came to be established by 1870. It is interesting to note that these early institutions had to face an unusual problem, namely, there were no women educated enough to qualify themselves for admission to them. They, therefore, set aside all the usual conventions and gave admission to adult women who had no qualification except the desire to become teachers. Some of these women, it has to be remembered, were even illiterate. The colleges, therefore, provided for their students, a condensed and intensive course of general education, and formal pedagogic training and sent out their raw recruits as teachers after a period of 3 to 5 years. This is obviously a very unorthodox approach to the problem of training of women teachers; but there was no alternative to it in these early days and in our opinion, this method has a certain utility and application even at the present time. It has to be remembered that a large majority of teachers employed in the girls' schools of this period were old men whose major qualification for the job was 'age' and who were neither efficient nor energetic enough to increase the enrolment of girls. Consequently, the encouragement which Mary Carpenter provided for the employment of women teachers and for their training gave a great stimulus to the education of girls. It also opened a very useful career to several women who were in need of some remunerative vocation to give a meaning and purpose to their lives.

It will be seen that it was only the primary education which had made some progress by 1882. Their secondary education, however, had only an humble beginning and women were just about to enter the threshold of higher education in 1882. In fact, the first woman to get the degree of an Indian University were two students of Bethune's school who graduated from the Calcutta University in 1883.

Indian Education Commission and After (1881-1901)

The Indian Education Commission discussed the problem of education of women with great insight and in considerable detail. It pointed out that, even in the most advanced State of India, 98 per cent of the female children of school-going were still outside the schools and that out of the total female population of 99.7 millions covered by its enquiries no less than 99.5 were returned as unable to read and write. It is, therefore, stressed the need to give special treatment to the education of women and recommended the provision of larger funds for it from all sources—municipal, local and provincial. In order to attract more girls to school and retain them therein for a longer period, it recommended the liberal grant of concession in fees, the award of prizes, and the institution of scholarships specially for those who are above 12 years of age. As an encouragement to private effort, it recommended that conditions for the grant of aid to girls' schools should be easier, and the rates of grant-in-aid higher than those prescribed for boys' schools. In order to encourage the employment of women teachers, it suggested the following:

* The adoption of pupil-teacher system;
* The establishment of additional normal schools under government control;
* The payment of liberal grant-in-aid to training institutions conducted by private efforts;
* The offer of liberal inducements to the wives of school masters to qualify them as school teachers;

* Training of widows as teachers for primary schools;
* The offer of liberal prizes to girls (as to the teachers who train them) who would agree to become teachers; and
* The grant of special assistance to the girls' schools with hostels attached.

Regarding the supervision of girls' schools, it recommended the organisation and strengthening of a special Inspectorate for girls' schools specially on the ground that women would agree to work as teachers more readily if the inspecting officers were also women. It also recommended the adoption of special measures to promote the secondary education of girls. As the general opinion at this period was strongly in favour of differentiation of curricula for boys and girls, the commission recommended:

1. that the standards of instruction in girls' schools whether primary or secondary, should be simpler than those for boys' schools;
2. that they should be drawn up with special reference to the requirements of home-life and the occupation open to the women; and
3. that special text-books should be prepared for girls' schools.

With the changes in the public opinion that have come about during last century, some of the recommendations of the commission, specially those that emphasise the establishment of separate schools at all for girls at all levels not excluding the lower primary or those that referred to the controversial issue of the differentiation of curriculum, have now lost much of their importance, but most of them are of great interest even today and can be adopted with advantage in several parts of the country.

Unfortunately, the two decades following the report of the commission were period of financial stringency, so that it was not possible for government to organise special programmes for the development of the education of women or to assign adequate grants for the purpose. But the expansion of private enterprise was so great that, in spite of the lukewarm support from the State, the education of women evinced some progress by the end of 19th century.

Even in 1901-02, the burden of providing educational facilities for girls lay heavily on private effort. Of the 12 colleges for women, only one, the Bethune college, was conducted by government. Of the 422 secondary schools, as many as 356 were conducted by private effort; and even at the primary stage, private effort accounted for 3,982 girls' schools out of the total of 5,305. Similarly, 32 training schools out of a total of 45 were under private management.

One significant development of the latter half of the 19th century was the opening of careers outside the home to women. The first career to be opened was that of teachers. A career in medicine was the next to be opened and in 1901-02, there were 76 women in medical colleges and 166 in medical schools. Besides there were a fairly large number of women undergoing training as nurses, midwives, etc. An important event of this period was the creation of Lady Dufferin Fund with the sole object of developing medical education among women. But very liberal encouragement from other sources also was available at this time. But as in the case of secondary and collegiate education most of the students in medical and art courses were Europeans, Anglo-Indians, Indian Christians or Parsis. The Hindu and Muslim women had not yet taken kindly to these careers.

A Period of Development (1921-41)

The Education of women showed a better progress during the next period of twenty years, mainly owing to the great public awakening created by the national struggle for independence and the First World War. The inauguration of Indian Women University in June 1961, virtually marked the beginning of new era in the history of women education in our country. The idea of inaugurating a university exclusively for women and its own special curricula generated variety of reactions in those days. Prof. D.K. Karve, the founder of the university had done experiment in women's education at Poona. The university maintained a college of some thirty persons. As said earlier, medical education for women also received the attention of the government and a scheme was formulated for a school to train Indian nurses and midwives. It was proposed in the scheme with a medical college for women in Delhi. Lady Hardinge Medical College for Women was opened in February 1916. The main object of this institution was to provide complete courses of instruction to Indian women who wished to qualify for a university degree in medicine or to receive full training as nurses.

Change in Attitude

By 1921 there was a definite attitudinal change in the educated Indians, who were eager to provide good education to their daughters for various socio-economic factors. One of the vital reasons, as stated above, was the social awakening and the freedom struggle. Versatile leaders like Mahatma Gandhi took the cause of women as a part of the freedom struggle. In *Young India* (28 June 1928) he had rightly observed: "The sooner it is recognized that many of our social evils impede our march towards *Swaraj* the greater will be our progress towards our cherished goal. To postpone social reforms, till after the attainment of *Swaraj*, is not to know the meaning of *Swaraj*." According to him *Swaraj* meant "not mere political awakening, but an all-round awakening—social, educational, moral, economic and political." Again in *Young India* (27 August 1925) he wrote:

> "I am strongly in favour of raising the age of consent not merely to 14 but to 16. I should heartily endorsed my movement whose object is to save innocent girls of tender age from man's lust. A so-called marriage rite ought no longer confer legally upon an immoral and inhuman act, which consummation even at the age of 14, undoubtedly. Sanskrit texts of doubtful authority cannot be invoked to sanctify a practice which is in itself immoral. I have seen the ruin of the health of many a child mother, and when the horrors of an early marriage is added enforced early widowhood, human tragedy becomes complete. Any sensible legislation in the direction of raising the age of consent will certainly will have my approval."

Thus, we see that social customs had greatly multiplied the difficulties in the way of female education. But upon this question opinion was slowly changing, and educated young men, of middle class were beginning to look for literate wives. But the percentage of female literacy was very poor in comparison with male literacy. So Mont Ford report sounded a note of warning. So long as education was confined to one sex, the social complexion of the country must react upon and retard political progress; and for this reason the great gulf between men and women in respect of education was one of the most serious problems which had to be faced in India. Rightly education was a great social problem of the country and until female education had made up a great deal more way it had lost under the restraints imposed upon it by Indian social traditions, India could not attain the place which she aspired as a modern nation. This was the feeling of many educated men and women in the country.

According to Prof. S.N. Mukerji,

"The present educational system of the country is the result of

> Macaulay's Minue and Wood's Despatch (1854). These two famous documents were inspired by the then utilitarian philosophy, a superiority of the West, and the administrative requirement of British India. While Macaulay was an empiricist utilitarian, James Mill who is supposed to have drafted Wood's Despatch was a rationalist utilitarian. The system aimed at preparing a class of people, who could understand the English language and sympathize with the culture of their rulers. Benthemite radicalism was also partially responsible for Macaulay's contempt for Arabic and Sanskrit. To a Whig like Macaulay, the classics had a decreasing utility in an educational scheme."[3]

Utilitarian philosophy was a deep-rooted conviction Western superiority and a contempt for the civilization of the East. British conquests and a rapid increase of wealth in England as a result of the nineteenth century had created in the majority of Englishmen a racial superiority and a contempt for Eastern nations. To Macaulay and his contemporaries, a single self of a good European library was worth the whole native literature of India and Arabia (Macaulay's Minute).

According to the Despatch of 1854, the total number of girls was 256 in Channai, 65 in Mumbai, 288 in Bengal and 17 in North Western Provinces. In the Punjab, the traditional education of women had continued an indigenous effort and the modern type of girls' schools had just begun to come into existence.

Sadler Commission, 1917

The Calcutta University Commission was appointed in 1917 under the chairmanship of a great educationist, Sir Michael Sadler, in connection with higher education in India. After the name of its chairman. It is also known as Sadler Commission. It formulated two principles in its report regarding female education—the modification of the curriculum to suit the needs of different classes, and the utilisation of the advice of the ladies in formulating a suitable scheme of instruction.

Education of Women under Indian Control (1921-47)

In 1921, education at the State level was transferred to the control of Indian Ministers under the system of Diarchy and in 1937, Provincial Autonomy was introduced. These changes made it possible to abandon the hesitant and over-cautious policies of the British Government, and the State now began to take a more active part in the promotion of the education of women. Other favourable factors of this period were: (i) the awakening in the people on account of the political struggle for Independence and the Second World War, (ii) a still further rise in the age of marriage, due partly to the Sarda Act but mainly to social and economic pressures; (iii) the teachings of Mahatma Gandhi who dominated the entire history of those days, and (iv) the phenomenal awakening of Indian womanhood which found its most striking and significant expression in the various representative organisations that rapidly sprang up all over the country and in the establishment of a number of pioneering institutions founded by prominent women for the advancement of women in educational and other fields.

On the negative side, we may mention that this was a period of general financial stringency up to 1937 and that, when the economic situation eased a little, the efforts of Government had to be concentrated on the War. Moreover, the Government of India was almost completely divorced from education during this period and did not give financial assistance to any educational developments. The Indian people also were mostly engaged in the political struggle and had little time for large scale constructive activities. In spite of these difficulties, the education of women had considerable progress during this period.

It will be seen that the total number of girls under instruction has increased from 12,24,128 in 1921-22 to 42,97,785 in 1946-47 (inclusive of those in unrecognized institutions). A large increase has occurred in higher education and the total number of girls reading at the collegiate stage has risen from 905 in 1921-22 to 23,207 in 1946-47. This increase also obviously implies that the higher education of women is no longer restricted to a few advanced communities. Even greater is the increase at the secondary stage where the number of girls enrolled rose from 26,163 in 1921-22 to 6,02,280 in 1946-47. At the primary stage also, there has been a very large increase of enrolment from 11,86,224 in 1921-22 to 34,75,165 in 1946-47. The increase of enrolment in special schools which open out different careers for women has also been large from 10,836 in 1921-22 to 56,090 in 1946-47.

The total number of education institutions in the country in 1946-47 was 2,18,165 out of which 28,196 were specially meant for girls. Of these, latter 59 were Arts and Science colleges, 2,370 were secondary schools (727 high schools and 1,643 middle schools), 21,479 were primary schools and 4,288 were institutions for professional, technical and special education. If these statistics are compared to those of 1921-

22 given earlier, it will be seen that there has been a considerable increase of separate institutions for girls at every stage except the primary, where the number of institutions has actually decreased from 21,956 in 1921-22 to 21, 479 in 1946-47. This fall is due to the adoption of co-education as a policy at the primary stage and is not significant, especially in view of the large increase in the enrolment of girls from 11.86 lakhs in 1921-22 to 34.75 lakhs in 1946-47. It is also necessary to point out that owing to the greater initiative shown by the State Governments and local bodies the burden on private effort was reduced considerably and it accounted for 16,979 institutions only out of a total of 28,196.

At the collegiate stage, for example, more than 50 per cent of the total number of girls enrolled were studying in mixed institutions in 1946-47. The same may also be said of colleges for professional education. In the primary stage, the number of girls studying in mixed schools is even larger than that in separate institutions. In the secondary schools as well as in the special schools for technical, vocational and special education, however, the enrolment in separate institutions is much larger than that in mixed schools. This is, of course, quite understandable. But taking the overall picture into consideration, we find that a little more than half of the number of girls under instruction were studying in mixed schools in 1946-47. This is a great change indeed because, in 1921-22, only about 35 per cent of the total number of girls under instruction were studying in mixed institutions.

By 1947 when the British power was withdrawn from India, the modern education of women was about a hundred and twenty-five years old. The evaluation of the achievements of this period can be done in two ways. The first is to compare the conditions that existed in India in 1800 to those that existed in 1946-47. This backward look shows a great achievement qualitative as well as quantitative. Educational opportunities had been opened to women at all stages during this period and their social status had been raised to some extent. Qualitatively, this education had brought women a new awareness of themselves and opened out to them a larger way of life. But if we compare the advance of the education of women with what was achieved in other progressive countries during the same period or with what ought to have been, we have a sense of great dissatisfaction. In 1946-47, even the education of men was backward when measured by the common standards that are now adopted in the West; and in spite of this the gap between their education and that of women was still very wide.

Hartog Committee (1927-29)

It was an auxiliary Committee which was appointed under Simon Commission under the presidentship of Sir Philip Hartog, who was one of the members of the Indian Statutory Commission and had served for several years in India as a member of the Calcutta University Commission and as the Vice Chancellor of the Dacca University. He submitted his report in September, 1929. Hartog Committee also expressed more or less the same view as endorsed by Sadler Commission in 1917. This Committee fully sympathised with the cause of female education. It said:

> "The education of women especially in the higher stage will make available to the country a wealth of capacity that is now largely wasted through lack of opportunity. It is only through education that Indian women will be able to contribute in increasing measure to the culture, the ideals and activities of the country."

In conclusion it said:

> "The whole case for women's education rests on the claim that education is not the privilege of one sex, but equally right of the both, and neither one sex nor the other can advance by itself without a strain on the social and national system and injury to itself. The time has come to redress the balance and we believe that the difficulties in the way of women's education are beginning to lose their force and the opportunity has arrived for a great new advance. We are definitely of opinion that, in the interest of the Indian education as a whole priority now should be given to the claims of girls' education in every scheme of expansion."

Thus, the committee made recommendation for its expansion and consolidation of female education.

Analysing the reason for slow advance in the direction of women's education the Report of the National Committee on Women's Education remarked as following:

> "On closer analysis, it is, therefore, quite evident that: (i) *the wide gap which now exists between the education of men and women is not being closed as rapidly as one would desire it*, and that (ii) *the pace of progress in the less advanced parts of the country leaves*

much to be desired. It is these two considerations that, in our opinion, are of extreme importance at the present time and one of the basic objectives of this Report is to analyze the causes that lead to these weaknesses and to suggest the remedies to eliminate them."

Causes of Slow Progress

According to the said report the reasons for slow advance of the education of women, for the wide gap that existed between it and the education of men, and for the comparative backwardness of rural areas were three:

1. The decision of government to take no direct action in the matter and to leave the education of women mainly to the private effort of the people, adversely affected the pace of expansion, especially because the people were preoccupied with the political struggle. Moreover, the expansion remained limited mostly to urban areas because hardly any private effort was available in rural areas which were generally neglected and more backward;
2. No adequate machinery was created to deal with the important and stupendous problem of the education of women. A significant advance in solving this problem would have been possible only if an adequate machinery had been created and if it had been created and if it had been helped by the support of the entire machinery of the government on the one hand and the full co-operation of the people on the other. The first of these was not possible under the over-cautious policy of social and religious mentality adopted by government and the second was more or less ruled out by the political conditions of the day; and
3. Education as a whole was starved for funds during the British period; but in particular a special problem like women's education needed very large funds which were never made available.

In spite of the several gains of this period, therefore, this is to be admitted that the progress achieved has been inadequate and unbalanced.

Contribution of Gandhiji

Among many other socio-political activities Mahatma Gandhi also worked for liberation of women. For him emancipation of women was an integral part of freedom struggle. He saw no difference between the two sexes. To him son and daughter stood on equal footing and any distinction between the two was unjust, and immoral. He wanted equal treatment to both. There was no reason for jubilation over the birth of a son and for anxiety over that of a daughter. Both are God's gift. They have equal right to live, and were equally necessary to keep the world going. In his *Ashram*, all the inmates engaged in physical and intellectual work were treated as equals and everyone was provided with facilities, according to his or her needs. He was a staunch supporter of women's right.

Gandhiji looked upon woman as the companion of man, gifted with equal mental capacities and she had the right to participate in very minutest detail in the activities of man. She was entitled to a supreme place in her own sphere of activity as man was in his sphere. He observed:

> "The wife is not the slave of the husband, but his comrade, otherwise known as his better-half, his colleague and friend. She is a co-sharer with him of equal rights and of equal duties. Their obligations towards each other and towards the world must be the same and reciprocal."

For the cause of women's education he took an active part in the movement of emancipation of women. Assessing the contribution of Mahatma Gandhi to this core S.N. Mukerji has rightly observed:

> "The greatest impetus to women's cause, however, came from the national movement launched by Mahatma Gandhi His appeal to Indian mothers for the country's cause fired their spirit of nationalism. Thousands of Indian ladies came out of the *purdah*, and suffered the same hardships as men did, whether it was in standing up to *lathi* charges or by police imprisonment in jail or for breaking intolerable laws. Numerous public gatherings of women are now annually held to discuss programmes of social and educational reconstruction. Sharda Act has also made child-marriage illegal throughout the country and is making it possible for many girls to enjoy girlhood, otherwise they used to pass from childhood to marriage all of a sudden. These factors have contributed a good deal to the growth of girls' education. All have fully realised that the education of the girl is the education of the mother and through her of her children."[4]

REFERENCES

1. S.N. Mukerji, *Education in India: Today and Tomorrow*, p. 252.
2. Sister Nivedita, *The Web of Indian Life*, pp. 90-91.
3. *Education in India: Today and Tomorrow*, p. 6.
4. *Ibid.*, p. 256.

8

COMMISSIONS AND COMMITTEES ON WOMEN EDUCATION

Besides good number of Constitutional provisions and Directives various Commissions and Committees have been constituted to frame suitable policies to eradicate educational disparities; in sexes. In a short chapter of its report, University Education Commission (UEC) 1948-49 recommended:

* To increase educational opportunities for women.
* To provide intelligent educational guidance to women so that they shall not try to imitate men; but shall desire good education as women.
* To frame men's and women's education which should not in general be identical in all respects.
* To give as much thought and consideration to the life needs of women as to those of men where new colleges are established to serve both men and women students.

Towards the end of Third Five Year Plan (1961-66), the Government set up a Commission on education to link it with the programmes of national development. To bring educational parity in sexes, the Commission 1964-66 in its report, Education and National Development, endorsed recommendations of the National Committee on Women Education 1958-59. And Smt. Hansa Mehta Committee on differentiation of curricula between boys and girls 1961-62. The members of the National Committee also took up the special studies and surveys as shown below:

(i) Wastage and stagnation—Shri J.P. Nayak
(ii) Co-education—Smt. Zahra Ahmed
(iii) Sample Survey of the leisure time of adult women in urban and

rural areas—Smt. O.C. Shrinivasan

(iv) A model syllabus of condensed courses for adult women—Kumari S. Panandikar.

After a span of just two years, the draft statement of the Parliamentary Committee on Women's Education in 1967 was adopted by the Government as the National Educational Policy 1967-68.

The policy (NEP 1967-68) in its resolution stated that the education of the girls should receive emphasis only on grounds of social justice but also because it accelerates social transformation. Reorganising the reduced enrolment gap in general education and the widening gulf in the field of vocational education the policy recommended to organise ITIs and polytechnics for women. At the end it clearly indicated to review the progress five yearly. But till 1976 no special effort was made to review it. Indeed at the time of every new Five Year Plan reviews were being made just to decide upon the programmes for the coming five years. But their impact was insignificant. Similarly, in the early seventies, assessments were made on Indian Women's Status by a Committee 1971-74. Recording major failure in bringing the parity in sexes the Committee in Chapter 6 of its report viewed that the educational system today has not even attempted to undertake this responsibility, it was in the year 1976 that a direct attempt was made by the Government to review the Education Policy. This ultimately resulted in National Policy on Education (NPE 1979) which translated the Article 45 of the Indian Constitution by emphasizing primary education by 1989 for all children in the age group of 6-14 through expansion of elementary schools and formulation of non-formal education scheme. The policy recommended for giving incentives such as mid-day meals, free text-books, stationery and uniforms for improving literacy among girls.

On the basis of recommendations of NPE 1986 the Government announced the appointment of a committee on 7th May, 1990, exactly after five years of the commencement of NPE-1986 to review the policy and its POA. The Committee for review of National Policy on Education (NPE) in its report (1990). Towards an enlightened and Humane Society, submitted to the Government of India in December 1990 recommended the following:

— For access to and retention of girls in school and quality learning, it is necessary: (i) to improve the access of households to water, fuel, and fodder; (ii) to provide full-fledged day care services for the 0-3 age-group during school hours; and (iii) to implement decentralized and participative mode of planning and management for removing regional disparities in education of both sexes.

— Gender perspective should be brought into the curriculum through projection of a positive image of the role of women, strengthening science and mathematics education among girls, and elimination of sexist biased concepts and gender stereotypes from all text-books.
— Gender equality and empowerment of women should be promoted through all media channels. Vocational training for women should be encouraged in non-traditional occupations following on undifferentiated curriculum for boys and girls.
— The teacher's training programmes should be restructured through decentralization in curriculum planning, conduction of training programme for teacher educators and teachers to sensitise them to women issues, and diffusion of information for educational administrators.
— For research and development of women's studies, women's study centres should be organized in both universities and institutions. Besides women's studies each findings should be incorporated into curriculum revision and teach training programme at all levels of education.
— The foundation courses introduced by University Grants Commission should be reviewed to incorporate women's dimensions.
— Women's Development Centres should be given funds to conduct extension services such as awareness programmes, workshops and seminars at both school and community levels.
— The proportion of women teachers in primary, middle, and high schools should be increased to at least 50 per cent.
— Mahila Samakhya (empowerment of women) would be implemented with organic linkages with the Early Childhood Care Education (ECCE) programme and universalization of girl's elementary education. Relevant adult education programme should be developed for illiterate women in the 15-35 age group.
— Allocation of resources should be increased in both plan and non-plan sectors of elementary, secondary, vocational and higher education.

Central Advisory Board of Education

Management of all school based programme should be decentralized through Panchayati Raj and heads of primary, middle, and higher secondary schools. The recommended measures on NPERC (1990) were further reviewed by the Central Advisory Board of Education (CABE) Committee under the Chairmanship of Janardana Reddy. Submitting its report in January 1992, the committee in its Chapter 3—Education and Women's equality—view that the NPERC's perspective is very much in tune with what NPE-1986 envisaged in respect of women's education. It very clearly recommended that the coordination between girl's school and access to water, fuel, and fodder can be better discharged by the Department of Women and Child Development and the Planning Commission at the centre, the corresponding agencies at the State level, and the agencies responsible at the district and non-district level than merely by Department of Education.

With respect to resources it said that earmarking of funds may not be administratively feasible as the problems of women's education cuts across caste and regional barriers. In accordance with its recommendation a POA was evolved and the CABE endorsed the document in August, 1992. The POA 1992 viewed that the actions of POA 1986 to promote education for women's equality can hardly be improved upon except modification of the contents whatever appropriate. Accordingly it developed a full chapter for actions relating to empowerment of women, research and women's studies, Universalization of elementary education and adult education women's access to vocational, technical professional education and emergent technologies, media and management structure at centre and State levels.

In addition to the policies framed by different commissions and committees sustained efforts have been made to look into the problems of women education since the inception of the Indian Planning in 1951-52. Opening a separate chapter on women and development Sixth Five Year Plan (1980-85) proposed a centrally sponsored scheme on 50-50 basis with the State government for construction of hostels for encouraging SC and ST girls education. The Seventh Five Year Plan (1985-90) accorded priority to free education for girls up to the end of higher secondary, functional literacy for rural women, and open learning system for talented girls to pursue higher education. Universalization of elementary education for girls, women's literacy, sustainability of literacy skill and attainment of minimum levels of learning are the thrust areas of the current Eighth Five Year Plan (1992-97).

Here we would like to give critical appraisal of various Commissions and Committees appointed from time to time soon after the independence, *i.e.*, from 1948 to 1986 and highlight their important role for emancipation of the girls and women by enhancing various programmes and policies for the education of the fair sex.

University Education Commission (1948-49)

The rapid advancement of women is the most significant fact in developing India. As K. Natarajan wrote:

> "If a person who died a hundred years ago came to life today, the first and most important change that would strike him is the revolution in the position of women." (*Indian Social Reformer*, 1937)

The University Education Commission, with Dr. Radha Krishnan as its Chairman, was appointed by Government of India on the 4th November, 1948, to report on Indian University Education and suggest improvements and extensions that may be desirable to suit present and future requirements of the country. The Commission presented its study on University Education before the Government of India in August 1949.

The University Education Commission (1948-49) included a short chapter on Women's Education but did not pose any special issues relating to it. Regarding higher education, it observed, women's and men's education should have many elements in common, but should not generally be identical in all respects.

Regarding the importance of women's education, the Commission observed:

> "There cannot be an educated people without educated women. If general education had to be limited to men or to women, that opportunity should be given to women, for then it would most surely be passed on to the next generation." (UEC 1948-49)

Considering this point, it can be argued that if a woman has open mindedness, inquiring and alert mind, capable of seeing behind rumour and tradition to find facts behind the happenings, has the curiosity to know the nature of the world around her, and has interest in history and literature and also enjoys and values them, then her children will learn these interests and attitudes from her. For an educated mother who lives and works with children in the home is the best teacher in the world of both character and intelligence. As Arthur Mathew wrote:

> "If the Government by the initial exclusion of the masses accentuated the segregation of the masses from the privileged few, by their initial restriction of their educational efforts to the male population, they brought a line of division where it had never existed before, within the household." (UEC 1948-49)

General education is very important not only for men but also for women because it is the education that makes men's and women's living interesting and intelligent. It also makes a person a good citizen of his society. General education means those phases of learning which should be the common experience of all men and women (Good, 1973). The purpose of general education at the college level are much the same as those at the high school level. The college general education programme attempts to give some broad experiences in the social sciences, humanities, and natural sciences needed by a well-educated man. It seeks intellectual development in the sense that a person can think critically for himself. It seeks to form socially valuable attitudes, not attitudes of rigidity and inflexibility. It is clear that 'general education is concerned with the development of a balanced individual who can take his place as a well-adjusted person in society and who can approach with intelligence the social and cultural problems of his day (Anderson, 1956).

The University Education Commission had made the suggestion that the education of women should be such as to suit them as women, that women's education should lead them to pretty accomplishments such as drawing, painting or the like—skills which will enable well-to-do women to pass their time harmlessly while their husbands do the early important work. This, however, is not accepted to those these days who feel that women should share with men the life and thought and interests of the times. For they are quite capable of carrying on the same academic work as men, with no less thoroughness and quality. The distribution of general ability among women is approximately the same as among men, but it does not follow that in all things men's and women's education should be identical. The University Education Commission wrote:

> "Indian universities for the most part are places of preparation for a man's world. Little thought has been given to the education of

women as women. Women must share the same programme as men, or go without. There are many ways in which women's interests or fields of work diverge from those of men and educational programmes should, therefore, take these facts into account."

(UEC 1948-49)

Not only in India but also in other countries of the world, husbands and wives commonly play different roles. In general practice, the husband earns the livelihood and the wife maintains the household. But many women who desire to raise their standard of living also want to work outside to augment family income. Education, therefore, comes handy, for it helps the women in successfully running the household in better looking, after her children and in functioning as a better human being in and outside the home.

In order, therefore, to better coordinate the relationship between the man and the woman, it becomes the responsibility of any form of government to frame the educational system in such a way that the discrimination between men and women can be removed. But while designing the curriculum it should also be kept in mind that everyone—both man and woman—has certain special potentialities of his which should be given full scope for development.

As far as preparation for home family life is concerned, the University Commission emphasized: "Her education as a woman should include practical laboratory experience in the care of a home and family. Equipment for girls' education might well include":

1. A baby home.
2. A nursing school, which incidentally would relieve nearby mothers during a part of the day.
3. A club for school children and adolescents.
4. A little home for convalescents.
5. A small home for old people.
6. A home-setting where students may have experience in maintenance and operation and where they may act as hostesses. (UEC 1948-49).

The above recommendations of the University Education Commission are however, not to our entire satisfaction. For, we are living in India which is not as developed as U.S.A, U.S.S.R., Japan, etc. If we want to implement any programme of educational reform, we must keep all the problems and disparities regarding the society and its economy in our mind. The Commission's recommendations do not relate to the large number of women, about 70 per cent of the population who are living in the most backward rural areas. These suggestions relate more suitably to the women in the urban areas.

There had been inadequate training for women's education and inadequate provision for full education for women in our colleges and universities. At that time only the Women's Christian College and Queen Mary's College for women—both at Chennai—and the Isabella Thoburn College at Lucknow were conducting some kind of training programme. Therefore, the educational system at all levels should make men and women to overcome all the complexities and disparities and should also make them very adjustable in the society.

The Commission has recommended the following special courses for women in order to enable them to fit themselves well in their social set up: (UEC 1948-49).

(a) Home economics
(b) Nursing
(c) Teaching
(d) Fine arts.

The home economics, according to the Dictionary of Education, is:

(1) College instruction offered at the undergraduate and graduate levels to prepare students for home-making and for a variety of professional fields such as teaching, dietetics, management, food service, certain business careers, home economics extension and research.
(2) A discipline that draws from the biological, physical and social sciences and the humanities the content needed to help people solve problems of food, clothing, shelter, and relationships and that deals with the development of understanding, skills, and attitudes, essential to the improvement of the ways of living of individuals, families, and community groups. (Good, 1973).

The Commission observed that:

"A mastery of home-economics is useful both to the homekeeper and to the woman who, from choice or necessity, is to practice a profession outside the home." (UEC 1948-49). According to one of the schools in this field, "Courses in Home Economics deal with the effective feeding and clothing of the family and others; the care and guidance of children, the family relationships, the growth of artistic sense, and taste which brings beauty into the home; the organization and running of the home on a sound economic, social and hygienic basis, and the care and use of equipment." (UEC 1948-49)

But now-a-days we find that with the relation of Home economics the author thought women students generally shun this course and insist on the same courses as men, such as engineering, agriculture, medicine and veterinary science, etc. It is being stressed that in order to bring our country in the row of developed countries, there should be a special provision for women's education in the same field as in the case of men. In keeping with the spirit of our constitutional provisions, they should be given the same opportunities of education and employment as enjoyed by men.

In the ancient time, in families at all social levels, all these types of art regarding home-making or home economics was transferred most informally from the mother to the daughter through the generations. A home economics course can help to preserve and transmit the best of those ancient arts with the integration and correlation of modern arts. As Confucius (551-479 B.C.), the father of Chinese history, said:

> ". . . The ideal is the harmony of the perfect individual and well ordered society based on the mutual moral objections of the fine human relations between ruler and minister, father and sons, older brother and younger brother, husband and wife and one friend and another, with filial piety and brotherly respect as the two fundamental virtues." (Edwards, 1967)

As it is indicated by Confucius, the author feels that there should be the best relationship between husband and wife. And this relationship can best be developed through education. In brief, occupations within the general field of home economics include child development, family relations, food and nutrition, home economics, housing and designing, institution management and textiles and clothing.

The Commission has also observed: A well-designed course in Home Economics will include:

1. The elements of a general education, except as they have already been acquired in secondary schools.

2. 'Core courses' which are desirable for everyone in the field; and
3. Specialized courses as needed or desired by the individual students. (UEC 1948-49)

The New York State College of Home Economics at Cornell University, Ithaca, New York, recommended the following 'Core Courses' in Home Economics:

> "The Individual and his relations with others, Household processes, Economic conditions in Relations to the Welfare of Families, Management in Homes, Elementary Food and Nutrition, Home Furnishings, and Clothing Selection, Purchase and Core." (UEC 1948-49)

It is observed that the study of Home Economics is only for women, but its very important aim is to help women and men to see the true dignity of home-making and to give it an ideal value. This is the need for men as well as for women. In the field of Institutional Management, men share the field with women. Even today there is a big scope for large extension of Home Economics teaching in Indian Higher Education.

Regarding the nursing course for women, the Commission observed:

> "To become professional nurses, students should begin their training after high school, should do work equivalent to that required for the B.Sc. degree and should receive the degree of B.Sc. in Nursing. . . . The nursing course should be combined with actual practice at caring for the sick. The duration of the course should be the same as required for the B.Sc. degree." (UEC 1948-49)

In Western countries nursing profession is an honoured profession for women and it will be entirely in the interest of our country, if it has the same standing here. Today, even 51 years after the Independence, there is still a lack of general facilities regarding nursing profession in our country. There is urgent need of large expansion of nursing service in our hospitals, both urban and rural. Nursing is not only good for women as a profession, but also good for the health of the country.

It is universally accepted that mother is the first school of child. Women are the first and the natural teachers for the child and lay the foundation of his formal education. Teaching profession is thus one of the best professions for women. On this point, the Commission has rightly remarked:

"With the expansion of education in democratic India, the call for well-educated and well-trained teachers for elementary and secondary schooling will probably long exceed the supply. Specially for the teacher's calling it is important that education shall not be limited to narrow specialization, but that well proportioned general education shall provide a broad foundation for special interest." (UEC 1948-49)

Even today, we find that there is far greater need of well-educated and well-cultured teachers, specially women teachers, in our country than it was when the Commission made the above observations.

Women can be much better teachers than men particularly in the early years of schooling. For, they can teach children with greater love and affection than is possible for men. And this is an essential requirement for the healthy and normal growth of children. Therefore, up to VIII class preferably there should be women teachers.

Keeping in mind the social taboos in our country, there are different views regarding co-education. Traditionally, from the thirteenth or fourteenth years of age, till above the eighteenth years, the boys and girls are educated in segregation. This is a sound practice. Co-education at the secondary school level is undesirable. But after that there can be co-education, especially in the Universities.

"The modern trend is for equality of opportunity for women in all spheres, and it cannot be arrested. There should be no distinctions of any kind of women from men, after the matriculation." (UEC 1948-49)

Regarding co-education after the age of 18 years that at the degree level, the Commission wrote:

"As the age of entry to degree colleges would be approximately eighteen, college may be co-educational, as it is at present in many medical colleges. Separate institutions at this level would demand unjustified increase in expense. To maintain separate institutions for men and women side by side, duplicating equipment even when it is very inadequate would be an undue tax upon limited financial resources. Separate women's colleges commonly have poorer buildings, poorer equipment, and less able teachers. So far as possible co-educational institutions should be encouraged at the degree level." (UEC 1948-49)

The need for co-education at the university (degree) level, thus becomes quite obvious. We find that we do not have sufficient resources for financing education. We have only 2.2 per cent of our total national income to spend on education, (*Navbharat*, 1986), while we need to spend at least 6.0 per cent of our gross national income on education in order to uplift our people and to take them to the 21st century (*Competition*, 1986). Even this amount will be too meagre as compared to the amount being spent on education in other developing countries. Keeping this point in mind it will be advisable to encourage and facilitate co-education at the degree level so that expenditure on education may be reduced and the cost-benefit approach may get a desirable place in the field of education.

Recommendations

After prolonged and enlightened discussion on women's education, the University Education Commission made the following recommendations:

1. that the ordinary amenities and decencies of life should be provided for women in colleges originally planned for men, but to which women are being admitted in increasing numbers,
2. that there should be no curtailment but rather increase in the educational opportunities for women,
3. that there should be intelligent educational guidance,by qualified men and women, to help women to get a clearer view of their real educational interests, to the end that they shall not try to imitate men but shall desire as good education for women as men get for as men. Women's and men's education should have many elements in common, but should not in general be identical in all respects as is usually the case these days,
4. that women students in general should be helped to see and get their normal places in a normal society, both as citizen and as women. To prepare them for their life career, the college programme should be so designed as to suit them,
5. that through educational counsel and by example the prevailing prejudice against study of home economic, home management should be overcome,
6. that standard of country and social responsibility should be emphasized on the part of men in mixed college,
7. that where new colleges are established to serve both men and women students, they should be truly co-educational institutions,

with as much thought and consideration given to the life needs of women as to those of men. Except as such colleges come into existence there are no valid criteria for comparing segregated education with co-education, and

8. that women teachers should be paid the same salaries as men teachers for equal work. (UEC 1948-49)

After the critical analysis of above mentioned recommendations of the University Education Commission, the author feels that even at the end of nineteenth century in India women did not have easy access to formal schooling. Their battle to enter higher education, therefore, requires greater persistence still. This battle is still continuing, even much after the appointment of the University Grants Commission. Tables 8.1 and 8.2 reveal in this respect.

TABLE 8.1: Number of Male and Female Students in Universities in India (1979-80)

Males	*Females*	*Total*
27,50,175	10,10,146	37,60,321

TABLE 8.2: Number of Students of Graduate, Postgraduate and Doctorate Level (1979-80)

	Male	*Female*
Graduate	13,36,421	5,56,653
Postgraduate	1,70,363	71,162
Doctorate	16,770	6,939

It is noticeable from the above tables that at the level of higher education, the number of female students is less than the male students. The women should, therefore, be given greater facilities so that they may come up to the level of men. What Rosemary Deem points out about conditions of women in Britain is also applicable to India.

> "If women received higher education they might have their expectations about their lives raised and their perception of their role in the social relations of production altered, wit disastrous consequences for the capitalist mode of production." (*Deem*, 1978)

Of course, in India, too, if women get equal opportunity in every aspects, then they can raise their socio-economic status. This is essential for the proper growth and development of the country.

We find that in the rural as well as urban areas, the parents do not send their girls to get formal education. We also find that the prejudices against women as well as lack of financial resources with their parents go against women's higher education.

When the author considered the recommendation of the University Education Commission regarding the salaries of the women in various types of schools and colleges, he came to realise that even today the women teachers are getting comparatively low salaries in the private-managed institutions. But in the institutions under the Government control, women teachers are getting the same salaries as men. The University Grants Commission (U.G.C.) is playing a significant role in this respect. The grade of salaries of teachers, both men and women in the degree colleges as well as in the Universities, have been made uniform.

Secondary Education Commission (1952-53)

The true function of education is to build an integrated, enlightened personality and ensure a simultaneous, harmonious growth of body, mind, senses and spirit. The Secondary Education Commission Report does not have any separate chapter on women's education. Only the situation has been analyzed and some pertinent remarks have been made in it:

> "There is no special justification to deal with women's education because every type of education open to men should also be open to women. Many women have joined the Faculties of Engineering, Agriculture, Veterinary Science, Commerce, Law and Teaching as well as the Arts and Science and have taken to research." (SEC, 1952-53)

The fact that a large number of women have joined the Faculties of Science, Arts, Commerce and Teaching, etc. is also evident from Table 8.3.

While girls can take courses in Arts, Commerce and research along with boys in the same educational institutions, it is desirable that special arrangements should be made for them for the study of Home Science and Home Economics.

In Secondary Education Commission Report there are two divergent views regarding education of women and their role (1952-53):

TABLE 8.3: Number of Pupils in Institutions by Type (1978-79)

		Boys	*Girls*
Degree Level:	Arts	6,22,740	4,08,534
	Science	3,47,869	1,20,052
	Commerce	4,37,880	57,718
Postgraduate Level:	Arts	95,235	50,341
	Science	35,023	13,516
	Commerce	30,262	1,673
Doctorate Level:	Arts	9,844	4,743
	Science	8,121	2,272
	Commerce	617	40
Research	—	2,762	436
Higher Secondary Schools (10+2 pattern)	—	24,00,769	12,97,520
Higher Secondary Schools (Old pattern)	—	28,31,084	8,27,202
All Professional/Technical Education (School Standard)	—	1,45,567	98,789
Professional/Technical Education (College Standard)	—	75,943	1,68,241

Table 8.4 shows the number of trained women teachers.

TABLE 8.4: Number of Trained Teachers in Schools (1952-56)

(*in '000*)

	Men	*Women*
Primary Schools	574	117
Middle Schools	124	24
High/Hr. Secondary Schools	155	35

1. The only proper place for a woman is the home.
2. Education should seriously concern itself with the place that women occupy in public life.

Those who made the first point that the only proper place for a woman is the home, argued that there should be separate education for boys and girls, because it is the woman who looks after the management of home properly. If women are not given the proper education and training in Home Management, they cannot look after their families well. But the other school of thought does not accept this too traditional and old-fashioned view about woman education and their role in society. They rather want parity between sexes in education as well as other matters of life. They argue that education should be imparted in such a way that women come to occupy their due places in public life. They should come out in the field of social responsibilities. They should not remain confined to home and kitchen. They should share the social responsibilities. Proper and formal education should be made available to them so that they may develop into wholesome human beings and may also fight against injustices and disparities. Like bride burning, heavy dowry, sexual exploitation, etc.

When we see the plight of women we realize that education is essential for them not only for facing the complexities inside the homes but also for combating the disparities outside. On this important point, the Secondary Education Commission recommends: "Education needs to be more closely connected with the home and the community." (SEC, 1952-53)

In the rural areas, women are not given the social status as required for a normal woman. Sex-role differences are too conspicuous. As Amrit Wilson points out:

> "A man's role is within his control. He has to work hard in the fields. He may fail as a result of natural disasters but no one can blame him for that. But a woman's success or otherwise is not within her control. It is a matter of chance. She might not be able to produce only daughters or she might even be childless. She is encouraged by religion, mythology and custom to produce sons. A new daughter-in-law is greeted by her mother-in-law with the blessing "may you have seven sons" or urged formally "to bathe in milk and you'll have lots of sons." (Wilson, 1980)

But what if she fails? Society responds with oppression which it justifies by again invoking myths, scriptures, and proverbs, some ancient and some only a few years old, the women are not given the rights to fulfil the needs of every day of their lives. A woman with many daughters and no sons is considered not only unfortunate but a carrier of misfortunes. A woman with no children may well be regarded as a witch who must be ostracised and barred from celebrations. Therefore, it is necessary to provide educatio.. specially for women who are living in rural areas.

Population education in the rural areas can go a long way in bridging the gulf between the school and the life of the home and the community. Special emphasis should be put on practical work. After getting formal education in school, the girls can adjust not only well in their homes but also outside the homes in the community. They can share well the responsibilities of the society and thereby promote the development of economy of the country. This may also increase the social status of women in general.

Regarding coeducation, the Secondary Education Commission remarked:

> "So far as the primary and the University stages are concerned, co-education was generally favoured, but in regard to education at the secondary stage there was considerable divergence of opinion." (SEC, 1952-53)

As a matter of fact, as far as the Primary Stage is concerned, there is no need to open separate educational institutions for boys and girls. For, at the time of admission to the Primary School, the age of children is about 5 years or 6 years, and there is no marked sexual differentiation in their attitudes towards each other. As E.B. Hurlock points out:

> "Girls become sexually mature at about 13 years, when the first menstruation occurs. From 11 to 13, many physical changes take place. Boys reach sexual maturity—as indicated by the first nocturnal omission—at an average age of 14 years. Puberty changes begin between the age of 12 and 14 in boys and are completed by16 or 17." (Hurlock, 1978)

It means that boys and girls both complete their primary education before they reach the age of sexual maturity.

At the university stage also there can be co-education. For, boys and girls both become mature enough to understand the problems regarding sex. In the case of boys, sex-appropriate behaviour is more clearly defined and the adherence to the approved pattern brings boys greater prestige and social acceptance than is true of girls. A psycho-sexually mature person is one who makes adjustments to members of the opposite sex. He does so because he has healthy attitudes towards sex, toward members of the opposite sex as well as towards his own sex and because he is willing to play the role society expects members of his sex to play. The girls mostly take isolation from boys. They do not even mix up with boys of their own age-group. Thus, there seems to be no harm making education co-educational at the university stage.

Co-education at the university level is desirable both from the psychological and the financial view point. Instead of opening separate educational institutions for boys and girls, we should provide adequate facilities for education so that the educational standard may be raised.

In regard to education at the secondary stage, there was, as the Secondary Education Commission observed, considerable divergence of opinion. It was maintained by many educationalists and psychologists that during the period of adolescence, it is desirable that the education of boys and girls should be carried out in separate institutions. For, during this period adolescent changes create problems for boys and girls. Hurlock points out that:

> "In puberty, the changes are so pronounced that the established pattern of life is disturbed. Children feel uncertain, insecure and confused. Their behaviour is often unpredictable and unsocial. For that reason puberty is sometimes referred to as the 'negative phase'." (Hurlock, 1978)

The social and psychological consideration, therefore, do not favour co-education at the secondary level. However, if we consider the economic and the administrative view point, we must conclude that co-education is the only solution for the needed development of girls' education in the country. Otherwise we will have to wait for centuries before we can ensure cent per cent education of girls.

Recommendations

The Secondary Education Commission made the following recommendations in favour of co-education:

1. While no distinction need be made between education imparted to boys and girls special facilities for the study of home science should be made available in all girls' schools and in co-educational or mixed schools.
2. Efforts should be made by State Governments to open separate schools for girls wherever there is demand for them.
3. Definite conditions should be laid down in regard to co-educational or mixed schools to satisfy the special needs of girls students and women members of the teaching staff. (SEC, 1952-53)

Table 8.5 shows that after independence, rapid progress has been made in spreading education among women and in raising their status. The table also indicates that there has been considerable progress in girls' education after the University Education Commission (1948-49) and the Secondary Education Commission. The Indian Constitution has made several provisions for women's education. The Indian Constitution provides under Article 16(a) that "there shall be equality of opportunity to all citizens in matters relating to employment or appointment to any office under the State and that no citizen shall, on grounds only of religion, race, caste, sex, descent, place of birth, residence be ineligible for, or discriminated against, in respect of any employment or office under the State." We are however, still waiting the fullest implementation of this constitutional provision.

TABLE 8.5: Education of Girls (1950-65)

		1950-51	*1955-56*	*1960-61*	*1965-66*
1.	Classes I-V				
	(a) Total enrolment of girls (in '000)	5,385	7,639	11,401	18,145
	(b) No. of girls for every 100 boys enrolled	39	44	48	55
2.	Classes VI-VIII				
	(a) Total enrolment of girls (in '000)	534	867	1,630	2,839
	(b) No. of girls for every 100 boys enrolled	21	25	32	35
3.	Classes IX-XI				
	(a) Total enrolment of girls (in '000)	163	320	541	1,069
	(b) No. of girls for every 100 boys enrolled	15	21	23	26
4.	College and Universities				
	(a) Total enrolment of girls (in '000)	40	84	154	271
	(b) No. of girls for every 100 boys enrolled	14	17	23	24
5.	Vocational Courses				
	(a) Total enrolment of girls (in '000)	41	66	86	120
	(b) No. of girls for every 100 boys enrolled	28	31	25	23
6.	Professional Courses (College Standard)				
	(a) Total enrolment of girls (in '000)	5	9	26	50
	(b) No. of girls for every 100 boys enrolled	5	7	11	14

National Committee on Women Education (1958-59)

The problems of education of girls and women have acquired a new significance since the attainment of independence. Education panels of the Planning Commission at its meeting held in July 1957, recommended that:

> "A suitable Committee should be appointed to go into the various aspects of the questions relating to the nature of education for girls at the elementary, secondary and adult stages and to examine whether the present system was helping them to lead a happier and more useful life." (Biswas and Agrawal, 1971)

This recommendation was placed before the Conference of the State Education Ministers held in September 1957. The Conference also agreed that a special committee should be appointed to examine the whole question of women's education. A National Committee on Women's Education was accordingly set up by the Government of India in the Ministry of Education, under the Chairmanship of Smt. Durgabai Deshmukh, who was also the Chairman of 'Central Social Welfare Board'.

The major recommendations made by the National Committee on Women's Education under different sections are as follows:

Section A: Special Recommendations Needing Top Priority.

1. The education of women should be regarded as a major and a special problems in education for a good many years to come and a bold and determined effort should be made to face its difficulties and magnitude and to close the existing gap between the education of men and women in as short a time as possible. The funds required for the purpose should be considered to be the first charge on the sums set aside for the development of education.
2. Steps should be taken to constitute as early as possible, a National Council for the education of girls and women.
3. The problem of the education of women is so vital and of such great national significance that it is absolutely necessary for the Centre to assume more responsibility for its rapid development.
4. The State Government should establish State Councils for the education of girls and women.

5. Every State should be required to prepare comprehensive development plans for the education of girls and women in its area.
6. It is also necessary to enlist the cooperation of all semi-official organizations, local bodies, voluntary organizations, teachers organizations and members of the public to assist in the promotion of the education of girls and women.
7. The Planning Commission should set up a permanent machinery to estimate, as accurately as possible, the woman-power requirements of the Plans from time to time and make the results of its studies available to government and the public.

Section B: Other Special Recommendations.

1. *Primary Education (Age Group 6-11)*

(a) Concessions in kind (not in cash) should be given to the parents of all girls, whether from rural or urban areas, below a certain level.
(b) The Government should formulate a scheme for awarding prizes to the village showing the highest proportional enrolment and attendance of girls.

2. *Middle and Secondary Education (Age Group 11 to 17)*

(a) At the middle school stage, more and more co-educational institutions should be started.
(b) At the Secondary stage, however, separate schools for girls should be established specially in rural areas, at the same time giving parents full freedom to admit their girls to boys' schools if they so desire.
(c) All girls (all boys also) of parents below a certain income level should be given free education up to the middle stage.
(d) As far as possible, free or subsidized transport should be made available to girls in order to bring middle and secondary schools, within their easy reach.

3. *Curriculum and Syllabi*

(a) There should be identical curriculum for boys and girls at the primary stage with the provision that even at this stage subjects like music, painting, sewing, needle-work, simple hand-work, and cooking should be introduced to make the courses more suitable for girls.

(b) At the middle stage, and more especially at the secondary stage, there is need for differentiation of curricula for boys and girls.

4. *Training and Employment*

(a) Immediate steps should be taken to set up additional training institutions for women teachers in all such areas of the country where a shortage exists at present.

(b) With a view to inducing women from urban areas to accept posts of teachers in rural schools, women teachers serving in rural areas may be provided with quarters and a village allowance may be given to such teachers.

(c) The maximum age-limit for entry into service may be relaxed, and the age of retirement may be extended to 60 years provided the teacher is physically and otherwise fit.

5. *Professional and Vocational Education*

(a) The employment of women on a part-time basis, wherever feasible, should be accepted as a policy.

(b) Girls should be encouraged to take up courses in Commerce, Engineering, Agriculture, Medicine, etc. at the University stage by offering them scholarships and other concessions.

(c) It is important to organize campaigns to mobilise public opinion for creating proper conditions in offices and establishments in which women can work freely.

6. *Facilities for Adult Women*

(a) Educational facilities in the form of condensed courses;
   (i) that prepare women for the Middle School Examination, and
   (ii) those that prepare them for the High School or Higher Secondary Examination should be provided more extensively in all States.

(b) Provisions should also be made of condensed courses, which train women for suitable vocation after completion of necessary continuation.

7. *Voluntary Organizations*

The services of the voluntary organizations should be extensively used in the field of middle, secondary, higher, social and vocational education of women. The existing grant-in-aid codes of the State need a thorough revision. There should be a substantial and significant difference in the rates of grants-in-aid as between girls' institutions should be made easier.

Section C: General Recommendations

1. Wherever, primary education is not free, immediate steps should be taken to make it free. Whenever, new schools are started, the rural region should be given priority consideration.

2. Wastage and Stagnation:

(a) As a scientific study of the problem wastage on an all-India basis is needed the Ministry of Education should carry out special studies of this problem in all parts of the country.

(b) The following steps should be taken to reduce the extent of stagnation in class I:

  (i) All fresh admission to class I should be made in the beginning of the school year and not later than 60 days after the beginning of the first session.

  (ii) It should be a specific responsibility of teachers to see that proper attendance is maintained in the school.

  (iii) The age of admission should be raised to six plus.

  (iv) Standard of teaching should be improved.

(c) Stagnation in classes II to V can be reduced if:

  (i) Attendance of children is increased.

  (ii) Standard of teaching is improved.

  (iii) Internal examinations are introduced.

  (iv) Books and educational equipment needed by poor children are supplied in good time.

(d) About 65 per cent of the cases of wastage at the primary level are due to economic causes. This wastage can be eliminated only if provision for part-time instruction is made for those children who cannot attend on a whole-time basis.

(e) About 25 to 30 per cent of the cases of wastage at the primary level are due to the indifference of parents. This can be eliminated partly by educative propaganda and partly by a rigorous enforcement of the compulsory education law.

3. Employment of Teachers

(a) The present scales of pay of teachers should be suitably revised.
(b) There should be no distinction between the pay scales of teachers in the Government and the local or Municipal Board institutions and in the private-run institutions.
(c) The tripple benefit scheme called the Pension-cum-Provident Fund-cum-Insurance Scheme should be made applicable to every teacher who is employed permanently in the institution.

A. Smt. Hansa Mehta Committee Report on Differentiation of Curricula for Boys and Girls (1961-62)

The National Council for Women's Education in its meeting held on May 10, 1961, appointed a Committee, under the Chairmanship of Smt. Hansa Mehta, to examine comprehensively the problem of curricula for girls at all stages of education. The Committee made the following observations and recommendations:

> "In the ultimate democratic and socialistic pattern of society, education will be related to individual capacities, aptitudes and interests which are not related to sex. There would, therefore, be no need in such a society to differentiate curricula on the basis of sex." (Biswas and Agarwal, 1971)

In the transitional phase, certain, psychological differences between men and women as well as certain divisions of social functions based on them will have to be accepted as matters of and as practical basis for building up the curricula for boys and girls. It is on the fundamental assumptions that the proposals for a differentiation of curricula between boys and girls are based.

1. *Primary Stage*

(a) No differentiation should be made in the curricula for boys and girls at the primary stage.
(b) Women should be appointed on the staff of all primary schools.

2. *Middle School Stage*

(a) The curriculum of general education should be common to

boys and girls and no differentiation should be made therein on the basis of sex.

(b) In all Middle Schools, it is desirable to have mixed staff, but where girls do attend school ordinarily meant for boys, appointment of women teachers on staff should be obligatory.

3. *Secondary Stage*

(a) The accepted policy at the secondary level is to provide diversified curricula to meet the aptitudes and capacities of all adolescents. If properly implemented, this programme could provide for all the special needs of girls. Diversified courses such as for home science, fine arts, music, etc. should be increasingly introduced at the secondary stage to meet the special needs of girls. These electives should not, however be made compulsory for them.

(b) The introduction of home science in the secondary school curriculum has come in for a good deal of criticism, due mainly to bad implementation resulting from absence of text-books, lack of teachers, lack of the recognition by universities and defective designing of courses. Steps should be taken to improve the implementation.

(c) Sex education is essential at the middle and secondary stages.

(d) Special encouragement should be given to girls who study mathematics or science at the secondary stage, and special efforts should be made to prepare women teachers of mathematics and science.

4. *Text-books*

(a) In text-books dealing with languages and social studies, adequate attention should be paid to the needs, experience and problems of girls by including such topics as special festivals of women, games, popular with girls, lives of great women, etc.

(b) One of the important values which education should develop through proper text-books is the mutual respect of individuals.

5. *Vocational Education*

(a) Immediate attempts should be made to expand the provision of vocational courses at the secondary and higher stage of education, and to relate these courses with man and woman-power requirements of society.

(b) The possibilities of employing women on a large scale on a part-time basis, in as many vocations as possible have to be explored.

This committee also have some view points regarding sex differences and co-education.

According to the traditional view the mere biological difference of sex created different physical, intellectual and psychological characteristics between men and women and these basic sex differences necessitated the provision of differentiated curricula for them. But with regard to the intellectual differences between the sexes, it has now been established that women are in no way inferior to men and the differences in their academic and professional achievements are due mainly to lack of adequate opportunities or to influence of traditional cultural pattern.

The Committee remarked:

> "With regard to psychological differences between the sexes, the recent findings are that there are no psychological characteristics related to sex as such and that the different psychological traits which men and women exhibit are the result of social conditioning."

It is true in the present that there is no difference between boys and girls only on the basis of the point of view of psychology. In the intellectual field, women and girls are superseding men and boys. In the administrative services like I.A.S., P.C.S., etc. also they are coming up fast.

It has also been established that the physical differences between the two sexes are of minor significance. Most of the researches relating to determination of sex differences and their causes have been carried out in the Western countries and it is a matter of regret that no such studies have yet undertaken in India. The need of such investigations is imperative.

Regarding the aspect of co-education, the Committee made the following recommendations:

1. Co-education should be adopted as the general pattern at the elementary stage.
2. At the secondary and collegiate stage, there should be full freedom to the management and parents either to evolve common institutions or to establish separate ones for girls.
3. Steps should be taken to appoint women teachers in all educational institutions at the secondary and university stages,

which are ordinarily meant for boys. Similarly, some men teachers should also be appointed in separate secondary schools and colleges for girls.

B. Report of the Bhaktavatsalam Committee Appointed to Look into the Cause of Lack of Public Support Particularly in Rural Areas for Girl's Education and to Enlist Public Cooperation (1963)

The National Council for Women's Education at its meeting held in April 1963 appointed a Small Committee under the Chairmanship of M. Bhaktavatsalam, Chief Minister of Chennai to look into the causes of lack of public support, particularly in rural areas, for girl's education and to enlist public cooperation. The Committee made the following recommendations:

1. Direct cooperation of the public should be encouraged in the following fields:
   - (i) Establishment of private schools.
   - (ii) Putting up of school buildings.
   - (iii) Provision of suitable accommodation for teachers and students.
   - (iv) Popularization of co-education at the primary stage.
   - (v) Popularization of the idea of women taking up teaching profession.
   - (vi) Encouraging married women to take up at least part-time teaching in village schools and to work as school mothers.
   - (vii) Initiating action and participating in educative propaganda to breakdown traditional prejudices against girl's education.
   - (viii) Supplying mid-day meals.
   - (ix) Supplying uniforms, free text-books and writing materials to needy children.
2. The State should create public opinion in favour of girls education through:
   - (i) School improvement conferences;
   - (ii) Seminars;
   - (iii) Radio talks, audio-visual aids and distribution of literature.
   - (iv) Enrolment drives generally in June and special additional drives for girls' education during Dussehra.

(v) Assisting voluntary associations engaged in the field of education of girls and women.

3. It should be the endeavour of the State to provide a primary school in each habitation with a population of 300. However, in scattered, hilly isolated areas, primary schools should be provided where the population is even less than 300, so as to provide every habitation with school within a mile.

   A middle school in each habitation with a population of 1,500 and above, and within a radius of 3 miles should be provided. Generally, there should be a secondary school within a radius of 5 miles.
4. It should be the aim of all States to appoint women teachers in primary schools and a great number of women teachers in mixed schools. Financial incentives like special allowance for hilly, isolated or any other specific backward rural areas should be given to teachers.
5. Attempts should be made to bring back to the teaching profession married women who have left it in recent years. Condensed courses should be organized for adult women, so that they could take up teaching jobs in rural areas.
6. During selection of trainees for training schools and colleges, special preference should be given to women from rural areas seeking admission.
7. A separate women inspectorate will help to bring in more girls to school.
8. It is only by providing women teachers with quarters near the schools that many educated women can be attracted to the teaching profession.
9. Special programmes for girls education should be taken up as centrally sponsored schemes on the basis of hundred per cent grant outside the plan ceilings. The provision of suitable school buildings is one of considerable urgency. For this, either hundred per cent central assistance or long-term central loans should be provided.
10. All States should find ways and means of providing funds in order to make education free for all girls up to the secondary stage. In case resources are limited and do not meet the full requirements, the priority should be given to rural areas.
11. Compulsory Education Act should be introduced in States where it does not exist. In addition, State Governments should provide

sufficient incentives and carry on propaganda to attract all children to school.

Comments

If women in the urban areas are a disadvantaged group, in the rural situations they are mostly victims of serious religious prejudices and social economic exploitation. In the rural areas, a woman's duty is to meekly serve the family. Her own needs of education or nourishment and health-care are ignored and her share in the fruits of labour is denied to her.

Village women, whether they belong to farm families or are landless agricultural labourers put in 50 to 60 per cent more hours of work than the men folk. Women are also responsible for all sustenance and household task including fetching of drinking water, gathering of fuel, cooking, cleaning, raising of children and tending cattle. Besides, they work almost full time in fields where they have specific jobs assigned to them. How can we imagine that such poor and overworked women will be given opportunity to take education (adult education) and how can they send their children (girls) to schools to take formal education? On account of this and the prejudices against women in society even today, more than 82 per cent of village women are still illiterate. How can India move into the 21st century with such a large number of illiterate women?

Kothari Education Commission (1964-66)

"If education would help in understanding the natural environment, the social reality and human behaviour, if the competencies required for co-operative living and increased productivity would be paid due attention, education would be a strong factor in creating a more integrated and satisfied community." (*Yojana*, 1986)

The Kothari Commission did not include a separate chapter on women's education. But it considered the issue and made some recommendations under Chapter VI (Towards Equalization of Educational Opportunity) and Chapter XII (Higher Education Enrolments and Programmes). The Commission has broadly and essentially endorsed the recommendations of the National Council on Women's Education.

It has also made some suggestions and recommendations of its own.

According to Kothari Commission, there can be two strategies for the development of education of girls and women:

(a) The 'special' programmes recommended by the National Committee on Women's Education, and

(b) The 'General' programmes that is to give attention to the education of girls at all stages and in all sectors and for the expansion and improvement of education.

Recommendations Regarding the First Programme

1. The education of women should be regarded as a major programme in education for some years to come and a bold and determined effort should be made to face the difficulties involved and to close the existing gap between the education of men and women in as short a time as possible.
2. Special scheme should be prepared for this purpose and the funds required for them should be provided on a priority basis.
3. Both at the Centre and in the States, there should be a special machinery to look after the education of girls and women. It should bring together officials and non-officials in the planning and implementation of programmes for women's education. (*KEC*, 1964-66)

These special programmes were to be of transitional in nature and were made only to fill the gap between the education of girls and boys. But in considering the first aspect of the strategy (special programmes), the second aspect of the strategy (general programme) should not be neglected. In fact, if this had been done right from the beginning the need for the special programme would perhaps had not arisen. It is the responsibility of the States to implement these programmes properly.

Regarding the role of women outside the home, the Kothari Commission observed:

> "The role of women outside the home has become an important feature of the social and economic life of the country and in the years to come, this will assume large proportions affecting a majority of women. It will, therefore, be necessary to pay adequate attention to the problems of training and employment of women." (*KEC*, 1964-66)

Onc of the important needs of women today is enabling them to carry out their dual role of home-making and following a suitable career. Today, we can see and observe critically the situation of women who are working in the government and semi-government offices, factories, schools, colleges. They face a lot of problems in discharging their daily routine, like feeding their children, and looking after the half partners of their lives. The Census of 1981, shows that there are at present more than a million young women, below the age of 24 years and with a minimum qualification of high school and intermediate, who are working only as house-wives. And this number is bound to increase yearly.

The Commission also emphasized:

> "Side by side, opportunities for full-time employment will also have to be expanded. As the age of marriage continues to rise, full-time employment will have to be provided for almost all young unmarried women." (*KEC*, 1964-66)

It is being realised that teaching, nursing and social service are very well recognised areas where women can have a useful role to play. There is a growing emphasis on women being employed as teachers at the primary level. For, they can teach much better than men at that stage.

> "The rate of expansion of education of girls is much faster than that of boys, with the result that the gap between them is gradually and steadily narrowing. At the lower primary stage, the number of girls enrolled per 100 boys has increased from 12 in 1901 to 39 in 1950 to 55 in 1965. At the secondary stage the corresponding figures are 4 in 1901, 15 in 1950 and 26 in 1965." (*KEC*, 1964-66)

For the acceleration of women's education in the field of higher education, the Kothari Commission recommended two programmes as follows:

1. A programme of scholarships and financial assistance to women students in colleges, and universities on a liberal scale, and
2. A programme of the provision of suitable but economical hostel accommodation for women students with all the necessary amenities on a large scale. Liberal grants should be provided by the Government of India for this purpose as also by the State Governments. Both these programmes are particularly necessary to encourage girls from rural areas to take advantage of higher education.

It can hardly be overstressed that higher education should be made available to girls of rural areas. But unfortunately, more than 60 per cent of the girls belonging to the rural areas are working on their agricultural fields to share the burden of their parents. They are not getting even primary education. Then, how can they go for higher education?

Regarding co-education, the Commission remarked:

> "A uniform policy of co-education is not necessary for the level of education. Conditions vary from state to state."

In some States, like Maharashtra, co-education is preferred by women students and also their parents, and the number of colleges having co-education is much larger than that of separate colleges for women. On the other hand, States like Tamil Nadu, which are equally advanced in the matter of women's education. The matter of having co-educational institutions as separate institutions for boys and girls should, therefore, be better left to the States.

Regarding courses for women at the Higher education level, the Commission remarked:

> "As at present women students should have free access to courses in arts, humanities, science and technology, it would be wrong to restrict their choice or to compel them to take particular courses. The more academic type of girls with ambitions of pursuing careers of research or teaching at the colleges or university level or in professions such as medicine, or technology should have all the opportunities and incentives for doing so."

The Commission felt that there is a special need to link up higher education with specific avenues of employment not only for boys but also for girls. Women should be encouraged to enter the professional fields like teaching, social work, nursing, nutrition, and dietetics, institutional management, etc.. Home Science (and also general education) should enable women to equip themselves to work in the professional works of dietetics, food technology, family welfare and extension work in community development. Women should also be given opportunities of research work under the schemes of ICMR, ICAR, and Council of Child Welfare. The Commission emphasized that course in nursing should be introduced at the graduation level *i.e.* at the B.Sc. level. There should be separate institutions for women to prepare them for these professional and vocational fields. In our country, different types of women's polytechnics are functioning. In the Third Five Year

Plan (1961-66), there was a scheme to set up a National Institute for women for imparting high level training to women candidates in organization, administration and management.

The Commission also recommended: "One or two universities should set up research units to deal specifically with women's education. These should take up follow-up studies of educated women, consider women's education from the point of view of employment opportunities available to women, and ensure proper planning of women's education particularly at the stage of higher education.

The latest official document on 'Curriculum for the 10 years school' prepared by some progressive educationists, tries to resurrect the old restrictive view regarding women's role in the society.

> "Particularly for the girls in our society special attention has been given at the middle age. They have to be prepared for maternity and child care and for the development and maintenance of a home. Just as the boys have to be prepared for the world of work outside the home, the girls will have to be prepared particularly for the work inside. . . . In science and mathematics the student should have the competence to apply his knowledge to the solution of problems around him. he should have an understanding of the technological processes in agriculture and industry in his surroundings. He should be able to contribute meaningfully to environmental conservation, reduction of pollution, development of proper nutrition, health and hygiene in the community. Girls should particularly be able to help in the development of proper habits and attitudes in child care and in improvement of home."

The women thus gets restricted to home and its management. The commission, on the other hand, observes:

> "For full development of our human resources the improvement of homes and for moulding the character of children, during the most impressionable years of infancy, the education of women is of even greater importance than that of men. In the modern world, the role of woman goes much beyond the home and the bringing up of children. She is now adopting a career of her own and sharing equally with man the responsibility for the development of society in all its aspects."

The progress of girls' education in the field of higher education became much better in 1965-66 than before. The total enrolment of girls at the university stage in the year 1950-51 was 40,000 and in 1965-66 it rose to 2,71,000.

This shows that women are now taking higher education much more seriously than ever before and are also moving with men in different walks of life—familial, economic, political, social and educational.

National Policy on Education—1979

Education has always remained an area of debate and controversies in not only developing countries but also in the developed countries like U.S.A., Japan, Germany and the like.

In March 1976, the Janata Party formed the government. It devoted considerable thought to education and presented to the Parliament a statement on the National Policy on Education in April, 1979.

The National Policy on Education emphasized that highest priority must be given to free education for all up to the age of 14 as laid down in the Directive Principles of the Constitution. Education up to this stage should be general and not specialized. With the help of tool subjects, it should develop among students scientific attitude. Elementary education should be an integral stage.

Development of personality and character both of boys and girls should be the objective of the elementary education. The content of education at this stage should include language, arithmetic, history, simple elementary sciences with special reference to environment, cultural values and physical education.

Regarding the facilities for the elementary education, the National Policy on Education remarked:

> "While it is necessary to expand the facilities for formal education in elementary schools for all children, in the age group 6-14, it is also important to formulate schemes of non-formal education for dropouts and the older children in the age group who have not any schooling. The aim should be to cover all the children in the age group 6-14 in the next ten years. Steps should be taken to prevent children giving up schooling without completing the course. The problem of wastage should be studied in detail and remedial measures taken." (NPE 1979)

If we want to cater to the requirements of a wide range of learners and learning circumstances than the curriculum must be made rich and diversified accordingly.

For improving literacy among girls the National Policy on Education recommended to give suitable incentives to them for improving attendance. It wrote:

> "Incentives such as mid-day meals, free text-books, stationery and uniforms should be given to the education of girls and children of Scheduled Castes and Scheduled Tribes." (NPE 1979)

Obviously, if we have to improve the rate of literacy among girls we should provide all possible incentives to girls, especially to those who belong to rural areas.

Under the section of 'Adult Education', the National Policy Statement on Education, emphasised appointment of Women Instructors for effective running programmes of Family Planning and social awareness:

> "Since the programme is not only meant for removing illiteracy alone but its aim is also to create awareness about other problems, it would be desirable that such programmes as family planning, health and nutrition, child and mother care should be built into this programme. For this it would be desirable that the newly appointed instructors for this programme should be women as far as possible." (NPE 1979)

Since the adult literacy programmes are to be run more in the rural areas than in the urban areas, it is advisable to appoint as far as possible women instructors. They should be sent to the country-side and facilities like housing, electricity, water, education, transportation, should be made available to them, so that they may adjust themselves well in the environment of rural areas. Not only these, but also the adult teaching learning material like the low-priced books and literature, village libraries and the mass-media facilities should also be provided to them for enabling them to run their mass-literacy and social awareness programmes well, especially among women.

National Policy on Education, 1986

Unlike other Commission or Committee there was no Chairperson for this policy documents, nor any Commission was appointed for the purpose. To bridge-up the imbalance between expansion and performances, to meet the new challenges of modern science and technology, to meet needs of aspiration, and requirements of the people and nation at large; to give special dispensation to the needy sections who cannot pay for it, to cultivate moral, social and democratic values by developing linkages between education and culture and by introducing national core curriculum; to reduce the percentage of drop-outs and increase the percentage of retention, to improve the percentage of literacy through non-formal education, early child-care and open school facilities, etc. and to induct the principle of decentralization and accountability into the system of education through proper machinery of educational management and involving even non-governmental agencies NEP was enunciated in January 1985. In this connection so far the following documents have been released by Government of India:

1. Challenge of Education: Policy Perspective, August 1985,
2. National Policy on Education—1986, May 1986,
3. Programme of Action, August 1986.

All these documents contain the problems, policies and programmes of action respectively. Because of its richness in varied contents and educational statistics the first one, *i.e.*, 'challenge of education' has rightly been termed as 'Gold mine of information'. This document remarks about literacy rate as following:

> "The literacy rate during the post-independence era increased from 16.67 to 36.23 in 1981. The number of literates thus increased four-fold from six crores in 1951 to 24.8 crores in 1981. There is a glaring disparity between male and female literacy, the former being 46.9 per cent and the latter 24.8 per cent. This is more accentuated in rural areas (40.8 and 18 respectively) than in urban areas (65.8 and 47.8 respectively). Kerala had the best literacy percentage (70.4), while the lowest percentage was in Rajasthan (24.38). Only 5.46 per cent of the females in Rajasthan were literate." (COE, 2.25)

The second document contains specific and well worded policy statement in twelve parts running into 29 pages only. Its part IV deals with 'Education for Equality' which underlines the following provisions as far as women's education is concerned:

> "The new policy will lay special emphasis on the removal of disparities and to equalise educational opportunity by attending to the specific needs of those who have been denied equality so far. (4.1)
>
> "Education will be used as an agent of basic change in the status of women. In order to neutralise the accumulated distortions of the

past, there will be well-conceived edge in favour of women. The National Education System will play a positive, interventionist role in the empowerment of women. It will foster the development of new values through redesigned curricula, text-books, the training and orientation of teachers, decision-makers and administrators, and the active involvement of educational institutions. This will be an act of faith and social engineering. Women's studies will be promoted as a part of various courses and educational institutions encouraged to take up active programmes to further women's development. (4.2)

"The removal of women's illiteracy and obstacles inhibiting their access to, and retention in, elementary education will receive overriding priority, through provision of special support services, setting of time targets, and effective monitoring. Major emphasis will be laid on women's participation in vocational, technical and professional education at different levels. The policy of non-discrimination will be pursued vigorously to eliminate sex stereo-typing in vocational and professional courses and to promote women's participation in non-traditional occupations, as well as in existing and emergent technologies." (4.3)

The third document (POA) is the most important, not because it is several times bigger than the policy itself; but it provides the detailed strategies and programmes of each idea contained in the policy document. The HRD Ministry undertook an intensive exercise to prepare the promised Programme of Action. In the first place, 23 Task Forces were constituted and each was assigned a specific subject covered by the National Policy on Education (NPE). Of these 23 task forces one was assigned specific subject on women's education under the caption *Education for Women's Equality*. The whole programme under this section has been given in the appendix of this volume. The suggestions and programmes of action given over there are of very practical nature. In the context of Adult Education Programme it remarks:

> Mass scale adult education programmes for women in the age-group 15-35 should be developed to eradicate illiteracy amongst by 1995. As majority of women in this age-group are workers, literacy *per se* may not have any relevance for them. It is, therefore, necessary to develop adult education programmes for women linked with upgradation of their skills and income-generating activities.

Skill development for girls and women should be continuous process of learning starting from the NFE and AE centres. Continuing Education Centres should be set-up in a phased manner which should organize vocational training, provide opportunities for retention of literacy skills and application of this learning for improving their living conditions.

In the introduction of the POA it is mentioned that this Programme of Action is meant to provide an indication of the nature of actions which will be needed in order to implement the directions of the policy. It provides a broad strategy within which the detailed schemes will be subsequently drawn up; it will also facilitate the preparatory work which will be required before such schemes can be worked out fully and put into operational form. The detailed projects will be taken up for formulation by the various departments and agencies, in consultation with all concerned, once the strategy outlined in the Programme of Action has been examined and endorsed by the Parliament. It is necessary to stress that what is presented here is not an inflexible structure but only a projection of direction with varying degrees of detail. A certain amount of flexibility is assumed which will help the implementing agencies in tailoring the programme of action to suit their contexts and to make necessary modifications on the basis of experiences and emerging scenarios. Implementation of the programme will be a cooperative effort between the Centre and the States with full involvement of the community and the teachers and a constant process of consultations is envisaged.

As per the Action Programme (XXIV.6) the Government is committed to carry out the following functions:

(a) To determine national priorities
(b) To evolve strategies through participation of concerned agencies.
(c) To lay down guidelines for formulation of programmes and schemes.
(d) To provide continuous technical back-up and resource support.
(e) To undertake monitoring and evaluation.
(f) To create conditions for the maintenance of quality and efficiency.

In this way, we see that one of the noble features of the NEP is to promote a National System of Education.

Introduction of National Core Curriculum

A national core curriculum is evolved for the first time for the inculcation of values like secularism, nationalism, socialism, patriotism, etc. In modern education the term core has come to be applied to that part of the experience curriculum which is concerned with those types of experiences thought necessary for all learners in order to develop certain behaviour competencies considered necessary for effective living in our democratic society. According to Anderson, "The core curriculum is a way of organizing some of the important common learnings in the high school curriculum, using a problem solving approach as its procedure, having social and personal problems significant to youth as its content, and the development of the behaviour needed in a democratic society as its purpose. This represents a fundamental reorganization of the curriculum of the secondary school rather than just a combination of the subject-matter."

The National Policy statement on this point observes:

> "The National System of Education will be based on a national curricular framework which contains a common core alongwith other components that are flexible. The common core will include the history of India's freedom movement, the constitutional obligations and other content essential to nurture national identity. These elements will cut across subject areas and will be designed to promote values such as India's common cultural heritage, egalitarianism, democracy and secularism, equality of the sexes, protection of the environment, removal of social barriers, observance of the small family norm and inculcation of the scientific temper. All educational programmes will be carried on in strict conformity with secular values." (3.4)

Aims at Not Only Access But Success Also

The earlier policy document gave more stress on universalization, excessive enrolment, opening of more schools etc. But the present one aims at retention and successful completion of education by all. This will become quite clear from the following policy statement contained in National Education Policy:

> "The New Education policy will give highest priority to solving the problem of children dropping out to school and will adopt an array of meticulously formulated strategies based on micro-planning, and

applied at the grass-roots level all over the country, to ensure children's retention at school. This effort will be fully coordinated with the network of non-formal education. It shall be ensured that all children who attain the age of about 11 years by 1990 will have had five years of schooling, or its equivalent through the non-formal stream. Likewise, by 1995 all children will be provided free and compulsory education upto 14 years of age." (5.11)

An Agent for Basic Change

In one of his speeches the Prime Minister had remarked that the greatest beneficiaries of the NEP should be the youths and the women. The NEP will be used as an agent of basic change in the status of women. It is obvious that despite many efforts there exists disparity and distortion leading to inequality between men and women. It has been clarified in the NEP that every effort will be made through the instrument of education, to evolve a society which values the equality of sexes, removal of sex bias against women in the text-books and attendance scholarships will have to be called for.

Gandhiji used to say that if you educate a boy you educate only one individual but if you educate a girl you educate the whole family. A literate mother can never tolerate illiteracy in the house. Girls' education in rural areas has thus acquired a very special attention. Very special time-bound programmes are being chalked out to minimize the percentage of girls drop-outs. The following measures (PA XII.5) are proposed to be taken to widen the access of women in programmes of vocational, technical and professional education and to empower her for further development:

(a) Every educational institution should, by 1995, take up active programmes of women's development built around a study and awareness of the women's predicament and for promotion of communication and organisation among women.

(b) All teachers and non-formal Education/Adult Education (NFE/AE) instructors should be trained as agents of women's empowerment. Special training programmes will be developed by NCERT, NIEPA, Directorate of Adult Education (DAE), SCERTs, State Resource Centres (SRCs) and UGC to incorporate in all training programmes of teachers and NFE/AE instructors elements which would motivate them to work for women empowerment: Voluntary agencies and activist groups for women's development will be involved in these training programmes.

(c) Women teachers and women instructors in adult/non-formal education programmes should receive special orientation to enable them to play an activist role towards women's equality.

(d) Special programmes should be developed by research institutions, voluntary institutions and professional groups of artists to promote general awareness and self-image amongst women through variety of programmes like discussions, street plays, skits, wall papers, puppet shows, etc.

(e) An environment should be created in which practically all sections of the society will commit themselves and work for achieving this objective enunciated in the National Policy on Education. Keeping in view the important role played by media in this sphere, clear policy guidelines should be developed by radio and TV in 1986-87 and measures taken to pursuade films and other media on these lines.

(f) Preference in recruitment of teachers up to school level should be for women. This will create a greater confidence in the rural areas and motivate the parents to send girls to the school.

(g) The common core curriculum is a powerful instrument for the empowerment of women through the incorporation of values commensurate with the new status of women. The Women's Cell in the NCERT will be revived and given the responsibility for preparing the component of the core curriculum relating to women's equality. The Cell should also accelerate its work of eliminating sexist bias and sex stereo-types from school text-books. The Women's Cell of NCERT should take active help of all persons on playing its assigned role.

(h) Sensitisation of teachers, trainers, planners and administrators to women's issues will be taken up as a major programme by NIEPA and appropriate State level agencies, through initial training, in-service training and refresher courses. NIEPA should also have a strong cell for planning and execution of these programmes.

It seems that the government is determined to keep its promises and translate the plans into deeds and action. Very recent formation of Lady Battalion in Central Reserve Police Force (CRPF) is an indicative of the fact that the government wants to create dynamic managerial structure for women's equality through various channels of education.

9

CONSTITUTIONAL PROVISIONS FOR SEX-EQUALITY AND BETTERMENT

Women complain that they make the largest minority in India and yet they suffer from a variety of social and economic disabilities which prevent them from fully exercising their human rights and freedoms in the society. Though the circumstances have now changed but only up to some time ago child-marriage, especially of female children, was common. Widow marriage was prohibited, even if the widow somehow succeeded in escaping from the funeral pyre of her deceased husband where she was expected to be burnt alive. A divorce was generally looked down upon and the remarriage of a divorcee was socially disapproved.

If some of these problems still persist in varying degrees it is not due to any lacunae in the Constitutional provisions against them. For our Constitution has made explicit provisions against these social discriminations and evils against women and has been playing an important role in changing deeply rooted social attitudes. During the last three decades a number of laws have been registered with a view to ensuring equality of status and opportunity for women.

The following articles in the Constitution of India make specific provisions for the education of women:

Article 15(1) states: "The State shall not discriminate against any citizen on grounds only of religion, race, caste, sex, place of birth or any of them."

Article 15(3) states: "Nothing in this article shall prevent the State from making any special provision for women and children."

Article 16(1) states: "There shall be equality of opportunity for all citizens in matters relating to employment or appointment to any office under the State."

Article 39(a) states: "The citizen, men and women equally have the right to an adequate means of livelihood."

In the Indian Constitution it is assured that no one is discriminated against the basis of sex. But in reality social taboos have historically been retarding the progress of women, especially in the field of education. The following table shows the slow educational progress of women during 1921 and 1937.

Table 9.1 given is indicative of the slow educational progress of women in India. By 1947, the total enrolment of girls in all primary schools in the country was 34,75,165. Some of the States had no separate schools for girls and had adopted the pattern of co-education at the primary level. The number of secondary schools for girls was 2,370 and the number of Arts and Science colleges 59. The total number of girls on roll at the college stage was 23,237. There were only 56,090 girls in the special schools.

TABLE 9.1: Recognised Educational Institutions for Girls

Year	*Arts College*	*High Schools*	*Middle Schools*	*Primary Schools*	*Spl. Instns.*	*Total*
1921-22	12	120	548	22,579	258	23,517
1926-27	18	145	656	26,621	316	27,756
1931-32	20	218	787	32,564	380	33,969
1936-37	31	297	878	32,273	404	33,983

In 1946-47 for every 100 boys in the primary school, there were only 36 girls. The corresponding figure in the middle school was only 22 and in the secondary school only 14, and in the university only 7 (Kohli, 1983). This shows that before the Constitution of India came into force, the girls had far less opportunities for education than the boys.

Article 6(1) of the Constitution provides that there shall be equality of opportunity for women not only in the field of education but also in the field of employment.

At the time of India becoming a republic, the bulk of the women workers were engaged in cultivation. The condition of women peasants was miserable beyond description. In trade and commerce the sex ratio was even more dismal. There were in this field only 2.8 per cent women workers in comparison to 6.1 per cent of men workers.

In view of the deploring, low status and representation of women in various walks of Indian life and society, at the dawn of Independence and at the time of the drafting and promulgation of the Indian Constitution, it was felt necessary to make certain specific provisions in the Constitution and also to take certain practical measures, to rectify the discriminations and injustices of the past, and thereby to uplift women to the level of parity with men. The decades since Independence have been singular progress of women in various fields. The framers of our Constitution and the Members of the Constituent Assembly have shown tremendous insight and farsight in making suitable constitutional provisions for safeguarding the educational and other interest of women who have had suffered centuries of neglect.

Gender Justice

Gender Justice is called for in various situations but the subject requires further debate. Equality between men and women by and large is there on paper but the reality is often somewhat different. The feminisation of poverty is a fact of life. According to one estimate, one out of five of the world's 5.6 billion people who live in absolute poverty in respect of adequate food, safe drinking water, health care and education are women. Most of the world's single parent families are headed by women. Unhelpful customs of which there are many in India *Sati*, for instance, have to be fought. The media can certainly bring some of these to light. Perhaps this is a cause that women journalists must take up and tactfully reveal so that their efforts are not frustrated by being dubbed as propaganda. The Indian Constitution makes it mandatory to give equal protection to every citizen. But law alone is not enough. It must be effectively used.

For this a reform movement is necessary as is a sympathetic media and judiciary. It is first of all necessary to expose violence against women and cases of sex discrimination. Until recently women who were sinned against preferred to leave their jobs or opt out of a marriage rather than have their miseries publicised. The media could not come to their help.

The custody of children is an important consideration when women seek separation from their husbands. Sometimes the courts prefer men with a sound financial backing to take over the responsibility of children rather than their working wives. Here the emotional needs of women and their children are overlooked. When women are given maintenance, the position is not always satisfactory in actual practice. Recovery of the maintenance money is often a tortuous process. A divorced woman's crying need is for a shelter which cannot be fulfilled with the limited amount given to her by way of maintenance. Gender equality is largely a neglected subject in the media. Women's welfare organisations must press the point harder so that it becomes generally known. As things stand women find it difficult to obtain the right jobs as well as proper promotion. They still do not have a share in joint family property except in a few States. There is ample violence against women. The police needs to be sensitised to women's problems. This can be done through special educational courses at the time candidates enter the service. A word of praise for the judiciary is deserved. The Supreme Court has passed some helpful judgments concerning women.

According to Jaffar Sharif: Under Muhammadan rule *Qazi* acted as civil and criminal judge. At present, save that he often leads the prayers at the *Ramazan* and *Baqar'Id* feasts, he is little more than a marriage registrar. He has no right to demand a fee for the marriage service, because this is a solemn rite enjoyed by the law. Gifts and grants of land (*inam, jagir*) and salaries were conferred upon *Qazis* by the former kings, which the East India Company and the British Government—may its good fortune be perpetuated—have continued to them, solely for the discharge of the following functions:

To perform *Nikah,* to train children in the knowledge of Islam, to bury the helpless poor, to act as Imam or prayer leader daily at the five times of worship in the mosque and the *khatib* or preacher, to deliver the *Khutba,* the bidding prayer or sermon, on the feast day and at the Friday services, to appoint *Muazin* or caller to prayer, the *Mujawir* or *Khidmati* to sweep the mosque and provide water for ablution—all such charges the *Qazi* should defray from his own purse, or from contributions collected from the congregation.

If the *Qazi* neglects these duties the ruler may dismiss him and appoint another in his stead, for the object of his office is to give relief to the servants of God, and this is frustrated if the poor are required to pay exorbitant marriage fees. But in Muslim states the mosque officials are generally appointed by the ruler and as they receive pay from him they are not in *Qazi's* service, and he, therefore, they demand marriage fees. *Qazis* are appointed for the advantage of the ignorant, and the learned men have no occasion for their services, because they can perform the marriage, funeral, and other rites themselves, a practice against which there is no prohibition either by God or by His Prophet.

After the marriage the *Qazi* offers up a prayer on behalf of the bride and bridegroom; O Great God! Grant that mutual love may reign between the couple, as between Adam and Hawwa or eve, Ibrahim or Abraham, and Sarah, between Yusuf, Joseph, and Zulaikha, wife of Potiphar, Moses and Safura or Zipporah. His Highness Muhammad Mustafa and

Ayisha, between 'Aliu-i-Murtaza and Fatimtu-z-zura!' He then takes the contents of the tray and handing the sugarcandy and beads to bridegroom's mother or some other lady, he tells her to take them to the bride and inform her that from this day she consider herself married to so and so, son of so and so, that such and such a jointure has been settled upon her, that she is to wear this necklace as a sign of wedlock and eat the sugar candy as an emblem of the sweets of married life. On hearing this the bride weeps, or is supposed to weep. In the men's room bride-groom falls upon the necks of his friends, kisses their hands and receives congratulations. Even were he a slave, on this occasion he would be allowed to embrace the men present. On the departure of the *Qazi* the musicians strike up a loud, discordant peal in order to scare evil spirits, and the friends of the bridegroom are feasted.

The bridegroom accompanied by his blood and marriage relations, to whom the bride's friends offer sandalwood paste, enters the room, a red cloth being spread on the floor for him to walk on and a red cloth canopy is held over their head as they walk in. As a joke their mouths are smeared with some sandalwood and the guests enjoy a laugh at their expense. Betel is handed round and they are seated on the carpet. By way of a joke some bits of leather or pot-sherds are put under the carpet. A basin (*chilamchi*) and an ewer (*aftaba*) are brought. A red cloth is hung over them, a little *sherbet* is poured over their hands, and they are given water to wash.

According to *Quran* and the traditions marriage depends on three facts: the assent of the parties, the evidence of two witnesses, the marriage settlement. If any of these are wanting, the marriage is void. Men of wealth usually pay the whole or one-third of the settlement at the time of marriage, the poor by instalments. As it is fixed by divine command, they must pay it partly in jewels, clothes, or in some other way, or induce the friends of the bride to permit a portion. should the bridegroom not have received this immunity or has not caused the demand to be cancelled he is responsible, and should he die his father or son is obliged to discharge it. Should the wife die, her relations can demand it, or recover it by law. But if a woman of her own accord leaves her husband she forfeits the settlement, and if her husband turns her out of doors he must first pay it.

The recent judgement proclaimed by the Supreme Court of India on the Shah Bano case followed by the introduction of the Muslim Women's Protection Bill in the Parliament, by no less a person than the Prime Minister himself, has aroused a great deal of controversy in India which ultimately should lead to a review and rethinking of the status and position of Indian women in general. Though the judgment according to Section 125 of the Criminal Procedure Code (Cr.P.C. No. 125) of India, primarily involves Muslim women, as it is they who fall prey to such undesirable and unjustified treatment by husbands due to marriage laws existing under the Muslim Shariat or Personal Law, it has caused concern about the condition of all women, which in general opinion is definitely not a happy or desirable one. The recent completion of the UN Women's Decade (1975-85) and the end of the Decade Conference at Nairobi has given a further encouragement to such enquiries.

It is a matter of grave concern to find that a religion inspired common law, as is to be found in the *Shariat* or the Muslim Personal Law, admits that a marriage can unilaterally be terminated by either of the spouse without a valid reason for it. In most cases it is generally the husband who ends the marriage mostly to marry again; and thereafter bear no legal liability to maintain his former wife. Marriage under Muslim Law is essentially regarded as a contract which can be easily and wilfully terminated. It is not even necessary to justify adequate reasons or grounds for such a termination. The law merely provides that a dower (or *mehr*) should be given to the wife at the time of the divorce so that she is able to maintain herself, but nothing is specified about the amount. At the Magistrate's Court where Shah Bano had first filed her suit, the dower or *mehr* had been fixed at the pitiable amount of Rs. 25 per month only, which was enhanced after her appeal to the High Court to Rs. 179.20 per month. It was not stated on what calculation or either why the members of the judiciary arrived at the sums decided upon. At the turn of events which subsequently took place, the hearing of the Shah Bano case has receded to the background, throwing up many other vital considerations. However, this controversy has led to further deliberations and a certain amount of soul-searching. People, learned and judicious, think, that time has come when a secular country like India should have one single common civil code for all its citizens, which will go a long way in providing unity of its people.

A strong opinion is present also in opposition to the discussion of this controversy; and it is argued that the claim is being put forward by people for immediate gain. Whatever may be the view it certainly has given a push and a new thrust to review the condition of the average, ordinary Indian women in general. In spite of all the efforts by certain section of the Indian women, during nearly last hundred years, though small in number but educated and articulate, the condition of the general body has shown no sign of betterment. To a large extent the immediate cause may be identified as illiteracy and ignorance, leading to a mind bound by superstitions and dogmas; and the lack of economic independence for the majority of such women. It has to be impressed upon that unless some amount of financial security can be assured for the very ordinary women, it will be well nigh impossible to give to them that little bit of self-reliance which is necessary for them to face the world on their own. But perhaps one has to go far deeper to strike at the root of the malaise.

In a society like ours, steeped in faith and tradition, a women's strategy for achieving power in marriage is possibly based on what Constantina Safillios-Rothschild argued and chose to call the "love debt." That is, a marriage works only when a woman marries a man who is much more in love with her than she with him. In such cases only, she is accepted by the man in their household as totally reliable and supreme. In the initial years this amounts to a surrender on the part of the man which settles down as years go by and a normal relation is developed between the two. Otherwise the power arrangement in the marriage will collapse due to multifarious social obligations and controls, as well as due to the existence of suitable laws for the interested party. The male member usually controls all the economic levers and may thus be able to even physically coerce the weaker partner into agreeing to his demands. Persuasions and manipulations from different quarters have to be resisted by the wife and she needs all the wisdom to do so. In cases where money comes in as a decisive factor, women are generally the losers, as they have either little or no resource to fall back upon.

This leads up to a very vital question in our social set up. A totally asymmetrical pattern of distribution of wealth and resource is the starting point of power and strength, where women begin by being the losers. Let us take the case of the Hindu Law here. A daughter's inheritance rights are severely circumscribed in comparison to a son's. A son, from the moment of his birth, is considered a coparcener, that is, an equal owner of the family's joint property, with other male members. A daughter cannot be a coparcener in a Hindu undivided family. She can only get a portion of what her father inherits if and when the property is divided. An unmarried daughter has the right of maintenance from the family property. But once she marries, she has no right to maintenance from her natal family's property, not even if she is widowed, divorced or abandoned.

Maintenance Law in India is far from a satisfactory, whether under Cr.P.C. Hindu Law or Muslim Law. There is no way to ensure that the husband will regularly make payments. As neither the police or no such authority will come to the deserted wife's help, she will in such cases have to go to the court again, which is never an easy way out; as by and large, the majority of the Indian women hardly possess the necessary or requisite financial resources to do so. These women are not only poor, they are isolated from each other. They also lack class consciousness and are often subject to negative sanctions. Being highly dependent on a single individual for material support and human companionship they are discouraged in uniting together and forming a "power group." All these kinds of "non-decision making" moves, prevent in issues being raised and fought for. This is what Bacharach and Baratz, mention as structural suppression of issues. It is, therefore, not plausible to draw a comparison with women's movements for their welfare and well-being; to other socio-political movements existing in the Indian society, as for example, that of the peasantry, which again forms a distinctive class in India. The peasants can, if they so decide improve their condition, by forcibly eliminating their opponents, the landlords. A woman can never eliminate the man from her life. It cannot be even as a last resort the optimal strategy. The goal in marriage is not to tear down the existing structure but to bring about through emotional changes a co-operative and better life. In a balanced marriage not only is a woman not powerless but she often has "bargaining" powers, it is only when this balance is disrupted that problems crop up. Life long persistence of male/female relationship is the single most important fact in the life of most women, who may be termed average or ordinary, in our society.

Another problem starts from this point, the feeling of being "ordinary" and "average." Women, throughout history, have been told that their subordinate position is natural. It, therefore, needs some preparation to prick this bubble. Religious teachings, school text-books—all say the same thing. Manu, the great Hindu Law giver is quoted to have said:

> "A woman is under the control of her father in childhood; her husband in her youth; and her son in her advanced age."

This belief is not only held by the men in our society. Young girls are even told by their mothers and grand-mothers that they should be satisfied with their position as the 'second sex'. Therefore, it would be necessary to arouse first of all, a "subjective" interest in each and every woman as to the wrongness of her position. "Collective consciousness" will have to follow later. Unless each one, in her mind, is aware and conscious of the wrong done, no organisation will succeed. Therefore, the women's movements have to realize first that the most serious problem to overcome is to make the women realize that they are oppressed. In democratic societies, political parties are the primary agents for arousing public conviction and motivation. In all countries, these have been structured round different issues, but hardly have the problems relating women taken the central stage. And today in our country, we find to our dismay, that political parties are bent upon to misuse and suppress women. actually, in most countries, political parties have tried to avoid politicization of the above issue. It is only after 1975 that we have come across some pronouncements on these lines. When the liberal, democratic constitutions were established in Europe and America, women's right to participate in the political life was not discussed at all. It was simply not an issue worth considering. Women had first to be acknowledged by themselves and by some men at least as human beings, as individuals, before the demand for political right or suffrage could be raised. It was a case of suppression of an issue not by any agent, but by the entire social structure. After a time, of all the rights that women could claim the right to vote was the easiest to handle because solution to this demand was in the hands of the political authorities. Thus, grew up the suffragist movements. In those countries, where constitution liberally gave the women such rights, no one bothered to examine the question, whether it also gave the women 'equal rights' in the other aspects as well; or whether the codification of rights really meant that they could be used adequately and properly. It must also be realised that rights develop on its own basis and requirement, it is never the result of a contract or agreement: whether it is between individuals or between the individual and the polity.

In political theory, the movement from status to contract is examplified in the development of the great concept of the social contract and the claim that the State itself had its origin in a contract. In the seventeenth century discussions of the social contract and the marriage contract went hand in hand. The main criticism of the social contract came from Hegel, who further regarded that a purely contractual conception of marriage was shameful. William Thompson laid the foundation for subsequent criticism of the marriage contract can only be entered into by two parties of equal standing which in this case was not so. Secondly, the terms of a contracts is generally revisable and alterable, which also will not hold good in this case.

The marriage contracts was criticized less polemically, but no less forcefully, by John Stuart Mill in *The Subjection of Women*. Many of the reforms of marriage law demanded by Thompson and Mill have now been enacted, but much still remains to be done. Masculinity and domination, virility and violence have been frequently linked together. Politics and power rest on an understanding of necessity and freedom.

Let us once again revert back to the consideration of the Muslim Personal Law and its effect in our country.

Section 125, Cr.P.C. provides for maintenance upto a maximum amount of Rs. 500 a month for a needy wife, child or parent. Section 127(3)(b) provides that a maintenance order under Section 125 shall be cancelled where "The woman has been divorced by her husband and she has received, whether before or after the date of the said order, the whole of the sum which, under any customary or personal law, applicable to the parties, was payable on such divorce."

Mr. Justice Krishna Iyer had interpreted this clause to mean that if the amount paid under personal law was sufficient to save the woman from destitution, the maintenance order under Section 125 would be cancelled, but in case the amount paid under personal law was not sufficient to save her form destitution, then the order under Section 125 would stand. He argued that, Section 125 exists to protect people from destitution, and to see that the State is not burdened with their upkeep if they have close relatives who should look after them.

According to Maulana Maudoodi,

> "Similar is the case of the punishment for adultery and fornication, Islam prescribes a hundred stripes for the unmarried and stoning to death for the married partners in the crime. But, of course, it applies to the society wherein every trace of suggestiveness has been destroyed, where mix gatherings of men and women have been prohibited, where public appearance of painted and pampered women is completely non-existent, where marriage has been made easy; where virtue, piety and charity are current coins and where the remembrance of God and the hereafter is kept ever fresh in men's minds and hearts. These punishments are not meant for that filthy society wherein sexual excitement is rampant, wherein nude pictures, obscene books, and vulgar songs have become common recreations; wherein sexual perversions have taken hold of cinema and all other places of amusement, wherein mixed, semi-nude parties are considered the acme of social progress and wherein economic conditions and social customs have made marriage."[1]

However, this interpretation was challenged pointing out that Section 127 clearly states that if "the whole" amount payable under personal law has been paid, the woman is not entitled to relief under Section 125. Therefore, the Supreme Court had to decide whether Shah Bano had in fact received the whole amount payable to her under Muslim Personal Law.

Shah Bano's counsel argued that apart from these two payments, another payment known as *mataa* is also due to a woman on divorce, under *Ayat* 241 of *Sura* II (*Sura-al Baqr*) of the Holy *Quran*.

Shah Bano had not been paid *mataa*. In practice, it is equally extremely difficult for a woman to claim and get her right under Hindu personal law, just as it is extremely difficult to get the "generous payment" under Muslim Personal Law. The case is a civil one which means that the husband can amploy all sorts of dilatory tactics to drag the case out for years.

In practice, all the laws on maintenance are highly inadequate. It is not enough to state that a woman should get a "fair" or "generous" payment because the definition of generosity varies widely. Women have been too long dependent on the generosity of men.

The Bill on the rights of divorced Muslim women passed by the Lok Sabha on May 6, 1986 can easily be cited as one of the most controversial Bills to have been passed by the Lok Sabha in the history of India's Independent existence.

The statement of objects and reasons relating to the Muslim Women (Protection of Rights on Divorce) Bill, 1986 begins with a reference to the judgement of the Supreme Court in Mohd. Ahmed Khan *vs.* Shah Bano Begum and others which was delivered in 1985. This gives many the impression that it was for the first time that the highest court of the land had held that if the divorced Muslim wife is unable to maintain herself after the period of *Iddat* (three months), she is entitled to have recourse to Section 125 of Criminal Procedure Code, 1973. Section 125 Cr.P.C. lays an obligation on the husband who, having sufficient means, neglects or refuses to maintain herself. In that event the court can decree a monthly maintenance, and the ex-husband will have to pay the maintenance decreed by the court.

Another landmark verdict is that of Kerala High Court of 24th February 1995, striking down an unjust provision of the Indian Divorce Act, 1867, an exclusively Christian law, is significant; because it has advanced the cause of women and is another step towards bridging the gaps between personal laws in India. It has effectively removed the provisions which happened to be very torturing for the women, especially for the women, in the Christian community. The verdict of Kerala High Court made the grounds for dissolution of a Christian marriage similar to those in the divorce as of other religions. The landmark judgment also highlighted the tendency of Central and State legislatures to turn down genuine demands for changes in personal laws on the ground that such reforms would be against religious beliefs and practices. Though the recommendations had been made by Law Commission, the Supreme Court and High Courts, the Central Government failed to amend the divorce provisions for Christians similar to those in the laws for other religious groups.

The law of marriage for Christians in India is regulated by the Indian Christian Marriage Act, 1872. However, this Act is not applicable to marriages solemnized among Christians living in areas that came under the erstwhile Travancore-Kochin, Manipur and Jammu and Kashmir, where "the customs and practices prevalent among the community in the area," that is, the canon laws and other personal laws are applicable But for divorce, the law applicable to Christians throughout the country (except in Jammu and Kashmir) is the Indian Divorce Act. The application of the provisions of the Indian Christian Marriage Act has created difficulties as they clash with Christian Personal Law. Divorce is an alien concept under the personal law, which, however, recognises and enforces the concept of "nullity of marriage" through religious courts. The Indian Divorce Act provides for divorce.

For members of community difficulties arise when the orders of civil court and religious court are opposed to each other. For example, if a person gets a divorce sanctioned by a civil court but not a decree of nullity from the religious court, he or she can remarry under the provisions of the Special Marriage Act but may face excommunication on charges of bigamy. If these are the perils of personal laws, the existing civil law for divorce among Christians, brought in by the British on the lines of the law passed in England in 1857, has remained with all its infirmities. Especially "unjust, unfair and oppressive," as the High Court observed, was Section 10 of the Act, which discriminated between Christian men and women regarding grounds on which a divorce could be allowed.

According to this provision, the civil courts could allow a divorce for a man on the ground that his wife was guilty of adultery, but not for a woman whose husband was guilty of the same offence. The wife could be granted freedom from the marriage only if the husband was found guilty of "incestuous adultery," or of "bigamy with adultery," or of "marriage with another woman with adultery," or "adultery coupled with cruelty," or of "adultery coupled with desertion."

It was also not possible for a Christian wife to get a divorce even if the husband was found guilty of treating her with cruelty habitually and persistently or he had deserted her forever—two reasons recognised as independent grounds for divorce for Indian women of all other religions—unless adultery was also alleged and proved by her. For a century and a quarter, Christian women have suffered under this law because direct proof of adultery was almost impossible to get. But in the meantime, legislation regulating marriage and divorce in other religions underwent change. So did matrimonial laws applicable to Christians outside India, especially in England, The Matrimonial Causes Act, 1857 is now in force in England in a transformed version—The Matrimonial Causes Act 1973, identifies "irretrievable breakdown of marriage" as the sole comprehensive ground for judicial separation and divorce.

Under the Hindu Marriage Act, 1955, which applies to all Hindus Buddhists, Jains or Sikhs, or any person who is not a Christian, Muslim, Parsi or Jew, the grounds for the divorce are for the husband and wife. Independent grounds have been established under this law, which includes, among others, cruelty and desertion and voluntary sexual intercourse with any person other than his or her spouse. The courts can grant a divorce if any one of these is proved.

A Muslim marriage can be dissolved by the parties without recourse to the civil courts and on certain grounds by recourse to courts. If it is without recourse to the court, a husband is allowed to divorce his wife by *talak*, whenever, he desires so, without assigning any cause. A couple may agree to a divorce by mutual consent or through an agreement before or after a marriage which allows the wife to divorce herself from the husband under certain specified conditions "not opposed to Muslim law." The husband marrying a second time could be one such condition.

Judicial divorce for Muslim women is through the Dissolution of Muslim Marriages Act, 1939, which clarifies the provisions of Muslim law relating to suits for divorce by women married under Muslim law. The Act also allows cruelty and desertion as independent grounds for divorce, among several others. Significantly, before the introduction of this law, there was no provision allowing Muslim women to get a divorce on the failure of her husband to maintain her or on his deserting or ill-treating her.

Cruelty and desertion are also independent grounds for divorce under the Parsi Marriage and Divorce Act, 1936. The evolution of this law, which governs marriage and divorce among Parsis, is significant in this context. The Parsi Marriage and Divorce Act of 1865, a culmination of 20 years of effort by the community to have laws suitable to their social requirements, was also based on the Matrimonial Causes Act, 1857, of England, and its major effect was to make Parsi marriages monogamous.

But the law of 1865 was defective in many respects. For example, adultery by itself and adultery coupled with some other offence were the only grounds for divorce. Moreover, the Act empowered only the wife to ask for judicial separation on the ground of cruelty or because the husband brought home a prostitute. The husband had no remedy for seeking judicial separation. The Act of 1936 remedied these.

Further amendments were introduced by the Parsi Marriage and Divorce (Amendment) Act, 1988. The law now allows divorce by mutual consent or on charges of adultery, cruelty or desertion, among others.

Divorce by mutual consent is allowed also under the Special Marriage Act, 1954, which applies to all citizens of India, if their marriage was legalised under it. It also recognises cruelty and desertion as independent grounds for divorce. "Voluntary sexual intercourse with any person other than his or her spouse" is another independent reason. This Act as well as the Parsi Marriage and Divorce Act allows divorce if the couple had failed to live together in the one year after the court had passed a decree for judicial separation.

Another important law is the Foreign Marriages Act, 1969, relating to marriages of Indian citizens in a foreign country. It allows a Christian wife or husband divorce on the independent grounds of cruelty and desertion and does not require that adultery should be proved. But if the marriage was solemnised in India, Christian women till now could get a divorce only if they established the strict grounds of the Indian Divorce Act.

The Law Commission had, in a Bill, submitted alongwith its 15th report in 1960, suggested comprehensive amendments to the Indian Divorce Act, to give the right of divorce to Christians on almost all grounds mentioned in the Special Marriages Act. The Government finalised and presented the Bill, but it lapsed on the dissolution of Parliament. Since then several courts, including the Supreme Court, had pointed out the "antiquated and anomalous nature" of the Act.

It is in this context that the order of the Full Bench of the High Court, consisting of Chief Justice M.M. Pareed Pillay, Justice T.V. Ramakrishnan and Justice P. Shanmugam, is being widely welcomed. The court upheld the contentions in two writ petitions seeking divorce (by Mary Sonia Zacharia, assistant warden, Corpus Christi High School, Kottayam, and E.J. Ammini, a government high school teacher) that some of the provisions of Section 10 of the Indian Divorce Act were violative of Articles 14, 15 and 21 of the Constitution.

The court said that "the life of a Christian wife who is compelled to live against her will, though in name only, as the wife of a man who hates her, has cruelly treated her and deserted her, putting an end to the marital relationship irreversibly, will be a sub-human life without dignity and personal liberty. . . . On the whole, such a life can legitimately be treated as a life imposed by a tyrannical and authoritarian law on a helpless and cruelly-treated Christian wife quite against her will, which she is bound to lead till her death. . . ." The court said the conditions prescribed for allowing divorce under Section 10 of the Act were harsh and oppressive, making the law arbitrary and violative of the rights of the petitioners and Christian women in general, guaranteed under Sections 14 and 21 of the Constitution. These provisions personified discrimination on the grounds of religion and sex, it ruled.

The judgment has made it possible for a Christain women to seek dissolution of her marriage on any one of the grounds of adultery, cruelty and desertion, just like women belonging to other religions.

In 1994, the Kerala High Court has passed another important verdict regarding the divorce of Christian women, which said a divorce sanctioned by religious courts would not be legally valid unless and until it was sanctioned by a civil court—in short, that civil laws have precedence over canonical laws in Christian marriages. These two judgments are in conformity with an earlier order of the Supreme Court striking down the discriminatory laws that governed the succession rights of Christian women of Kerala.

The Kerala High Court has pointed out that it has made only a "limited attempt" to reform an antiquated law and thus called for a fresh look at the personal laws that govern Christians. The real issue is the delay in bringing a uniform law for all Indians.

Legal or Constitutional positions need not necessarily lead us to an improved situation; all around legal change is not to be confused with social change. Social change requires translation of such rights won by law into the social fabric of the society. People may accept legal changes yet resist their application in their personal lives. Faced with the basic truth in our own country we find that the vital statistics dealing with the life span of the women in India hardly gives an encouraging picture. Between 1901-71 the increase in the women population has been 4 per cent lower than the male. The proportion between men and women has also steadily declined during this period. Female life expectancy is lower; 45.6 against 47.1 for the male population; with a very high death-rate up to the age of 40, which generally tapers off with the child-bearing age.

Another point that was to be considered also is that among the women themselves, there is a great divergence. The Constitution of India recognizes the unequal position of women and children [Article 15-Section (iii)] and allows the government to create special provisions for them. But how does one assure the equality of status and opportunity among the different classes and groups of women placed in the different strata of society? Other Asian countries also face identical problems.

The same difficulty arises when an attempt is made to measure female participation even in a very restricted sector, like in different industries; because much of the workforce, actually the majority of the total number, function in the unorganised sector. There is not possible to have proper and reliable statistics, and these women are denied every protection of law. They become tools in the hands of *thekedars* as they are known in our country, who use and misuse them according to their whims. No Labour Law can protect them, no unions are there to fight for their cause. There is hardly any actual protection from either State or society, though these women have distinctive and accepted roles. A recent international compilation states that the percentage of women in the labour force is 29.1 per cent; of which women employers and own-account-workers constitute 18.6 and women employees 23.6 per cent. 45.2 per cent women can be classified under unpaid family workers.

On the home-front also their contribution is not assessed and realised properly. Their work is not given the status of an economic contribution and so is not even considered for computation in any measurement of national income. The women are conditioned into believing that it is their natural work and duty. Many a time, instead of being proud to be an efficient house-wife she is apologetic and defensive with a sense of inadequacy that she is not good enough for anything else. This peculiar situation has forced the women to be relegated to distinct class of their own and they are regarded as inferior, generally in all societies of the third world.

REFERENCE

1. Syed Abul-Ala Mandidi, Islami Law and Constitution, p. 55.

10

EMPOWERMENT OF WOMEN

The women in India are fortunate enough to get the political rights and civil liberties on an equal footing with men with the adoption of the Constitution on January 26, 1950. The Constitution not only guarantees 'equality before law' and 'equal protection before law', it also empowers the State to adopt positive measures to promote the interests of women in India. The Constitution also guarantees equality of opportunity in public employment and imposes a fundamental duty on every citizen to renounce practices derogatory to the dignity of women.

To uphold the Constitutional mandate, the Parliament in India has also enacted various laws from time to time to secure to all its citizens, justice, social, economic and political, liberty of thought, expression, belief, faith and worship, equality of status and opportunity and to promote among them all fraternity, assuring the dignity of the individual and the unity of the Nation. It has adopted various legislative measures to counter social discrimination and various forms of violence and atrocities against women. The legal edifice adequately takes care of women and their special needs.

The initial approach of the Government was to focus women as targets of welfare policies in the social sector. In action as far as women's issues were concerned. In the Fifth Plan (1974-78), there was a shift in the Government's approach from 'welfare' to 'development'. In the Sixth Plan, there was a separate chapter on women's development with a definite thrust on health, education and employment. The Seventh Plan aimed at raising their economic and social status and bringing them into the mainstream of national development.

The Eighth Plan (1992-97) realizes the need to develop special programmes so that the gains from development in various sectors do not bypass women. We now find a shift from 'development' to 'empowerment' of women. As such, the Government has reflected, articulated and seriously addressed the women's issues from a new perspective. It has adopted many women-specific policies. We also find a progressive increase in the planned outlays during the last 50 years. The outlay for women's needs was Rs. 40 million during the First Plan (1951-56), while it has gone up to approximately Rs. 20,000 million during the Eighth Plan.

In 1971, the Government appointed a Committee on the status of women in India which raised certain basic issues about the socialization processes inherent in a hierarchical society, resource and power distribution patterns and cultural values prevailing in India. It stressed the need to transform the *de jure* equality into *de facto* equality. A separate Department of Women and Child Development was set up in 1985 under the newly created Ministry of Human Resource Development. In 1988, the National Perspective Plan for Women was drawn to facilitate mainstreaming of women's issues in Government Programme and Policies. In 1990, the Parliament set up the National Commission for Women to monitor all matters related to constitutional and legal rights conferred on women.

As a signatory to the World Declaration on the Survival, Protection and Development of Children, the Government of India has drawn up an Action Plan for the Girl Child (1991-2000). In a recent legislation, the Government has now banned sex-determination test to prevent female foeticide. The crowning achievements of the current decade have been the 73rd and 74th Constitutional Amendments which guarantee one-third representation to women in all local bodies both in the rural and urban areas and also reserve in one single stroke, one-third of all posts of chairpersons for women. It is expected to be finalized soon. The Government is now planning to set up a National Resource Centre for Women to act as an apex body for promoting and incorporating gender perspective in Government Programmes and Policies.

Empowerment of Women

Women become empowered through collective reflection and decision-making. The parameters of empowerment are:

- building a positive self-image and self-confidence;
- developing ability to think critically;
- building up group-cohesion and fostering decision-making and action;
- ensuring equal participation in the process of bringing about social change;

— encouraging group action in order to bring about change in the society; and
— providing the wherewithal for economic independence.[1]

The policy of empowerment can be translated into action provided women also help themselves. Until and unless they are not well-equipped with their rights and duties, social awareness, etc., there empowerment is remote hypothesis. Equal opportunities are there; but they should be able and well prepared for availing them. Prof. M.S. Gore has rightly said:

> "If women have to be prepared for an equal status they must have more information on the factual position regarding the number of women in the work-force, the types of occupations in which they are distributed, the types of careers are likely to make upon their abilities and on their family life. It might even be useful to discuss—in co-educational classes of young persons—cases of successful adjustments and/or failures in the marriages where the woman is working."[2]

Though the Indian Constitution gives equal rights to men and women, Indian woman has not achieved absolute equality in actual practice. They find it difficult to achieve access to high-level jobs where men reach easily than them. This is one way of discriminating against women. However, women government servants are better off in this matter. Women in decision-making positions can be seen in various fields supported by the government. Women in the service—the IAS, IPS and the foreign service have been doing a commendable. The sphere of women's earning activity is no longer confined to teaching and medicine. Whether it is advertising or the arts architecture or any other man-sized profession like law, etc.

Rural Women

The draft National Policy on Empowerment of Women envisages:

(i) to set up councils at national and State levels to review the implementation of the recommendations of the national and State commissions for women;
(ii) the Centre and State to draw up time-bound action-plans to translate this policy into concrete action in consultation with the Central and State Commissions for women; and

(iii) every ministry at the Centre and in the State is obliged to ensure equal flow of benefits in physical and financial terms to women including the disadvantaged among them through different programmes and plans.

The Government of India also reiterated its commitment of women empowerment on International Women's Day, March 6, 1997 for setting up of Commissioners for Women Rights and National Resources Centre for women in order to create a conducive environment for the advancement of women.

In spite of numerous measures, the socio-economic status of women, more particularly rural women, is abysmally low as compared to that of urban women. However, it is recognized that the empowerment of rural women would in real sense hasten the pace of rural development.

The following are a few significant areas which calls for empowerment of rural women:

(i) Women and their work-force participation;
(ii) Women and their education;
(iii) Women and their health, and
(iv) Women and their political participation at the grassroot level to deal with atrocities on women and other development issues of rural women.

Rural women suffer mainly from economic, educational, hygienic, and backwardness. Out of these the first one that is economic backwardness is the root of other problems. This is the significant cause for wastage and stagnation of rural girls. Parents cannot afford the expenses incurred in the education of their children. Moreover, they often employ their children to supplement their income for livelihood. Thus, the poverty of the parents proves a potent cause for wastage and stagnation. Some other causes, *i.e.*, illiteracy and ignorance of the parents; social forces working against women education; domestic help given by the girls to their mothers; early marriage system; non-availability of separate girls school; socially deprived classes like scheduled caste, tribes, backward classes, etc. can be enumerated.

According to Prof. S.N. Mukerji:

"A century ago, girls' education had open enemies in India, but it is now a *sine qua non* of India's social and national development. It had to face many peculiar difficulties; the system of *purdah* and child marriage, indifference of parents to the education of their daughters, distrust in western system of girls' education, financial pressures on the middle classes, lack of suitable curricula for girls, absence of women teachers, and allied problems.[3]

The most potent cause was the political one. Under the rule of East India Company it was not considered necessary to educate the fair sex, perhaps because lady clerks or officers were not required for administrative purposes. In his report William Adams wrote about female education in 1838.

> "All the established native institutions of education exist for the benefit of male sex only, and the whole of female sex is systematically consigned to ignorance, and left wholly without even the semblance of a provision for their instruction." [4]

Because of such an attitude of the British towards the education of girls the progress was very slow. According to the census of 1961 the percentage of literacy amongst women is 12.9 per cent only. After independence due to tremendous awakening special attention was given towards the education of women and as such the speed of progress was accelerated. The greatest impetus to women's cause, however, came from the national movement launched by Mahatma Gandhi. On his call thousands of ladies came out of *purdah*, and suffered the same hardships as men did.

Committee on Women Education

Education panel of the Planning Commission at its meeting held in July 1957, recommended that, "a suitable committee should be appointed to go into the various aspects of the question relating to the nature of education for girls at the elementary, secondary and adult stages and to examine whether the present system was helping them to lead a happier and more useful life. This recommendation was placed before the Conference of the State Education Ministers who also agreed that a special committee should be appointed to examine the whole question of women's accordingly set up by the Government of India in the Ministry of Education.

Chairman	*Members*
Smt. Durgabai Deshmukh	1. Kumari S. Panadikar,
Central Social Welfare Board	2. Shri P.N. Mathur,

3. Smt. Kulsum Sayani,
4. Shri J. P. Naik,
5. Smt. Sahara Ahmed,
6. Kumari Sarojini Rajan,
7. Dr. Phulrenu Guha.

Terms of Reference

(a) To suggest special measures to make up the leeway in women's education at the primary and secondary levels;

(b) To examine the problem of wastage in girls' education at these levels;

(c) To examine the problem of adult women who have relapsed into illiteracy or have received inadequate education and who need continuation of education so as to enable them to earn a living and participate in projects of national reconstruction;

(d) To survey the nature and extents of material and other facilities offered by voluntary welfare organizations for the education of such women and to recommend steps necessary to enable them to offer larger educational facilities to them;

(e) To examine the possibility and methods of encouraging a large number of women to go into vocational trades by providing suitable vocational training as a part of formal education or through special courses designed for adult women.

Major Recommendations

A. *Special Recommendation Needing Top Priority*

1. The education of women should be regarded as a major and a special problem in education for a good many years to come and a bold and determined effort should be made to face its difficulties and magnitude and to close the existing gap between the education of men and women in as short a time as possible. The funds required for the purpose should be considered to be the first charge on the sums set aside for the development of education.
2. Steps should be taken to constitute as early as possible a National Council for the Education of Girls and Women.
3. The problem of the education of women is so vital and of such great national significance that it is absolutely necessary for the Centre to assume more responsibility for its rapid development.

4. The State Governments should establish State Councils for the education of girls and women.
5. Every State should be required to prepare comprehensive development plans for the education of girls and women in its area.
6. It is also necessary to enlist the cooperation of all semi-official organizations, local bodies, voluntary organizations, teachers organizations and members of the public to assist in the promotion of the education of girls and women.
7. The Planning Commission should set up permanent machinery to estimate, as accurately as possible, the women-power requirements of the Plans from time to time and make the results of its studies available to Government and the public.

B. *Other Special Recommendations*

1. *Primary Education*

(1) Concessions in kind should be given to all girls, whether from rural or urban areas, of parents below a certain income level.
(2) The Government should formulate a scheme for awarding prizes to the village which shows the largest proportional enrolment and average attendance of girls.

2. *Middle and Secondary Education*

(1) At the middle schools stage, more and more co-educational institutions should be started.
(2) But for the secondary state, separate schools for girls should be established specially in rural areas, at the same time giving parents full freedom to admit their girls to boys' schools if they so desire.
(3) All girls of parents below a prescribed income level should be given free education up to the middle stage.
(4) As far as possible, free subsidized transport should be made available to girls in order to bring middle and secondary schools, within easy reach.

3. *Curriculum and Syllabi*

(1) There should be identical curriculum for boys and girls at the primary stage with the proviso that, even at this stage, subjects

like music, painting, sewing, needle work, simple hardwork, and cooking should be introduced to make the courses more suitable for girls.

(2) At the middle school stage, and more especially at the secondary stage, there is a need for differentiation of curricula for boys and girls.

4. *Training and Employment*

(1) Immediately steps should be taken to set up additional training institutions for women teachers in all such area of the country where a shortage exists at present.

(2) With a view to including women from urban area to accept posts of teachers in rural schools, women teachers serving in rural areas may be provided with quarters and a village allowance may be given to such teachers.

(3) The maximum age limit for entry into service may be relaxed, and the age of retirement may be extended to 60 provided the teacher is physically and otherwise fit.

5. *Professional and Vocational Education*

(1) The employment of women on a part-time basis, wherever feasible, should be accepted as a policy.

(2) Girls should be encouraged to take up courses in commerce, engineering, agriculture medicine, etc., at the university stage by offering them scholarships and other concessions.

(3) It is important to organize campaigns to mobilize public opinion for creating proper conditions in offices and establishments in which women can work freely.

6. *Facilities for Adult Women*

(1) Educational facilities in the form of condensed courses: (a) That prepare women for the middle school examination, and (b) those that prepare them for the high school or higher secondary examinations should be provided more extensively in all States.

(2) Provision should also be made of condensed courses, which train women for suitable vocation after completion of necessary continuation education.

7. *Voluntary Organization*

(1) The services of the voluntary organizations should be extensively used in the field of middle, secondary, higher, social and vocational education of women. The existing grant-in-aid codes of the States need a thorough revision. There should be a substantial and significant difference in the rates of grants-in-aid and between girls' institutions and boys' institutions at all levels. The conditions of aid for girls' institutions should be made easier.

General Recommendations

Whenever primary education is not free, immediate step should be taken to make it free. Whenever, new schools are started, the rural region should be given priority consideration.

Wastage and Stagnation

(1) As a scientific study of the problem of wastage on an all-India basis is needed, the Ministry of Education should carry out special studies of this problem in all parts of the country.
(2) The following steps should be taken to reduce the extent of stagnation in class I: (i) all fresh admission to class I should be made in the beginning of the first session; (ii) it should be a specific responsibility of teachers to see that proper attendance is maintained in the school; (iii) the age of admission should be raised to six plus, (iv) standards of teaching should be improved.
(3) The stagnation in classes II to V can be reduced if (i) attendance of children is increased; (ii) standards of teaching are improved; (iii) internal examinations are introduced; (iv) books and educational equipment needed by poor children are supplied in good time.
(4) About 65 per cent of the cases of wastage at the primary level are due to economic causes. This wastage can be eliminated only if provision for part-time instruction is made for those children who cannot attend on a whole time basis.
(5) About 25 to 30 per cent of the cases of wastage at the primary level are due to the indifference of parents. This cause can be eliminated partly by conducting propagandas and partly by a rigorous enforcement of the compulsory education law.

Environment of Teachers

(1) The present scales of pay of teachers should be suitably revised.
(2) There should be no distinction between the scales of pay and allowances paid to teachers in Government and local board or municipal institutions and those that are paid to teachers working under private managements.
(3) The triple-benefit scheme called the Pension-*cum*-Provident Fund-*cum*-Insurance Scheme should be made applicable to every teacher who is employed permanently in an institution.[5]

Education in Human Rights has been stressed in all Human Rights Documents and has been viewed as an essential contribution to the development of Human Rights Culture. United Nations Charter (1945) and UNESCO constitution have been designed with a view to make major human rights documents accessible to the large body of personnel involved in various sectors of education, like policy-formulation, curricular development, classroom and out of classroom teaching-learning activities to enrich the human rights education programmes wherever and in whatever way they exist. Such education will go a long way in creating and promoting awareness of current issues and controversies relating to human rights.

To create awareness in Human Rights, National Policy on Education (NPE) 1986 has included a special chapter on *Core-Curricuium*. Another term for core-curriculum, according to the Western educationists is 'common learning'.

> "What does this title "Common Learnings" mean? It means that this course consists of learning experiences which everyone needs to have, regardless of that occupation he may expect to follow or where he may happen to live. "Common Learnings" extends through the three years of high school and two years of community institute. It meets for two period daily, in grades ten, eleven, and twelve, and for one period daily, in grades thirteen and fourteen. It is required of all students."[6]

In the Indian set up it includes: the history of India's freedom movement, the constitutional obligations and other contents essential to nurture national identity. These elements will cut across subject areas and will be designed to promote values; such as, India's cultural heritage, equalitarianism, democracy and secularism, equality of sexes, protection of environment, removal of social barriers, observance of small family norms and inculcation of scientific temper. All curricular programmes will be implemented in strict conformity with secular values.

Activities Suggested

For developing awareness about Human Rights amongst boys and girls at school level the following activities are hereby suggested:

Mock Parliament

The desired training in the working of parliament, legislative assemblies, etc. can be imparted to the young generation. Ministry of Parliamentary Affairs has launched the programme of disseminating the requisite information and procedure of the Parliament by conducting the Mock Parliament throughout the country involving Kendriya Vidyalayas spread throughout the country. It is being conducted at three levels— Regional level, Zonal level, and National level. Every year about 200 Kendriya Vidyalayas participate in this programme. The performance of the best Vidyalaya is displayed at Delhi in the presence of the dignitaries. The students and trainers are awarded suitably. This activity should be introduced in the States also.

Besides Mock Parliament, many other co-curricular activities can also be arranged at school level for promoting awareness in the human rights.

Human Rights Clubs

Human rights club and centres of human rights education should be opened in all educational institutions.

- Survey of child labour by students volunteers;
- Arranging extension lecture on Human Rights;
- Officials of NGOs can be invited to apprise the students of the contribution of reputed leaders working in the area of Human Rights. From time to time students should be informed about various issues of human rights;
- Creating Awareness about the role and function of reputed leaders working in the area of Human Rights Commission and other Non-government organizations for achieving the goals of UN Decade for Human Rights Education 1995-2004;

— In some of the good schools we find UNO corner in their libraries. Here some literature on Human Rights can also be displayed so that everyone may have easy access to it.

A significant landmark began in the history of Indian women with the Constitution of India, guaranteeing equality opportunity to men and women this was, no doubt, a silver lining in the dark clouds. The UN Charter Declaration on the right to development, equal remuneration against women, etc., ensure equal rights to women. For protection of women rights a number of acts were passed, as elaborated earlier. The Hindu Marriage Act, Hindu Succession Act-1956, Sati Prevention Act 1929, Dowry Prevention Act 1961, though passed, in fact, have little or no effect in reality.The year 1989 was declared year of the girl child by SAARC countries, UNESCO also brought the issue of girls and women on National and International agendas One of the objectives of WARLAT (Women Action Research and Legal Action Trust) established in 1992 in asserting of gender equality and taking recourse to the special protection laws already designed to empower women, the other objectives, to examine factors, which perpetuate the inferior status of women; to promote conception of Human Rights established in the Universal Declaration of Human Rights 1948 and other related International Convention and to work towards the elimination of discrimination against women.

Women's conference held in Beijing in 1995 discussed important issues of women Human Rights, property rights. Reproduction rights were broadly discussed. But in spite of all these provisions, violation of Human rights of women are on the rampant and a strong and urgent growth of NGOs to create awareness of the Human Rights and also to sensitize the need of exercising one's rights alongwith duties is very much needed.

Women and Political Participation

The Universal Declaration of Human Rights states that everyone has right to take part in the Government of his or her country. The United Nations Economic and Social Council endorsed a target of 30 per cent women at all levels of decision-making by 1995. However, women who constitute fifty per cent of total population are meagrely represented in political scenario. It has been rightly remarked that although the recent years have witnessed an increase in female voters, changes in voter participation have not been accompanied by changes in similar magnitude in the number of women occupying decision-making positions. Globally, women constitute only 10 per cent of legislative bodies and less in parliamentary positions.

The extent of power in taking or making positive decisions leading to the assumption of power which would ultimately determine effective, dominant and authoritative position in the society would have to be considered as well. One has to rely on statistical indicators such as literacy, education, employment, and political participation also. In India the 1962, 1967 and 1971 women members in Lok Sabha were 13, 13, and 17 respectively; but over the years it registered a considerable increase, and in the year 1996 there were as many as 32 women members out of 544 total numbers in the Lok Sabha.

Political empowerment of women does not imply just a right to vote silently, but to discuss, share politics by knowing its pros and cons and thereby to influence policies and decision-making. In recent years there has been increased participation of women. In other words, female representation appears to be increasing at the local level and minimal at the central level. The 73rd and 74th Constitutional Amendments of India which introduce Panchayati Raj Institution throughout the country and ensure reservation of one-third seats for women in Panchayats and municipal bodies is a good example of women political empowerment at the grassroot level. A recent countrywide survey conducted by the Centre for the study of Developing Societies revealed that 70 per cent of men and 79 per cent of women favour active participation of women in politics and 75 per cent of men and an equal percentage of women favour reservation for women in legislature.

Another Constitutional Amendment which proposes reservation of one-third seats for women in the parliament and State assemblies. It was discussed also in the parliament very recently; but for want of consensus of opinion amongst various political parties it could not be passed. It is hoped that a good sense will prevail on the political parties and they will review their own decision and they will give their positive contribution to the empowerment of women by ensuring their political participation.

In South Africa due to 33 per cent of reservation of seats for women in parliament and party structure 110 women have been elected to the South African Parliament out of the total membership of 450. Mr. Govender, South African delegate for the Inter-Parliamentary Union's specialised conference on *Towards Partnership between Men and Women in Politics* held at New Delhi in February 1997, opined that as a large number of women in their parliament are from rural areas, therefore, their performance, particularly the powerful manner in which they articulate their demands, has brought a fresh perspective to the parliamentary debates. In India also by reserving one-third seats in legislature, India will have one hundred eighty women in Lok Sabha and these women representatives largely elected from rural areas would put forth various issues of rural development in the parliament and make parliament debate a balanced, vibrant and healthy one.

To fulfil this purpose appropriate training needs to be given to these women about different aspects of rural development from time to time. These members are required to be involved at the planning, implementation, monitoring as well as evaluation stages of policies and programmes directed towards rural development of their area. The Panchayat members are needed to be financially empowered to carry out some of the rural essential rural developmental activities at the grassroots. Further the women political leaders are needed to be legally empowered to deal with the physical and sexual abuse on women and curb and menace of *nasa* and *jua* (*wine and gambling*) at the grassroots with full protection of police. They need to work for raising the age of marriage of girl child and empower women to take care of their reproductive health by acquiring MCH and family planning services by themselves if possible by overlooking unnecessary interference.

For this purpose women will have to be much more active in constructive social activities and equip themselves with the mental make-up. Women political leaders should take initiative for the formulation of Mahila Mandals at the grassroots for dealing with important women issues like, women illiteracy, girl child labour, women reproductive health care, economic empowerment of women, wage discrimination and other social evils and atrocities on women. They need to be empowered to monitor the different developmental programmes especially earmarked for women development and more particularly social and economic uplift of women belonging to scheduled castes, scheduled tribes, economically weaker sections, minorities and other backward caste communities.

Here a word of caution needs mention, *viz*., cultural identity of women. While making all efforts for empowerment of women their cultural identity should not be relegated to the background. Women are required to be more cautious to this core. In this context Mahatma Gandhi has rightly observed:

> "I believe in the proper education of women. But I do not believe that woman will not make her contribution to the world by mimicking

> or running a race with man. She can run the race but she will not rise to the great heights she is capable of by mimicking man. She has to be complement of man.
>
> "In my opinion, it is degrading for man and woman, that woman should be called upon or induced to forsake the hearth, and shoulder the rifle for the protection of that hearth. It is a reversion to barbarity and beginning of the end. In trying to ride a horse that man rides, she brings herself and him down. The sin will be on man's head for tempting or compelling his companion to desert her special calling. There is much bravery in keeping one's home in good order and condition, as there is in defending it against attack from without."

As far as the political participation is concerned Indian women have been better off than their western counterparts since they achieved the right to vote much earlier than some Western women. They played a commendable role in the freedom struggle by going to jail and suffering hardships and facing many odds and obstacles. They earned their right to be the equals of men. The law has not been kind to Indian women. Though protective legislation has made some headway there are still some shortcomings either in the law itself; but mostly in the non-implementation of protective measures the government has initiated over the years since Independence. In the matter of property, for instance, action needs to take to ensure a woman's right to part of her ancestral property. Though the amended Hindu Law has given the Indian woman many new rights, she cannot be a member of the coparcenary and cannot ask for a partition. What she and her husband acquire during their marriage including a house if it stands in his name, she cannot be a claimant legally. But judicial activism particularly at the higher levels, has been of help. The need for a shelter for the estranged wife has been recognized in some of their pronouncements.

Violence against women whether it is rape or harassment for dowry has been a serious matter. The number of dowry deaths are increasing day by day. The Dowry Prohibition Act, 1961, was amended in 1986 to make the effective. The period of filing a complaint was then left open. The court has now powers to act on its own knowledge or on a complaint by a recognized welfare organization. The offence has been made cognizable for the purpose of investigation. A new section on dowry murder has been introduced in the Indian Penal Code.

The sex-ratio between males and females in the population is 1000 : 927 respectively. This is a matter of great concern since child-deaths among girls are higher than among boys. Also the drop-out rate of girls from school is higher and their admission to schools is lower as compared to boys. However, there are positive and encouraging signs for improvement in women's position. The number of women job-seekers through employment exchanges has gone up sharply. The average age of women at marriage has also gone up.

The year 1993 achieved a milestone in India with the passing of the 73rd Constitutional Amendment which provides for 33 per cent compulsory reservation for women in Panchayati Raj Institutions (PRIs). After this enactment, all the States have formulated by and large, a uniform PRIs Act. Accordingly barring one or two States, all others have held elections. By this, there are not only about seven lakhs elected women representatives at various tiers of PRIs, but quite a number of them are holding chair-persons as well. This situation is definitely going to empower women substantially.

Present Scenario

As women have no control over economic resource (money) and since they also lack in decision-making power at the household level, they are naturally unable to contest elections on their own free will. Without the consent and cooperation of the male-sponsor, which is rare to come forth many women aspirants dare not enter the political battle-field. Fighting an election proves to be too costly and hence it is difficult to get the consent of a male sponsor to invest in favour of a woman. Without 5 to 15 lakhs of rupees, no one can dream of winning an assembly or parliament seat. Only a few rich men who have tasted what 'political power' really is, and what it can bring in at the shortest time-span, would go to any extent to grab political power by adopting any means.

Though women form a little less than 50 per cent of the population, their strength either in the State Legislatures or Parliament has been pathetically low ever since independence. Though women's political participation in Parliament is less than males in all countries, India's position is pretty bad as compared to the situation in the erstwhile USSR, Finland, Sweden and China. Since 1952 the highest women representatives during 1985-90, with 8 per cent and lowest was in 1979-80 with 3.4 per cent. Similarly in the Rajya Sabha it was about 7.3 per cent in 1952 which reached 15.5 per cent in 1991. The State Assembly positions are none the better, irrespective of which Party is in power.[7]

Because of this, political empowerment of women has not been a reality, so far. The political parties, national or regional, never bother to give party tickets to women. It is reported that tickets are allotted most undemocratically by the party presidents, based on some parameters particularly favouring those having well established political link. By caste lobbying, muscle power political loyalty and other political inputs quite a number of aspirants succeed in securing party tickets. Unfortunately no political party has been an exception to this informal cult called the 'modern political culture'.

Holistic Approach

The planners have to realise that the needs of the women are holistic and responses to their problems shall have to take note of their needs. The present sectoral and fragmented approach in our responses to the problems of poor women has to be replaced by holistic and integrated approach. Poverty among women is both a cause and effect of the backwardness of women. Poverty reduction appears to be the right approach for raising the status of women in general but alongside these strategies, other schemes for promoting literacy, social awareness, better nutrition and health, social security, etc. should be strengthened to improve the conditions and status of women in India.

Thus, the need of the hour, on the one hand, is to ensure better management of the existing programmes and, on the other hand, enhance the capabilities of women to overcome the problem of low self esteem so as to enable them to perceive the various social services as instruments redressing their social inequities. The process of awareness generation would not only improve the effective demand for services but also generate clientele-orchestrated co-ordination of services. It would enhance community participation and trigger off appropriate behavioural changes leading to sustainable development. The rural women would need to get mobilized into sub-village and village level groups. The groups perception about their health, nutritional, educational and economic status and needs should determine the mode and content of the services and interventions. They should manage and monitor the programmes. This would enable them to reduce not only operational costs but also opportunity costs for using those services. They could through their committees oversee the functioning of non-women specific essential services having a bearing on their status and work as well as on the household food security such as water pumps and ration shops. These groups would provide a forum where women can discuss and deliberate such issues as discrimination against women, dowry, bias against girls, alcoholism, equal remuneration, etc. As a group, they would be in a better position to have improved access to extension services which today, by and large, ignore them.

A package of services having awareness generation; basic health and education for women and children; upgradation of skills; income, employment and self-employment opportunities and effective support services supported by family and community would go a long way to bring women out of the vicious circle of poverty and discrimination.

Successful programmes like the Integrated Child Development Services (ICDS) could be used as an entry point for such a comprehensive package of services with a marginally higher input. Integrated delivery mechanism would make development process not only cost effective but also more accountable and culturally acceptable if women get the right to orchestrate such a convergency. PRA, as Mosse (1993) argues, in certain circumstances, could become the means to empower women. This would require a strong input of awareness generation and conscientisation for women in general and poor women in particular. An animator or catalyst from among the rural women could take up the task of conscientisation of women about their social, economic and political rights. They would need to be made aware that their overall emancipation would eventually depend upon their economic independence. It would also improve their access to various social services through improved knowledge and ability to utilise them.

The approach paper to the Ninth Five Year Plan has identified *empowerment of women* as an objective of the plan. The Agricultural Ministry has made a break through in this direction by setting up a special committee, comprising officials, experts and representatives of voluntary organisations, to see how a gender perspective can be imparted to the agricultural programmes being drawn up for the Ninth Five Year Plan.

Empowering women with economically productive work will enhance their contribution to rural development. The women need to be empowered both in the ownership as well as management aspects of the agricultural and allied services, *i.e.*, poultry, fishery, orchard, etc., which would help to raise their income and justify their importance and contribution to rural economy. A special Women Development Cell needs to be constituted in District Rural Development Agency (DRDA) to look after this task. At least thirty per cent of loan under the IRDP scheme need to be sanctioned to women mostly belonging to scheduled castes, scheduled tribes, economically weaker sections and other minorities. This is needed to be strictly monitored by the district authorities through Gram Panchayat or Village Development Committee and if possible by external agencies.

Women work participation in the secondary and tertiary sectors operating at the village need to be empowered to work in these two sectors operating at the grassroots in order to enhance their contribution in rural development. Moreover, women need to be provided loan for opening locally based small-scale and cottage industries. DWACRA and other social security and welfare schemes, *i.e.*, old age pension, maternity benefits and compensation for the sudden death of family earner launched for the women need to be strictly implemented. However, women should also be given benefits under Indira Awas Yojana and Jawahar Rojagar Yojana which would entitle them of ownership right as well as raise family income.

The human resource development programme for women on different aspects of rural development and their valuable role on it need to be regularly imparted to them by the village level workers (VLW) through the help of village Pradhan, Mahila Mandal Members, Village School Teachers, health workers and other village level society members. They should be provided training on modernisation of agriculture allied services, rural administration, etc., from time to time.

Moreover, NGOs engaged in women developmental programmes and activities may play a key-role in empowering women at the grassroots. Political leaders, *i.e.*, MP, MLA, Members of Panchayati Raj institutions and other leaders may also help to generate awareness on women economic empowerment through their mass meetings at the grassroots level.

These suggestions may work out when there is an honest will in all concerned, may it be a political leader, bureaucrat or social worker. Moreover, the society and male members need to have a positive attitude toward empowerment of women. They should let women to work independently relying upon their worth. It will empower women to act freely and develop autonomy and skill among them.

REFERENCES

1. National Policy on Education 1986, *Programme of Action* (POA), p. 105.
2. M.S. Gore, *Indian Education: Structure and Process*, p.116.

3. S.N. Mukerji, *Education in India: Today and Tomorrow*, p. 252.
4. *Ibid.*
5. Introduction, "Report of the National Committee on Women's Education." pp. 1-3.
6. N.L. Gupta, *Mulya-Parak Shiksha*, p. 57.
7. *Kurukshetra*, March 1996, pp. 22-23.

11

CHANGING SCENARIO AND FUTURE PROSPECTS

Action by UNESCO

In his inaugural speech, Rene Maheu, Director-General of UNESCO, at the Third Regional Conference of Ministers of Education, rightly remarked: "The access of girls to education is also a direct consequence of the fundamental rights to education... the requirements of economic progress also make it necessity." Further he added that "No country can afford to leave half its population in relative ignorance, which makes them a brake on development instead of a motive force in it."

The United Nations Educational, Scientific and Cultural Organization (UNESCO) which long ago as 1945 was entrusted with the task of promoting education, has always drawn the attention of the Member States to the need to educate girls and women. In 1948 the Organization was called upon to watch over the implementation of the Universal Declaration of Human Right in respect of those articles which came within its particular sphere, and more especially the following:

Article 1: All human beings are born free and equal in dignity and right. They are endowed with reason and conscience and should act towards one another in a spirit of brotherhood.

Article 2: Everyone is entitled to all the rights and freedoms set-forth in this Declaration, without distinction of any kind such as race, colour, sex, language, religion, political or other opinion, national or social origin, property, birth or other status.

Article 26: 1. Everyone has right to education. Education shall be free, at least in the elementary and fundamental stages. Elementary education shall be compulsory. Technical and professional education shall be made generally available and higher education shall be equally accessible to all on the basis of merit.

2. Education shall be directed to the full development of the human personality and to the strengthening of respect for human rights and fundamental freedoms. It shall promote understanding, tolerance and friendship among all nations, racial or religious groups, and shall further the activities of the United Nations for the permanence of peace.

3. Parents have a prior right to choose the kind of education that should be given to their children.

Today this Declaration still constitutes a common standard of achievement for all peoples and all nations, as is stated in its preamble:

> "However it is not so long ago since the idea that anyone of either sex should have a right to education was considered revolutionary. Over vast areas of the world the idea that the male population should be given an education was a new one which completely upset people's habit and way of thinking. And now the female population had to be educated too: As to those countries that had introduced general education, most of them felt that the need to give the same education to the two sexes meant radical change in their way of life, since girls and women were backward—sometimes very much so as compared with men."[1]

The need remains, and so does the backwardness. Yet—and this shows how much progress has been made—nearly all countries are addressing themselves to the problem of the education of girls and women. Their backwardness, which is less and less regarded as being inevitable and 'normal', now poses with ever-greater insistence a serious problem that threatens the balance of the whole of society and constitutes a brake not only on economic development, but also on human progress.

The realization of this fact was clearly manifested when, on 14 December 1960, the General Conference of UNESCO adopted the Convention and Recommendation against Discrimination in education. In defining discriminations 'any distinction, exclusion, limitation or preference, which being based on race, colour, sex, language, religion, political or other opinion, national or social origin, economic conditions or birth, has the purpose or effect of nullifying or impairing equality of treatment in education'. This text expressed clearly in concrete terms the requirements that were implicit in the proclamation of the right to education. Ten years later, fifty-four Member States of UNESCO are parties to the Convention.

In 1966 an inter-governmental conference, attended by delegates from seventy-five states, adopted a recommendation, concerning the status of teachers. Several paragraphs of this recommendations were devoted to the need to trained women teachers and to eradicate discrimination against married women teachers and women with a family to look after.

Another step forward was taken when, on 7th November 1967, the General Assembly of the United Nations adopted the Declaration on the elimination of Discrimination against women. This emphasized in the most definite manner the requirements set out in Article 1 of the Declaration of Human Rights, namely, that 'All human beings are born free and equal in dignity and rights'. It also drew attention to a fact that is too often ignored, namely, that none of the spheres of women's life education, occupation, family and social status, etc.—can be disassociated from the others.

Giving girls and women educational opportunities equal to those of men presupposes a series of coherent measures going beyond the sole realm of education and amounting to a complete revision of the status of women in society. Similarly, the granting to women of full professional and matrimonial rights entail a revision of the educational system and of the content of education. It is towards this end that the international agencies and women's organizations are working. Gradually, the Member States of the United Nations have come to recognize the reality and the extent of discrimination against women. And gradually they have manifested their determination to work towards the ideals enshrined in the various texts adopted by them within the United Nations and UNESCO. By putting the question of the status of women on the agenda of their general assemblies and conferences, the United Nations and UNESCO have helped to show that this is not a minor problem, to be solved after more important ones, but a question of world-wide importance.

The UN declared 1975 as an International Women's Year and 1980 as the year for Development of Women. The UN member-countries too declared 1975-85 as the Women's Development Decade. The Fourth UN World Conference on women was concluded in September 1995 at Beijing finalising an Action Plan to be concretized and implemented in each country. The theme of the conference was Equality, Peace, and Development. India played a crucial and commendable role in this conference. In India too Women Decade was observed, during which women started mobilizing and activating for getting redressal to their century-old problems of gender-discrimination. These actions implied the Government of India to appoint a committee on the status of women in India in 1977 which suggested establishing Statutory Women's Panchayats so as to ensure greater political participation. Subsequently, a National Plan of action for women was formulated. Later a National Committee with the Prime Minister as its head was set up. In 1992 a National Commission for women was constituted. As a culmination effort, a National Perspective Plan for 1988-2000 was formulated.

All these aforementioned initiatives have, however, failed to realise the policy intents fully and therefore women, by and large, remained far behind men in all sectors of society. There is gender disparity in respect of educational attainment, level of employment, nutritional level, sharing of political decision-making power, administrative, military, para-military, judiciary or executive positions, etc. Cumulative effect of all these have deprived women of equity and equality, resulting in an iniquitous unjust social order, unfavourable to women.

Role of Women's Commission

The Women's Commission has been holding *Mahila Adalat* (a counter-part of Lok Adalats) to resolve cases of domestic disputes which result in speedy justice. The commission has called for strengthening laws to protect women in various ways. For instance it is pressing for the passing of a law making rape a non-bailable offence. The bill has been pending for two years. The problem of child prostitutes aged between eight and sixteen years is a pressing one. According to Ms. Mohini Giri, Chairperson of the Women's Commission there are as many as forty thousand child prostitutes in Mumbai alone. Every district of India has two thousand five hundred child prostitutes. Quite a few of them are from Nepal, Bangladesh and Sri Lanka. Their entry into India through pimps and sale to brothels must be stopped.

Similarly, the condition of women prisoners in some of larger cities is deplorable. The Women's Commission emphasises the findings by UNDP and published in its Human Development Report for 1995 concerning gender equality. It says: "Women's work is greatly undervalued in economic terms. The value of household and community work transcends market value, " Various other studies concerning women are throwing up interesting facts. One of them concerns the decline of the female ratio as against men.

One study points out that "the decline appears to have been significantly more pronounced among disadvantaged castes. In 1991, the female-male ratio among some scheduled castes was 922 women per thousand males compared to 927 women for the population as a whole.

The Women's Commission is pressing the need for women's participation in political processes at all levels to enlarge their access to education, health care, employment opportunities and to impart legal awareness of their rights to them. In relation to media the Commission regret that "the growing privatisation and commercialisation in particular of television, causes grave concern. A cheep portrayal of women is often there. Women in distress are a continuing factor for various reasons.

Sex Education

Sex education has been one of the controversial issues in the arena of prevalent system of education. It has been more so because of our conservative nature of thinking, a part of composite culture . Sex education is still considered as a novel concept in our country whereas in Western countries this has been in practice since long. Sex instruction aims at proper planning and implementation of such educational measures which prepare human beings to deal with life-situations and social relationship gracefully and in socially accepted manner. There are no organized instructions at home. Of course, there is code of ethics, religion, stress on chastity, monogamy, etc. The main aim of sex instruction is to influence the attitude and behaviour. For this purpose some educationists think that school is an ideal place whereas many thinkers take it as parents' responsibility.

Some of the Western educationists also think that formal sex education is not necessary. T. Dilworth Harrison observes that "Teaching sex in schools will aggravate the malady. It is better for children to talk about sex among themselves and feel ashamed than be given a sex instruction in schools, often by teachers, whose outlook is inevitably that of the world." In a traditional set-up of homes, where discussion of sex is still taboo, parents can do very little in imparting sex education to the children. This taboo is there partly because of our cultural tradition and partly because of inbuilt inhibitions. The obsessive hush-hush of the parents rubs-off on the child and the child start learning the facts of sex through the back-alley approach. The child may get the facts right; but the values are all wrong. Therefore, schools have to come to the rescue. According to one of the expert opinion the right time to start it is at the age of 12. The sex education or instruction imparted at this age will prepare girls to face puberty without confusion and promote healthy outlook of sex. This will also break down the barrier that prevents communication on sex-matters between parents and the adolescent children.

In some of the cosmopolitan cities of our country some schools and women organizations are arranging sex education. However, precaution should be taken that sex education should be informal and not the formal, implicit and not explicit. We should not forget that the sex instinct is not the same in man as in women—physical in one and physical in the other. One should not think of sex education as a cataloguing of dangers and should not warn the child unless really necessary.

Today we are living in the age of transition of values that are deteriorating very fast. The signs of the danger of moral retrogation brought about by the wide use of contraceptive measures for control of population growth are clearly visible. Undeniably, scientific knowledge about contraception is an essential part of education and should be included in the higher classes of the schools, as it is found in some of the developed countries. Mr. Wilson has rightly observed: "In many cultures, and in some cultures for many centuries, the sexes were carefully segregated, and the occasions of their coming together were subject to close social control. Even so, illicit unions and casual sexual encounters were common place and at sometimes, in some societies illegitimate offspring may have outnumbered children conceived in wedlock. Yet a 'legitimacy principle', that is to say, a preference for legitimate offspring has been the normal demand of most societies from the primitive to the most advanced, and illegitimate children have generally suffered various social handicaps, whether legally instituted or merely conventionally imposed, because of the breach of the moral norms committed by their parents. The ubiquity of the legitimacy principled indicates a profound if unconscious awareness of the potentially disruptive consequences for illegitimacy to the normal operation of the social order. The often vigorous taboos against even innocent association between the sexes, the enforcement of sexual segregation, chaperonage, and the mythology (largely by male) about the opposite sex are all indications of the effort that has been required to counter the power of sexual attraction."[2]

Abortion

From the view point of preventing further population growth, abortion seems not only permissible, but also inevitable. Very often voices are being raised for legalization of abortion. One of the studies reveals that the number of yearly abortions in Japan is equal to the number of children born. In our country the condition is not so precarious. With the view point of humanism abortion is a sin. Moreover, other factors like personal health of the mother, etc. are also related to it. It is "wrong to terminate artificially an already initiated life and thus to condemn it to darkness before it has ever seen the light. Furthermore, abortion is physically and mentally cruel to the mother and, if performed often, can render her barren."

With the humanistic point of view many humanitarians are totally against abortion. There are several socio-economic reasons behind such humane approach. Mr. Willson has enumerated such reasons in the following manner:

> "Like many other people in the West, I find the very idea of abortion abhorrent. Like you, I would strongly support a campaign to increase knowledge of contraceptive techniques throughout the world. Our problems arise, of course, when we are faced with pregnant mothers and who reject all the implications of that role. In general, I, too would favour a policy in which women were encouraged to have their babies, even if the mothers subsequently relinquished them to the care of orphanages. In practice, in the West there is still a demand for babies for adoption, and many of these children might find excellent homes and foster-parents. I do not see that abortion can ever be an acceptable policy directed towards the limitation of population. That goal must be sought through the extension of contraceptive methods, which are cheaper, safer, more humane, and in the interest of women—to say nothing of what some regard as the evil of abortion towards the human foetus."[3]

Except the selfishness and cruelty there is hardly any point for which we may feel reluctance in agreeing with the view point of Mr. Wilson. In India, moreover, as per the religious or cultural tenets "killing of a foetus is a great sin (*maha-pap*), as per the opinion of many law-givers including Manu, Yajnavalkya, Apastamba, Atri and so on.

Indira Mahila Yojana

Women and child welfare schemes have been accorded a high priority in the national development plans. The Government of India is taking keen interest in the development of women and children and is anxious to see that their welfare is ensured through systematic planning.

In 1995 the new programme of Indira Mahila Yojana (IMY) for women's welfare launched on the late Rajiv Gandhi's birth anniversary was announced by the Prime Minister Mr. P.V. Narasimha Rao in his Independence Day address. Indira Mahila Yojana has ushered in a new chapter in women's welfare programme as it will seek to integrate components of all sectoral programmes for women.

Objectives

The IMY is aimed to empower women through a sustained process of awareness generation and their direct access to resources, thereby they can share and demand social and economic development. The main objectives of IMY are:

(i) To generate awareness in women through provision of information on different developmental programmes and issues of specific concern to women;
(ii) To ensure convergence of sectoral services at the Panchayat, block and district levels through active involvement of women;
(iii) To optimize the utilisation of scarce resources in speeding up the process of mainstreaming women in development;
(iv) To initiate the process of awareness generation/education to enable them to understand and analyse their problems and find solutions through their collective interactions; and
(v) To help women become self-reliant and independent by their economic empowerment through income generation activities.

Initially, the IMY would be implemented in 200 blocks of the country. The blocks will be identified on the basis of presence of an active NGO, infant mortality rate (IMR), female literacy, poverty and other social disabilities. The IMY will initially be sanctioned for a period of seven years starting from 1995-96. The IMY is a centrally sponsored scheme and it will be implemented through the Indira Mahila Kendras (IMKs) and funds shall also be released to IMK for the implementation of IMY. NGOs working in the field of women and child development will be actively involved and these NGOs are identified by the State Governments.

Indira Mahila Kendras (IMK)

The social mobilization would be initiated by the formation of Indira Mahila Kendras at the Anganwadi level. The Indira Mahila Kendra will be registered under the Registration Societies Act/Charitable Societies

Act and will comprise a number of homogeneous groups, each having 20-25 members. All the members of the group would be adult women, *i.e.*, above 18 years of age. The President of IMK will be elected by the members of groups from amongst themselves. There would also be an elected Vice-President of the Kendra and the Anganwadi worker shall be the secretary of IMK.

The IMK will have an executive body consisting of 8-10 members. Each group will elect a leader amongst its members who will be represented in the executive body of the IMK. The executive body of IMK will also have some ex-officio members such as primary school head, *patwari*, village postmaster, ANM, *Gram Sevak* and Panchayat member representing the area. These village-level functionaries will work only as facilitators.

Each member of the group shall contribute Rs. 5 as membership fee and will continue to contribute Re. 1 per month to the Kendra. An amount of Rs. 5,000 as one-time grant shall be provided to each IMK to initiate social mobilization activities/training of members. The Anganwadi worker shall be paid Rs.100 per month as additional honorarium.

At the Gram Panchayat Level, Indira Mahila Gram Panchayat Samiti (IMGPS) will act as a nodal committee for guiding and assisting the IMKs in their activities. The IMGPS is headed by the chairperson of Gram Panchayat. It will consist of the Presidents of all IMKs in the Gram Panchayat.

Poverty Reduction Schemes for Rural Women

Till the early seventies, the main emphasis of the planned development was on the growth of the economy and overall development. A sound industrial base had been created particularly after the II Plan. The Green Revolution resulted in phenomenal increased agriculture yields. This reliance on the 'trickle down' effects of growth, however, did not bring fruits of development to the masses in equitable measures. In the face of poverty and malnutrition, an alternative strategy of 'direct attack on poverty' was adopted. The IV and V Plans saw the launch of area development and target oriented programmes. The eighties also saw the launch of the Minimum Needs programme for providing the rural poor the basic services like elementary education, health, water supply, housing, environmental improvement and nutrition. The services of adult education, domestic energy, sanitation and public distribution system were also included as part of the sector allocations. It is useful to recall this brief history over here as in the changed policy environment of the nineties, poverty reduction programmes have increasingly been judged on the criteria of allocative efficiency though they were initially conceived to address redistributive concerns.

Strategies

Poverty reduction programmes for women in rural India have been conceived with the following strategies in mind:

(i) awareness generation initiatives;
(ii) promoting self-employment through credit and training ;
(iii) providing lean season wage employment;
(iv) promoting savings habit among women;
(v) providing a range of support services to meet gender needs; and
(vi) addressing minimum needs such as nutrition, health, sanitation, housing and education.

Awareness Generation Initiatives

In recent years, efforts have been, on the one hand, made to break the vicious circle of existing 'undesirable' images of girls and women and on the other hand, project them as potential human resources and assets with a view to trigger off changes in social attitudes towards women, an integrated media approach projecting a positive image of women and girls has been followed. The focus of this initiative is both on women themselves as well as society in general. Women themselves has to be made aware of their importance in the society. A number of programmes now include initiatives to improve the low self-image and respect among women/adolescent girls.

Policy-makers, planners, enforcement machinery are also being sensitised about the gender issues and needs of women. Special campaigns to combat atrocities against women have been launched throughout the country in collaboration with the State Home Departments and NGOs.

Self-Employment for Rural Women

There are a number of programmes which seek to promote self-employment among rural women. Some of them are exclusively for women, while others have specific targets for women as proportion of the total beneficiaries. In the first category, there are programmes like

Development of Women and Children in Rural Areas (DWCRA). Support to Employment Programmes for Women (STEP), employment-cum-income generating training-cum-production centres (NORAD). Under DWCRA, groups of women are provided with suitable avenues of income generation suiting their skills and local conditions. Launched in 1982-83, the scheme covers, at present, 18,000 women's groups.

In the second category, there are programmes like the Integrated Rural Development Programme (IRDP). Training of Rural Youth for Self-Employment (TRYSEM) which envisage that 40 per cent beneficiaries shall be women. Poor women are identified and given assistance for acquisition of productive assets or appropriate skills for self-employment to enable them to generate sufficient income to cross the poverty line. The scheme also subsidises (between 25 and 50 per cent depending upon the occupation and economic status) the acquisition of initial capital assets.

Measures to Promote Girls' Education (Primary Stage)

A number of measures have been suggested to the members of the National Committee on Women's Education (May 1958 to January 1956) with a view to promoting the education of girls at the primary stage. They may be broadly classified under the following heads:

(i) *Providing school facilities where they do not already exist* by opening new school, bringing schools within easy reach of the children; starting girls section in boy's schools, starting night schools for children not expected to attend day schools; increasing the teacher-pupil ratio; and encouraging private efforts in the field of education by liberal financial and other help.

(ii) *Improving the existing schooling* by providing the better, more qualified and adequate staff including a larger number of women teachers; appointment of school mothers in mixed school, better building and educational equipments and alongwith it a wide choice of subjects, a more flexible, varied and rich educational programme both within and outside the classroom and including what are commonly called co-curricular activities so as to make the education imparted less bookish and more practical as well as useful.

(iii) *Making education free where it is already not so and granting concessions* in the form of scholarships to poor and meritorious students. Free supply of books and stationery and free or subsidized uniform.

(iv) *Effectively enforcing compulsion and educating public opinion* so as to mitigate social prejudice against women's education and also make the enforcement of compulsion easier. Parent-school co-operation, education of adult women, organization of enrolment drives. Women's education days, Weeks and rallies and use of audio-visual aids are some of the means which have been suggested to help arouse a favourable public opinion in regard to education of girls.

(v) *Providing other convenience and inducements:* Such as adjusting school timings and vacation to suit local needs and conditions, free or subsidized mid-day meals, free medical and health facilities for the school children, establishment of creches, special enrolment grants to schools, institution of attendance prizes to students, and reward to individuals and villages for distinguished work in the field of increasing enrolment in schools.

(vi) *Bringing primary education under the charge of women as far as possible both in regard to teaching as well as inspection and administration.* Women are not only better teachers of children but also prove more efficient and responsible administrators in this behalf as they should have much better appreciation of children' problems and needs.

Out of the measures suggested above many are being implemented in different states and of the rest some are proposed to be taken. As regards free education the National Committee opined as following:

> "Education at primary stage is generally free. We are of the opinion that wherever it is not so immediate steps should be taken to make it free and the government should compensate the private schools for the loss of revenue resulting from the introduction of free education in case they are the only schools available in a particular area."

Regarding new schools the committee observed:

> "Whenever new schools are started, the rural region should be given priority consideration. In fact, a definite plan based on survey should be followed by the government concerned so that there would be no unnecessary duplication and the distribution of schools would not be lopsided."

Co-Education

The Committee recommended that co-education should be adopted at the primary stage as a general policy. It also referred to the fact that social opinion and attitudes are generally favourable to it, but we should not forget that the there would still be found a body of opinion in the country particularly in rural areas and the more tradition ridden sections of society and in respect of the final classes of the primary stage, which even if it is not opposed to co-education and would reconcile itself to it, would, however, welcome separate schools. This is an example of an old prejudice still lingering. For such cases we make two recommendations:

(i) Separate schools for girls may be permitted as an exception in places where there is a strong public demand for them and the enrolment of girls is large enough to justify their establishment;
(ii) Educative propaganda should be recognised in all such areas to remove the existing prejudice against co-education and create a positive opinion in its favour.

Middle and Secondary Stage

At the middle and even more so at the secondary stage co-education is not recommended as a general rule, though for the middle we have recommended that more and more co-educational institutions should be started.

For bringing all girls of the relevant age-group to school the Education Ministers' Conference suggested:

1. The construction of quarters for women teachers;
2. Improvement in the training facilities for women teachers;
3. Recruitment of women teachers on a large scale and, as an interim, appointment of school mothers;
4. Provision of hostels for girls for rural areas;
5. Provision of free education to girls till the end of secondary stage to increase the supply of teachers;
6. Utilisation of the services of adult women on a part-time or whole-time basis; and
7. Provision of suitable incentives to students wherever necessary.

The conference further recommended that the special programme of girls' education should be taken up as a centrally sponsored scheme on the basis of 100 per cent grant outside the State plan ceilings. (*Education in India,* 1959-60, Vol. I, p. 33).

Administration

As recommended by the National Committee, inspection, supervision and administration of girls' schools should be carried out by female officers as far as possible. Girls' education in India is greatly handicapped for want of a proper organization, which is mainly due the weakness of administrative machinery. Practically no state has a separate post of a deputy directress: Administration of girls' education is carried on mostly by the inspecting agency of the other sex.

The progress of education depends a good deal on careful planning, and hence, the administration of girls' education cannot be entrusted exclusively to the male sex which is already over-loaded with multifarious works and has practically no time to pay attention to the education of girls. Hasty and ill-advised schemes are often put forth and thus the cause of girls' education suffers.

National Committee on Women's Education has suggested that an administrative machinery should be set up at the Centre and in the States which would be specially concerned with the implementation of girls' education programmes in different sectors. On the recommendations of the Committee, a National Council for Women's Education was set up at the Centre in May, 1958. It consists of a Chairman and 23 members— a representative of each of the fourteen States (initially), a representative of CABE, two members of the parliament, two representatives of the Union Ministry of Educational representative of Union territories, and a representative of each of the following ministries; Community Development, Health, and Labour. Non-official members will hold office for two years. Councils for Women's Education have also been established in all States and Union Territories except Tripura.

> "It will also be desirable for every State to have a deputy directress for directing the educational policy of girls' education. She should be helped by an adequate number of inspectresses. Every district ought to have at least one inspectress, and woman supervisors must be employed by local bodies for looking after primary education of girls. In short, girls; education cannot progress without wise advice, careful council and efficient control."[4]

REFERENCES

1. Jacqueline Chabaud, *The Education and Advancement*, UNESCO, 1970, p. 138.
2. Bryan Wilson and Daisaku Ikeda, *Human Values in a Changing World*, pp. 239-40.
3. *Ibid.*, p. 247.
4. S.N. Mukerji, *Education in India: Today and Tomorrow*, p. 260.

APPENDICES

APPENDIX-I

EDUCATION FOR WOMEN'S EQUALITY

The Present Situation

Provision of educational opportunities to women has been an important programme in the education sector since independence. Between 1951 and 1981, the percentage of literacy amongst women improved from 7.93 per cent to 24.82 per cent. However, in absolute numbers, illiterate women have increased during this period from 158.7 million to 241.7 million (excluding Assam). Women comprise 57 per cent of the illiterate population and 70 per cent of the non-enrolled children of school stage are girls. In spite of the efforts made so far, the education system has not been able to make sufficient contribution towards women's equality.

Targets

(a) A phased time-bound programme of elementary education for girls, particularly up to the primary stage by 1990, and up to the elementary stage by 1995.
(b) A phased time-bound programme of adult education for women in the age group 15-35 (whose number is estimated to be 6.8 crores) by 1995.
(c) Increased women's access to vocational, technical professional education and to existing and emergent technologies.
(d) Review and reorganization of the educational activities to ensure that it makes a substantial contribution towards women's equality, and creation of appropriate cells/units therefor.

Policy Parameters and Strategies

3. The National Policy on Education (NPE)* envisages that education would be used as a strategy for achieving a basic change in the status of women. The National education system would (i) play a positive interventionist role in the empowerment of women, (ii) contribute towards development of new values through redesigned curricula and text-books, and (iii) women's studies will be promoted as part of various courses.

* From National Policy on Education (NPE-1986), Programme of Action, Ministry of HRD, New Delhi, August 1986, pp. 105-10.

The main features of the targets and implementation strategy will consist of the following:

(i) to gear the entire education system to plan a positive interventionist role in the empowerment of women;
(ii) to promote women's studies as a part of various courses and encouragement to educational institutions to take up active programme to further women's development;
(iii) to widen the access of women in programmes of vocational, technical and professional education;
(iv) to create dynamic managerial structure to cope with the targets envisaged.

Strategy Enunciation and Programme of Action

Empowerment of Women

4. Women become empowered through collective reflection and decision-making. The parameters of empowerment are:

— building a positive self-image and self-confidence;
— developing ability to think critically;
— building up group cohesion and fostering decision-making and action;
— ensuring equal participation in the process of bringing about social change;
— encouraging group action in order to bring about change in the society;
— providing the wherewithal for economic independence.

5. The following measures will be taken for the achievement of the above parameters:

(a) Every educational institution should, by 1995, take up active programmes of women's development built around a study and awareness of the women's predicament and for promotion of communication and organisation among women.
(b) All teachers and Non-Formal Education/Adult Education (NFE/AE) instructors should be trained as agents of women's empowerment. Special training programmes will be developed by NCERT, NIEPA, Directorate of Adult Education (DAE),

SCERTs, State Resource Centres (SRCs) and UGC to incorporate in all training programmes of teachers and NFE/AE instructors elements which would motivate them to work for women's empowerment. Voluntary agencies and activist groups for women's development will be involved in these training programmes.

(c) Women teachers and women instructors in adult/non-formal education programmes should receive special orientation to enable them to play an activist role towards women's equality.

(d) Special programmes should be developed by research institutions, voluntary institutions and professional groups of artists to promote general awareness and self-image amongst women through a variety programmes like discussions, street plays, skits, wall papers, puppet shows, etc.

(e) An environment should be created in which practically all sections of the society will commit themselves and work for achieving this objective enunciated in the National Policy on Education. Keeping in view the important role played by media in this sphere, clear policy guidelines should be developed by radio and TV in 1986-87 and measures taken to persuade films and other media on these lines.

(f) Preference in recruitment of teachers up to school level should be for women. This will create a greater confidence in the rural areas and motivate the parents to send girls to the school.

(g) The common core curriculum is a powerful instrument for the empowerment of women through the incorporation of values commensurate with the new status of women. The Women's Cell in the NCERT will be revived and given the responsibility for preparing the component of the core curriculum relating to women's equality. The Cell should also accelerate its work of eliminating sexist bias and sex stereo-types from school text-books. The Women's Cell of NCERT should take active help of all persons on playing its assigned role.

(h) Sensitisation of teachers, trainers, planners and administrators to women's issues will be taken up as a major programme by NIEPA and appropriate State level agencies, through initial training, in-service training and refresher courses. NIEPA should also have a strong cell for planning and execution of these programmes.

Women Studies

6. Women's studies programme has 4 dimensions—teaching, research, training and extension. In teaching, the following activities will be taken up:

(i) Incorporation of issues relating to women's status and role in the foundation course proposed to be introduced by University Grants Commission for all undergraduate students;
(ii) Incorporation of the women's dimension into courses in different disciplines;
(iii) Elimination of sexist bias and sex stereo-types from text-books.

7. Under research, the following steps will be taken:

(i) Encouraging research on identified areas and subjects which are crucial in advancing knowledge in this area and to expand the information base;
(ii) Critical appraisal of existing tools and techniques which have been responsible for the disadvantages suffered by them and where necessary reformation of research methodology.

8. The following measures will be taken under training:

(i) Dissemination of information and interaction through seminars/ workshops on the need for women's studies and its role in university education;
(ii) Orientation of teachers and researchers to handle women-related topics and to incorporate women's dimension into general topics;
(iii) Workshops for restructuring the curriculum.

9. Under extension, it is proposed to encourage educational institutions to take up programmes which directly benefit the community and bring about the empowerment of women.

10. These would include actual implementation of development programmes directly aimed at women's empowerment such as adult education, awareness building, legal literacy, informational and training support for socio-economic programmes of women's development, media, etc.

Universalisation of Elementary Education and Adult Education

11. The present programme of non-formal centres for girls on 90 : 10 pattern will be extended to all educationally backward pockets of the country. NFE Centres should be community based. Responsibility of planning, selection of instructors and monitoring should be with the community including parents. Increased assistance to voluntary agencies to run non-formal education centres for girls should be given.

12. In the rural areas, girls are kept busy at home in sibling and household care, in fetching fuel, fodder and water, or in earning a day's wage. Therefore, special support services referred to in the Policy need to cover all these areas up to 1995. Early childhood education centres are important support service in increasing enrolment and retention of girls in schools. Programmes of social forestry, drinking water supply, mid-day meals and other nutrition programmes, smokeless *chullahs* and other devices aimed at eliminating drudgery from women's lives should be formulated by the Ministry and organisation concerned up to 1990 to converge with the objective of universalisation of education.

13. Skill development linked to employment or work opportunities in the villages or local areas are required to be given overriding priority so that there is an incentive on the part of the parents to educate the girls.

14. Mass scale adult education programme for women in the age group 15-35 should be developed to eradicate illiteracy amongst women by 1995. As majority of women in this age group are workers literacy *per se* may not have any relevance for them. It is, therefore, necessary to develop adult education programmes for women linked with upgradation of their skills and income generating activities.

15. Skill development for girls and women should be continuous process of learning starting from the NFE centres and AE centres. Continuing Education Centres should be set up in a phased manner which should organise vocational training, provide opportunities for retention of literacy skills and application of this learning for improving their living conditions.

16. The skill development given by the Continuing Education Centres will be supported by other programmes of non-formal, vocational training and skill development to be administered by a variety of organisations and institutions, such as Polytechnics, Community Polytechnics, ITIs, Shramik Vidyapeeths, Central Social Welfare Board, State Social Welfare Advisory Boards, Voluntary agencies, Krishi Vigyan Kendras, Women's Centres in Agricultural and Home Science Colleges

as part of their extension activities. Besides, industries which employ women should themselves run non-formal vocational training courses. For effective learning and monitoring Women's Bureau is to be set up in the Department of Education.

Women's Access to Vocational, Technical and Professional Education and to Existing and Emergent Technologies

17. At each stage in school education; or a part of work experience or vocationalisation, girls should be exposed to a variety of vocational training activities. The method of vocational training should be both through the formal and non-formal courses. The choice of skills to be taught will depend on the natural resources, traditional occupations and new activities being taken up through government and private investment.

18. There are 104 ITIs functioning exclusively for women and 97 wings in general ITIs reserved for women. It is proposed that these institutions be revamped during the period 1987-90 on the following lines:

(i) Diversification of trades and courses, will be done, keeping the job potential of the area in mind. There will be an efficient placement system which will enable the institutions to have continuous dialogue with employers. The idea behind this diversification is that while girls will continue to receive preferential treatment in trades/occupations, for which they are particularly well suited (*e.g.*, teaching and nursing), this will not become a barrier for their participation in technical and professional courses of higher level and equal opportunities will be provided for them in all vocational, technical and professional courses.

(ii) There will be a strong element of vocational counselling in each ITI/RVTI/NVTI, polytechnics, suitable orientation should also be provided in the schools as preparation for motivating the girls to choose non-traditional courses.

(iii) Information about credit, banking, entrepreneurial development, etc. will be provided by the ITI/NVTI/RVTI/Polytechnics and community polytechnics alongwith practical on-the-job training. The implementation of the apprenticeship scheme will be strengthened to increase the coverage of women.

(iv) In order to substantially enlarge the opportunities to women for craftsmen's training, shift system will be introduced in existing

ITIs—one in the morning and the other in the afternoon.

(v) DGE&T office should have a separate Directorate of Women's Vocational Training.

(vi) The women's access to technical education will be improved qualitatively and quantitatively. The choice of trades/disciplines offered to women at Certificate/Diploma/Degree levels in all types of technical education institutions, will be made keeping in view the objective of bringing about women's equality. Necessary incentives, as spelt out in the section of Technical Education will be provided.

Management Structure at Centre and State Level

19. The interventions and programmes referred to above will be planned, coordinated, monitored and evaluated continuously both at the national and State level. Each of the organisations responsible for the programme will have to be strengthened. The Women's Cell in the NCERT will be revived and strengthened. NIEPA and Directorate of Adult Education will have strong cells to plan and administer Women's training programmes. The Women's Cell in the UGC will be strengthened in order to monitor the implementation of various programmes at higher education level.

20. At the State level, Women's Cell should be set up in all the States with adequate supporting staff to be headed by an officer of at least Joint Director's status.

APPENDIX-II

THOUGHTS OF MAHATMA GANDHI ON WOMEN AND THEIR EDUCATION

Of all the evils for which man has made himself responsible, none is so degrading, so shocking or so brutal as his abuse of the better-half of humanity to me, the female sex, not the weaker sex.

I have regarded woman as an incarnation of tolerance. A servant wrongly suspected may throw up his job, a son in the same case may leave his father's roof, and a friend may put an end to the friendship. The wife, if she suspects her husband, will keep quiet, but if the husband suspects her, she is ruined.

Woman is the embodiment of sacrifice and, therefore, non-violence.

Let it be man's privilege to protect woman, but let no woman of India feel helpless in the absence of man or in the event of his failing to perform the sacred duty of protecting her.

The real ornament of women is her character, her purity.

Women do not know what influence for good they can exert on their husbands.

Domestic slavery of woman is a symbol of our barbarism.

If by strength is meant moral power, then women is immeasurably man's superior.

If by strength is meant brute strength, then indeed is woman less brute than man.

If the will to die rather than to yield is there, no monster can make the woman yield.

I do not believe in women working for a living or undertaking commercial enterprises.

I have worshipped woman as the living embodiment of the spirit of service and sacrifice.

I passionately desire the utmost freedom for our women.

The privilege of awakened woman should be to stop and eradicate age-long evils.

Let not women ever despise their sex or deplore that they were not born men.

Silent and dignified suffering is the badge of her sex.

Man and woman are of equal rank, but they are not identical.

Pure woman is mightier than man.

Women, in the new order, will be part-time workers, their primary function being to look after the home.

Would that woman realise the power she has latent in her for good, if she has also for mischief?

Dear sisters, the future of India lies on your knees, for you will nurture the future generation. You can bring up the children of India to become simple, God-fearing and brave men and women, or you can coddle them to be weaklings, unfit to brave the storms of life and used to foreign fineries which they would find it difficult in after-life to discard.

The female sex is the nobler of the two, for it is even today the embodiment of self-sacrifice, silent suffering, humility, faith and knowledge.

A woman's intuition has often proved truer than man's arrogant assumption of superior knowledge. There is method in putting Sita before Rama and Radha before Krishna.

To call a woman a member of the weaker sex is a libel. In what way is woman the weaker sex, I do not know. If the implication is that she lacks the brute instinct of man, or does not possess it in the same measure as man, the charge may be admitted. But then, woman becomes, as she is, the nobler sex. If she is weak in striking, she is strong in suffering.

A woman no more loses her honour or virtue, because a brute renders her senseless and ravishes her, than a man loses his because a wicked woman administers to him a stupefying drug and makes him do what she likes.

She won't better humanity by vying with man in his ability to destroy life, mostly without purpose. Let it be her privilege to wean the erring man from his error, which will envelop in his ruin that of woman also.

Very few woman come out to serve their fellow-countrymen. Women are the very incarnation of service, but at present they minister only to their own families. Why should they not extend the field of their ministry so as to embrace the whole of India?

Multitudes of women live in idleness; who will induce them to take to industry?

I am deeply pained when I see women heavily bedecked with ornaments. Who will explain to them that these trinkets are no aid to beauty?

Women in the West are doing much work that was supposed to be reserved for men. I do not mean that all their activities are worthy of imitation, but they have certainly upset many calculations of man.

Where there is a non-violent atmosphere, where there is the constant teaching of *ahimsa*, woman will not regard herself as dependent, weak or helpless. She is not really helpless when she is really pure. Her purity makes her conscious of her strength.

I have always held that it is physically impossible to violate a woman against her will. The outrage takes place only when she gives way to fear or does not realise her moral strength. If she cannot meet the assailant's might, her purity will give her the might to die before he succeeds in violating her.

It is my firm conviction that a fearless woman who knows that her purity is her best shield can never be dishonoured. However, beastly the man, he will bow in shame before the flame of her dazzling purity.

A woman is worthy of condemnation only when she is a willing party to her dishonour. In no case are adultery and assault synonymous terms.

When woman, freed from man's snares, rises to the full height and rebels against man's legislation and institutions designed by him, her rebellion, no doubt non-violent, will be none-the-less effective.

I will far rather see the race of man extinct than that we should become less than beasts by making the noblest of God's creation the object of our lust.

Woman, I hold, is the personification of self-sacrifice, but, unfortunately, she does not realise what a tremendous advantage she has over man. As Tolstoy used to say, they are labouring under the hypnotic influence of man.

Woman is the companion of man, gifted with equal mental capacities. She has the right to participate in very minutest detail in the activities of man, and she has an equal right of freedom and liberty with him.

Women must cease to consider herself the object of man's lust. The remedy is more in her hands than man's. She must refuse to adorn herself for men, including her husband, if she will be an equal partner with man. I cannot imagine Sita ever wasting a single moment on pleasing Rama by physical charms.

If you want to play your part in the world's affairs you must refuse to deck yourself for pleasing man. If I was born a woman, I would rise in rebellion against any pretension on the part of man that woman is born to be his plaything. I have mentally become a woman in order to steal into her heart. I could not steal into my wife's heart until I decided to treat her differently than I used to do, and so I restored to her all her rights by dispossessing myself of all my so-called rights as her husband.

Equality of the sexes does not mean equality of occupations. There may be no legal bar against a woman hunting or wielding a lance. But she instinctively recoils from a function that belongs to man. Nature has created sexes as complements to each other. Their functions are defined as are their forms.

Woman is nothing if she is not self-sacrifice and purity personified.

I am uncompromising in the matter of woman's rights. In my opinion she should labour under no legal disability not suffered by man, I should treat the daughters and sons on a footing of perfect equality.

Hindu culture had erred on the side of excessive subordination of the wife to the husband, and has insisted on the complete merging of the wife in the husband. This has resulted in the husband sometimes usurping and exercising authority that reduces him to the level of the brute.

Man has regarded woman as his tool. She has learned to be his tool, and in the end found this easy and pleasurable to be such, because when one drags another in his fall the descent is easy.

I suggest that before you put your pens to paper, think of woman as your own mother, and I assure you the chastest literature will flow from your pens, even like the beautiful rain from heaven which waters the thirsty earth below. Remember that a woman was your mother, before a woman become your wife. Far from quenching their spiritual thirst, some writers stimulate their passions, so much so that poor ignorant women waste their time wondering how they might answer to the description our fiction gives of them. Are detailed descriptions of their physical form an essential part of literature, I wonder? Do you find anything of the kind in the *Upanishads*, the *Quran* or the *Bible*? And yet, do you know that the English language would be empty without the *Bible*? Three parts *Bible*, and one part Shakespeare is the description of it. Arabic would be forgotten without the *Quran*. And think of Hindi without Tulsidas. Do you find in it anything like what you find in the present-day literature about women?

I believe in the proper education of women. But I do not believe that women will not make her contribution to the world by mimicking or running a race with man. She can run the race but she will not rise to the great heights she is capable of by mimicking man. She has to be the complement of man.

Man has converted her into a domestic drudge and an instrument of his pleasure, instead of regarding her as his helpmate and better-half. The result is a semi-paralysis of our society. Woman has rightly been called the mother of the race. We owe it to her and to ourselves to undo the great wrong that we have done her.

In my opinion, it is degrading both for man and woman, that woman should be called upon or induced to forsake the hearth, and shoulder the rifle for the protection of that hearth. It is a reversion to barbarity and the beginning of the end. In trying to ride the horse that man rides, she brings herself and him down. The sin will be on man's head for tempting or compelling his companion to desert her special calling. There is as much bravery in keeping one's home in good order and condition, as there is in defending it against attack from without.

There is as much reason for man to wish that he was born a woman, as for woman to do otherwise. But the wish is fruitless. Let us be happy in the state to which we are born, and do the duty for which nature has destined us.

Woman is described as man's better-half. As long as she has not the same rights in law as man, as long as the birth of a girl does not receive the same welcome as that of a boy, so long we should know that India is suffering from partial paralysis. Suppression of woman is a denial of *Ahimsa.*

Would that woman realize the power she has latent in her for good, if she has also for mischief. It is in her power to make the world more livable both for her and her partner whether as father, son or husband, if she would cease to think of herself as weak and fit only to serve as a doll for man to play with. If society is not to be destroyed by insane wars of nation against nation and still more insane wars on its moral foundations, the woman will have to play her part not manfully, as some are trying to do, but womanfully. She won't better humanity by vying with man in his ability to destroy life mostly without purpose.

More often than not a woman's time is taken up, not by the performance of essential domestic duties, but in catering for the egoistic pleasure of her lord and master and for her own vanities. To me, this domestic slavery of woman is a symbol of our barbarism. In my opinion, the slavery of the kitchen is a remnant of barbarism mainly. It is high time that our womankind was freed from this incubus. Domestic work ought not to take the whole of a woman's time.

APPENDIX-III

WOMEN FIGHTERS FOR FREEDOM

Years of slavery and humiliation that husbands, sons, brothers and fathers suffered stirred Indian women to their very depths. The circumstances that forced these men to take up the challenge of an attack against foreign rule resulted in wrenching them away from their hearths and homes and this created a deep vacuum in their lives.

In the sheltered life of Indian women, as mothers, wives or daughters, sharing the duties of the man of the house was their proud privilege. When these men were gone, their sorrow caused them to step out, to lend their shoulders to the duties opted for by their menfolk.

So it was that an onrush of the unseen, spontaneous and unexpected force gushed out. Infuriated by the humiliation of their menfolk, distressed by their suffering and motivated by the urge to share their burden, the hitherto cloistered women rushed out of their cloisters.

Tender feet that glided so softly, so silently that only the tinkling of their ankle bells echoed their movements, now thumped the streets shaking the foundations of an Empire. Feet that were picturesquely lined with henna were now lacerated and blistered by long marches.

Here are a few models.

Lakshmi Bai

"Lakshmi Bai, the name stands out above others and is revered still in the popular memory, was Rani of Jansi, a girl of twenty years of age who died fighting. 'Best and bravest' of the rebel leaders, she was called by the English General, who opposed her." (*Courtesy: Vivekananda Kendra Patrika*, Madras, August, 1974).

Mata Maha Rani Tapasvini

A contemporary of Rani Lakshmi Bai was Mata Maha Rani Tapasvini, who was also the niece of the famous Queen. She was the link between the first war of independence of 1857 and the Revolutionary Movements of later days.

A child-widow, Mata Maha Rani stayed with her father, Narayana Rao. Endowed with a knowledge of the Scripture, she was also bequeathed a proficiency in physical training and martial arts. When her father died, she devoted her time to the development of the defence of his fort. The British, intent upon uprooting opposition, soon noticed this and put her in confinement at Trichy. After her release, she took to spiritual life and as the disciple of Gauri Shankar came to be known as Mataji Maha Rani Tapasvini. It was Mataji's fertile brain that was responsible for the idea of the Arms Factory in Nepal. She suggested it to Tilak when she met him in 1901 who sent his close and devoted friend K.P. Khadilkar in 1902 to Nepal to open negotiations with the Nepalese Commander-in-Chief on the topic. It was agreed to open an Arms Factory in collaboration with the German firm 'Krupps' under the disguise of a tile manufacturing unit. Khadilkar stayed back in Nepal—registered as an innocent citizen under the name of Krishna Rao. But the plan floundered. Krishna Rao's identity was revealed and the scheme came to a dead end. No one ever guessed that the brain behind the whole plan was Mataji.

Sarala Devi

Sarala Devi was the niece of the great poet Rabindranath Tagore. Her contact with Sri Aurobindo in 1902 drew her towards the Revolutionary Movement. In collaboration with Jatindranath Bannerjee, whom Aurobindo sent to her, she started organising the Revolutionary Movement in Bengal under the direction and guidance of Sri Aurobindo.

She was impressed by the spirit and physical prowess of the Maharashtrians displayed in the religious festivals, and on her return to Calcutta introduced festivals and related rituals that called for the development of physical prowess. Through such rituals, she awakened the Kali aspect of Indian womenhood, the warring, terrible, aspect that was the prime necessity for strengthening the nation in the freedom struggle. The Bharati Samiti and Shakti Samiti of Calcutta, the Sevak Samiti of Dacca and eighteen other similar organisations all over the country, imparted training in boxing, wrestling, dagger and sword-play.

To Rambhaji Datta Chaudhuri, who was then a prominent member of the Lahore Chief Court Bar, and a well-known Congressman, she was married in 1905. Both husband and wife took active part in the political movements of the day. The Datta Chaudhuris were in the forefront of the movement against the Rowlatt Act; her husband was exiled while she was spared.

From her earlier, violent revolutionary trends, Sarala Devi slowly deviated and finally came completely under the influence of Gandhian ideology, to which she remained dedicated to the end.

Vidyavati

Vidyavati, the heroic mother of the Sardar Bhagat Singh who smilingly embraced death, so that posterity may live and breathe the pure air of freedom was the daughter of Waryam Singh, a resident of Moranwali village, Hoshiarpur District in Punjab.

Born in 1887, she was married to Sardar Kishan Singh, son of Arjan Singh, a resident of Kattar Valam near Jullundhar. From his boyhood Kishan Singh was a social worker. He saved thousands of innocent Hindus from conversion by the missionaries of other faiths. He was a revolutionary, too. And for forty-five years, he was a member of the A.I.C.C.

Vidyavati and Kishan Singh had four sons. Bhagat Singh, Kulbir Singh, Rahim Singh and Rajinder Singh, and three daughters, Amar Kaur. Sumitra and Shakuntala. All of them were social workers. The entire family was dedicated to the service of the nation.

Vidyavati was a worthy wife to Kishan Singh. She shared willingly his revolutionary activities. When he was fighting the Britishers with his friends. Vidyavati exhibited rare courage and resourcefulness. She gave protection and succour to the revolutionaries hunted by the police. This was no easy task. It was like playing with fire. But undaunted, she provided food and shelter to them. Many were the times when she moved about armed and attired as a male.

When Bhagat Singh, who, by his revolutionary ardour and activities, made it hot for Britishers, was born, both his father and uncle were behind British bars.

Vidyavati, like Jija Bai, trained Bhagat Singh and turned him into a soldier of the revolution. She narrated to the boy adventures of his father and uncle. She instilled in him indomitable courage, spirit of sacrifice and faith in the Sikh Gurus.

This was not all, Vidyavati was in no way inferior in courage to any man.

Those were the days of 1931. Her eldest son was in goal. The husband was behind the bars, due to Ludhiana disturbances. The dacoits waiting for this opportune moment raided the house. Like an enraged lioness she faced them single-handed and forced them to beat a hasty retreat.

Her indomitable will was put to test again and again. Kulbir Singh and his brothers were arrested in 1940. Protesting against the inhuman prison conditions they started a hunger strike. The mother in Vidyavati felt a deep longing to see her children. But the cunning authorities laid down a condition that she could visit her children only if they gave up their hunger strike.

Her heroic motherhood gained the upper hand. Addressing a mammoth gathering, she thundered: "Let my children die in the hunger strike; I would rather welcome their death than allow them to stop the ordeal just to see me. Let them continue the hunger strike till their demands are conceded."

She was a mother to the large family of revolutionaries. Sukh Dev, Raj Guru and Chandra Sekhar Azad the bosom friends of her son, were like sons to her.

Basanti Devi

There was a new development on the morning of the 7th of December 1921. Basanti Devi, Desh Bandhu Das's wife, and Urmila Devi, his sister, decided to take the lead in hawking *khadi*. When they were doing so, a police sergeant approached Basanti Devi and asked her, "Madam, what are you doing?" Basanti Devi replied that she was selling *khadi* and asking people to observe *hartal* on the 24th of December. The sergeant then said that she was under arrest and asked her to go with him to the police station. She did so willingly. The arrest of Basanti Devi had an electrical effect on the people. Immediately, more than a thousand young men offered themselves for arrest. They also developed a new militancy. When a trial magistrate asked them for a statement, the young men replied that they had come to serve their country. Among those who courted arrest at this stage was Hiralal Gandhi, the eldest son of Mahatma Gandhi.

Basanti Devi's arrest had in fact stirred up the whole of Bengal. Muslims as well as Hindus joined the national movement in thousands. There were stirrings even among the police. While Basanti Devi and her companions were being carried to the prison, a number of police constables saluted her and vowed that they would resign their jobs. Factory workers also joined as volunteers and offered themselves for arrest. The government was disturbed by these new developments, and orders were issued that the wages of policemen would be forthwith increased.

When Desh Bandhu Das heard of Basanti Devi's arrest, he took it calmly and advised all Congressmen to devote themselves even more resolutely to the national programme. In his heart he exulted at this evidence of the courage and spirit of sacrifice that was moving the women of India. He told some of his friends that he was now sure that the Government would be shaken to its very foundations. The Government, however, had no intention of keeping these ladies in prison. They were released at dead of night and sent home. Desh Bandhu Das felt that this was an insult and became even more determined that the struggle should continue.

Nellie Sen Gupta

In 1933, while Jetindra Mohan was in the Medical College Hospital as a prisoner-patient, it was proposed that the annual session of the Congress should be held in Calcutta. The Congress was, at that time banned by the Government. Office-bearers elected by the Congress were arrested and jailed. Nellie Sen Gupta was then asked to be the next President. There was a great element of risk involved in accepting this offer, as the situation was by no means normal. After consulting her husband, she consented to accept the honour, and became the President of the Indian National Congress. She was the third woman to be the President of the Congress, the first two being Annie Besant (1917) and Sarojini Naidu (1925). The time and place where Nellie was to read the Congress manifesto were not declared, as it was feared the police would break up the proceedings.

On the appointed date, people began to gather in groups at the Esplanade Tram Depot, but not openly as they knew that the police would be waiting. The police had closed all open spaces so that the Congress session could not be held in town. The Tram Depot was, therefore, chosen as the venue. Suddenly, at 4 p.m. sharp, bugles were sounded from Chittaranjan Avenue, Bentinck Street, Dharam Tala Street, and thousands of Congress volunteers ran to the *goompti* in the Tram Depot shouting 'Bande Mataram'. Nellie had arrived by car a little earlier together with her brother-in-law, Ranendra Mohan. When she heard the bugles, she stepped out of the car and went quickly to the place where the people were shouting *Bande Mataram*. Hundreds ran to the meeting place and she was proposed and seconded as President. Quickly Nellie started reading the Congress pledge in a loud and clear voice. She had hardly uttered a few words when the police, who were hiding in all corners, swooped down on the Congress crowd and dispersed them by charging them with staves. Truck-loads of police came from Lal Bazaar and surrounded the meeting place, and mercilessly lashed out at the assembled people. A large number of people were arrested.

Ranendra Mohan was in the midst of this turmoil and helplessly saw the policemen take his sister-in-law away to jail in a waiting Blace Maria. Though the meeting had been perfectly peaceful, the police struck people across their faces with canes and cruelly beat them up. Blood flowed freely, but the people continued to shout 'Bande Mataram'. They were again and again attacked but they never retaliated with any form of violence. It was a soul-stirring scene. The great courage which Nellie Sen Gupta showed was worth recording in letters of gold, for she knew that the police would resort to violence, and yet she accepted the role of the Congress President and read out the Congress pledge.

Ranendra Mohan went home and received a telephone message from the Police Commissioner informing him that his sister-in-law could be released if she agreed to sign a bond acquiescing to appear before the Magistrate when required. Ranendra Mohan took this message to his brother in the hospital. Jatin instructed that his wife was to undertake no agreement. Accordingly, she refused and was taken to prison, where she put in a tin shed alongwith many other Congress prisoners. When Ranendra Mohan went to see her, she was in a pitiable state in the heat of the prison. Those days in prison she actually went through hell. Sushil Sinha, I.C.S., was then the Presidency Magistrate and the trial was held in his court. He ordered the release of all the prisoners and Nellie was once again free.

For twenty-four years, she had worked at Jatindra Mohan's side sharing all the risks and poverty and distress. Never had she felt that she was an English woman and that the freedom struggle in India was not hers. She had become an Indian the moment she married her illustrious husband.

Kasturba Gandhi

If Madam Cama was the mother of revolution, the nation itself gained a mother in Kasturba Gandhi. As husband and wife, the great Gandhis shared the responsibilities of a nation in the same simple, accepted manner as a couple would share the responsibilities of their family. The tribute paid to Kasturba Gandhi described her life as "the greatest sacrifice made by India to the moloch of British imperialism."

When she was married to Mohandas Karamchand Gandhi, she was instructed, as was every Indian bride at the time of her going to her in-laws, that it was her duty to serve him faithfully in all aspects of life. No one realised the mightiness of the responsibility it meant to serve Gandhi in all aspects. And in her success in achieving this mighty task, Kasturba

Gandhi made the greatest contribution to the cause of the nation; she helped Gandhiji's transformation into a true Mahatma and gave this gem of unsurpassed brilliance to the world.

Much against her orthodox convictions were the policies of the Mahatma, yet to each of them she contributed her share. And she carried out his plans and his campaigns, whenever he was whisked away from them half-way through—seven gruelling years of privation in South Africa that broke her health to the point of death; and the years of storm and struggle in India when she stuck through it all and stood by her husband through all his fasts and his *satyagrahas*; the banner of Mahatma Gandhi and the mantle of leadership she carried, spreading the national spirit from village to village, touching the hearts of the peasants with her simplicity, thus evoking in them the spirit of nationalism, which gave them the capacity to rise equal to the challenge of the occasion; all these were the silent silhouettes of a great woman leader, who became the Mother of the Nation.

The memorable event on the 9th August brings to one's vision the picture of a frail form, her face radiant with the joy of a married life that was a true companionship; a form from which vitality was fast fading away, but the soul was still burning aglow, a face on which every line was a line of determination. And determined she was, to deliver the address at the meeting that was to have been addressed by her husband. When the police threatened her with arrest if she carried out her decision—they knew the answer from her firm set lips, even before she worded it. She was taken away in the police car. That was also her last journey.

Kamala Nehru

Remembering the frail, dainty fair form of Kamala Nehru one always thinks of her as a bride,—a bride with tinkling ankle-bells, soft whispers and softer tread, delicate and dainty in every aspect. If Kasturba was the Mother of the Nation, Kamala to her last was the beautiful *Bahu* and *Bhabi*. Somehow from all that is said about her by all who knew her, including some of the touching details given by her fond husband, she only emerges as a bride. That is why perhaps Nehru had to say, that in all his years of association with Kamala, though he understood as much of her, yet so much still was there to be understood.

She was delicate and yet she wanted to share the arduous tasks of the National Movement with her husband. To be left out of it would have been the denial of a part of him to her. Nehru understood this, and so they worked together.

When the Nation shook with the storming movement of Civil Disobedience—when most of the men were crammed into prisons—it was then that the Government was taken by surprise. The women rushed out from their homes. They gathered together, formed into an indomitable force. Each woman, who took part, had two motivating forces—the love for Motherland which the actions of her man kindled, and the urge to share his life in every respect and carry on the task he was whisked away from. The simple peasant's wife and the great leader's wife,—both were prompted by the same impulse, and the same flame burnt in the hearts of all.

The Nehru family witnessed their daughters and daughter-in-law go out of the house and follow the path that led to the goal upon which the entire Nation set its heart. At first Motilal Nehru was adverse to these delicate creatures taking up a task of such great strain both mentally and physically. He grudgingly gave in, and was delighted at the outcome in the end.

"In this upheaval Kamala had played a brave and notable part and on her inexperience shoulders fell the task of organizing the work in the city of Allahabad,when every known worker was in prison. She made up for that inexperience by her fire and energy and, within a few months, she became the pride of Allahabad,"says Jawaharlal Nehru.

More difficult, and heart-rending was the other aspect of Kamala's contribution to the national struggle. She had to suffer continuous pangs of separation from her beloved husband many a time, and she bore this with a brave smile. Not a man to show the softer side of his nature too openly. Nehru said very little of the agony the couple have suffered in their separations. Yet the little he expressed here and there reveals that which is unsaid. This was the silent, sublimated part of the great struggle for Freedom which the Nehrus and Gandhis and all others who took part in it suffered.

In 1936, when news of Kamala's deteriorating health reached him, Nehru sped to Germany. Later, when she seemed better and improving after her transfer from Badenweiller to Lausanne in Switzerland, Nehru had to make preparations to leave; he was elected a second time the President of the National Congress, which was to meet in April. He even toyed with the idea of resigning from the Presidentship, but Kamala persuaded him not to, though she knew in her heart, that she may not live long enough to see him again when he would be back. Even the doctors sensed this, though outwardly from her physical condition there was nothing to suggest an immediate crisis.

Four or five days before his due date of departure, Nehru was informed by the doctors to postpone his trip. This he did, and as though to do her last bit to make things easy for him, to give him the satisfaction of being with her in her last moments, and yet to enable him to respond to the National Call in time, she breathed her last on the 28th of February, 1936, content in the knowledge of her beloved's presence by her side. This was Kamala the strong, silent one.

Bharati Devi

When Prof. N.G. Ranga was in prison he anxiously awaited news of his family, especially his wife; not regarding her health, or welfare; but whether she was making enough progress in contributing her share to the national cause and as to when she would join him as a worthy partner in prison life too. Such was the love of the husband for his wife and for the Mother Land. And such was the devotion the couple had for their country's cause. Bharathi Devi responded to her husband's nationalistic fervour—and it was a proud moment in Professor Ranga's life when he received in prison the news of Bharathi Devi's arrest. She had organised the peasant women and marched them on to protest against Foreign Rule, by picketing before the shops that sold foreign merchandise and cloth. She was arrested as the responsible leader of women *Satyagrahis*, and fined Rs. 500 and sentenced to a year's imprisonment.

Those were days when wives were true "partners." They were not merely house keepers with a decent designation. They truly shared the woes and welfare of their husbands, understood the enthusiasm of the patriotic spirit that burnt the frames of their men. Some came out of their abodes and took active part, suffered side by side with their menfolk. Others, though bound perhaps by some responsibilities to the home. contributed their share to the struggle by functioning like the oil which constantly fed the flame of patriotism in their men's hearts.

A resolution of Remembrance was passed at thousands of Public Meetings on January 26, the anniversary of India's Independence and a part of lit related to the Women of India. "We record our homage and deep admiration for the womanhood of India, who, in the hour of peril to the Motherland, forsook the shelter of their homes, and, with unfailing courage, stood shoulder to shoulder with their menfolk in the front line of India's National Army to share with them the sacrifices and triumphs of the struggle."

BIBLIOGRAPHY

Asthana, P., *Women's Movement in India*, Vikas Publishing House, Delhi, 1974.

Altekar, A.S., *Position of Women in Hindu Civilization*, MLBD, New Delhi, 1995.

Anjana Kumari and Anju Dube, *Women Parliamentarian*, Har Anand Publication, New Delhi, 1994.

Ahmad, Karuna, *The Social Background of Women*, Delhi University Press, 1968.

Anagrika Dharmapal, *The World's Debt to Buddha*, Mahabodhi Society of India, Calcutta.

Ain-i-Akbari, Translated by H. Blochman.

Baig, Tara Ali, *India's Women Power*, S. Chand, New Delhi, 1976.

Bagil, J.C., *Women's Education in Eastern India*, The World Press, 1956.

Buch, M.B., Second Survey of Research in Education (1972-78). The Society for Educational Research and Development, Baroda.

Bapat, P.V. (ed.), *2500 Years of Buddhism*, Publication Division, Govt. of India, New Delhi, Fourth Reprint, 1976.

Bryan Wilson and Daisaku Ikeda, *Human Values in a Changing World*, Macdonald & Co., London, 1984.

Bernier, F., *Travels in Moghul Empire*, (Translated by A. Constable).

Chitnis, Suma, *Traditional Stereo Types and Roles of Women*, Bombay University Press, 1975.

Chiplumkar, G.M., *The Scientific Basis of Women Education*, Hudlikar, Poona, 1930.

Comek Margaret L., *The Hindu Women*, Asia Publishing House, Mumbai, 1961.

Chattopaddhyaya, *The Awakening of Indian Women*, Calcutta, 1939.

Elise, B., *Women in the Twentieth Century World*, Wiley, New York, 1977.

Gupta, N.L., *Educational Ideals and Institutions in Mahabharata*, Mohit Publications, New Delhi, 1977.

———, *Education and Values in Mahabharata*, Concept Publishing Co., New Delhi, 1995.

Gupta, N.L., *Current Trends and Problems of Progressive Education*, Krishna Bros., Ajmer, 1985.

———, *New Education Policy: A New Era in Education*, Krishna Bros., Ajmer, 1987.

———, *A Search for Human Values*, Arya Book Depot, New Delhi, 1992.

Gandhi, Mahatma, *Views on Women*, New Delhi, Govt. of India, Ministry of Social Welfare and Culture.

Gandhi, Indira, *My Truth*, Autobiography.

Giri, V. Mohini, *Emancipation and Empowerment Women*, Gyan Books Pvt. Ltd., New Delhi-2, 1997.

Gore, M.S., *Indian Education: Structure and Process*, Rawat Publications, Jaipur, 1994.

Jafar Sharif, *Islam in India or the Qanun-i-Islam*, Translated by G.A. Herclots, edited by William Crooke, Curzin Press, II issue, 1975.

Jafar, S.M., *Education in Muslim India*, 1936.

———, *Islam in India.*

Jacqueline, Chabaud, *The Education and Advancement of Women*, UNESCO, 1970.

Keay, F.E., *A History of Education in India and Pakistan*, OUP, 3rd Edition, 1959.

Kautilya's Arthashastra, (Translated by R. Shamashastry).

Kapadia, K.M., *Marriage and Family in India*, 2nd Edn., OUP, Mumbai, 1958.

Law, Rajendra Nath, *Promotion of Learning under Muhammadan Rule.*

Mathur, Y.B., *Women Education in India* (1913-1966), Delhi University Press, 1973.

Mathur, V., *A Study of Political Attitudes and Alienation among Female College Students*, Ph.D. Psychology, Rajasthan University, 1985.

Mishra, L., *Education of Women in India from 1921 to 1955*, Ph.D. Education, Sagar University, 1961.

Max Muller, F. (Ed.), *Sacred Books of the East*, Vols. I and XV.

Mukherjee, Radhakumud, *Ancient Indian Education: Brahminical and Buddhist*, MLBD, New Delhi.

Mishra, Lakshmi, *Education of Women in India : 1921-1966*, Mumbai, 1966.

Mujeeb, M., *The Indian Muslims*, George Allen & Unwin Ltd., London, 1967.

Narayan, K.S., *Women and Polity in India*, Deccan Herald, Bangalore, 4th Dec., 1994.

Narullah Syed and Naik, J.P., *A History of Education in India*, Macmillan & Company, Mumbai, 1951.

Nehru, S.K., *Our Cause: A Symposium by Indian Women*, Kitabistan, Allahabad, 1936.

Nehru, J.L., *The Discovery of India*, OUP, Ninth Impression, 1989.

Paul, Brunton, *A Search in Secret India*, Rider & Co., London, 18th Impression, 1957.

Sharma, R.P., *Women in Hindu Literature*, Gyan Publishing House, New Delhi-2, 1995.

Siddiqui, Mujibul Hasan, *Women Education*, Ashish Publishing House, Punjabi Bagh, New Delhi, 1993.

Singh, U.K. and Nayak, A.K., *Women Education*, Commonwealth Publishers, Ansari Road, New Delhi, 1997.

Sister, Nivedita, *The Web of Life*, Advaita Ashram, Calcutta, 3rd Impression, 1996.

Sukhia, S.P., *Woman Education in India—Retrospects and Prospects*, DET, Women Training College, Dayal Bagh, Agra, 1972.

Talesra, Hemlata, *Higher Education Among Women National*, New Delhi, 1989.

Vedanta, Kesari, *Monasticism: Ideals and Traditions*, Shri Rama Krishna Math, Chennai, 1991.

Verma, H.N. and Amrit Verma, *Women through the Ages*, Indian Publishers, New Delhi, 1976.

Wells, H.G., *Short History of the World*, Pelican Books.

Yusuf, Hussain, *Glimpses of Medieval Indian Culture*, Asia Publishing House, reprint, 1962.

Books in Hindi

Natthoolal Gupta, *Mahabharata: EK Samaj-Shashtriya Anusheelan*, Chetna Prakashan, New Shukrawari, Shirke Road, Nagpur, 2nd Edition, 1994.

———, *Mulya-parak Shiksha*, Krishna Bros., Ajmer, 1988.

———, *Jain Baudha Shikshan Paddhati*, Vishwa Bharati Prakashan, Sitabuldi, Nagpur, 1980.

———, *Shiksha-shashtriya Nibandha*, Chetna Prakashan, Nagpur, 1997.

———, *Sanskriti ke Sat Sopan*, Radha Publications, Ansari Road, Daryaganj, New Delhi, 1997.

———, *Manava-mulya*, Sahitya Aur Sanskriti, Mohit Publications, Daryaganj, New Delhi, 1995.

Swami Ghananand, *et al.*, (ed.), *Purva aur Paschim ki Sant Mahilayen*, Publications Division, Government of India, 1962.

Book in Urdu

Maulvi Abul Hasnat Nadvi, *Hindustan Ki Qodim Islami*.

Reports

Challenge of Education—A Policy Perspective, Ministry of Education, New Delhi, August, 1985.

National Committee on Women Education (1958-59), Ministry of Education, Government of India, New Delhi, 1959.

National Education Policy (1967-68), Ministry of Education, Government of India, Delhi.

National Policy on Education (1979), Ministry of Education, Government of India, Delhi.

National Policy on Education 1986: Programme of Action, Government of India, Ministry of Human Resource Development, Department of Education, New Delhi, November, 1986.

National Policy on Education 1986, Ministry of Human Resource Development, Government of India, Dept. of Education, New Delhi, May, 1986.

Programme of Action (National Policy on Education—1986), Ministry of HRD, New Delhi, August, 1986.

Report of the Bhaktavatsalam Committee, Ministry of Education, Government of India, 1965.

Report of the Committee for Review of National Policy on Education, 1986. Final Report, 26th December, 1990.

Report of the Committee on Policy Department of Education, Ministry of Human Resource Development, Government of India, January, 1992.

Report of the Secondary Education Commission, 1952-53, Government of India, New Delhi.

Journals/Magazines

Asian Studies, Netaji Institute, Calcutta.

Education in Asia (Bhopal), January-March, 1998.

Femina.

Frontline, March 1995.

Kurukshetra, May 1996, June 1998 and March 1998.

Yojana, Republic Day, 1997. Special, October, 1997, *Yojana*, July 1998.

INDEX